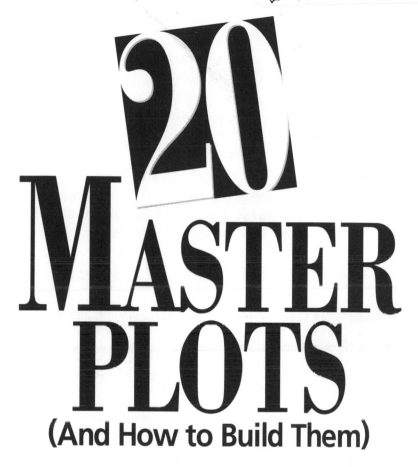

20 MASTER PLOTS

(And How to Build Them)

RONALD B. TOBIAS

WRITER'S DIGEST BOOKS

CINCINNATI, OHIO

Dedication

To Valerie, As Always

"Sue's Got a Baby" appearing on page 176 is reprinted from
Collected Verses of Edgar A. Guest, by Edgar A. Guest, © 1934.
Used with permission of Contemporary Books, Inc.

20 Master Plots (and How to Build Them). Copyright © 1993 by Ronald
B. Tobias. Printed and bound in the United States of America. All rights
reserved. No part of this book may be reproduced in any form or by any
electronic or mechanical means including information storage and retrieval
systems without permission in writing from the publisher, except by a
reviewer, who may quote brief passages in a review. Published by Writer's
Digest Books, an imprint of F&W Publications, Inc., 4700 East Galbraith Road,
Cincinnati, Ohio, 45236. 1-800-289-0963. First paperback edition 2003.

07   06   05   5   4   3

Library of Congress has catalogued the hardcover edition as follows:

Tobias, Ron
        20 master plots (and how to build them) / by Ronald B. Tobias.—1st ed.
            p.   cm.
        Includes index.
        ISBN 0-89879-595-8 (hardcover) ISBN 1-58297-239-7 (pbk.: alk. paper)
            1. Plots (Drama, novel, etc.) 2. Fiction—Technique. I. Title. II. Title;
        Twenty master plots (and how to build them)
        PN218.T59   1993
        808'.02—dc20   93-21785
                                                                              CIP

Edited by Jack Heffron
Designed by Sandy Conopeotis

TABLE OF CONTENTS

Chapter One

Invisible Fiction

If a writer has to rob his mother, he will not hesitate; the "Ode to a Graecian Urn" is worth any number of old ladies.
— *William Faulkner*

The shelves of libraries are stacked with the stories of centuries, but out in the street, the air swarms with newly made fiction. These living stories are so much a part of us that we hardly think about their role in our lives: They are rumor, gossip, jokes, excuses, anecdotes, huge outrageous lies and little white lies—all daily inventions of fiction that create the fabric of life.

Stories thrive at the company water cooler, in the lunchroom, at the hairdresser's, in taxis and taverns, in boardrooms and bedrooms. Years of schooling have conditioned us to think about fiction as something either on the page or on the screen, so we overlook the fact that our everyday lives are steeped in stories: full of energy, inventiveness and conviction.

An example of a fiction that was passed along by word of mouth around the English-speaking world is a modern legend known as "The Choking Doberman." Modern legends are stories that pass from person to person as if they were true. ("I swear, it happened to a friend of a friend of mine. . . .") The story is both simple and simply told:

> A woman returned to her house after a morning of shopping and found her pet Doberman pinscher choking and unable to breathe. She rushed her dog to the vet, where she left it for emergency treatment.

When the woman got home, her phone was ringing. It was the vet. "Get out of your house now!" he shouted.

"What's the matter?" she asked.

"Just do it! Go to a neighbor's. I'll be right there."

Frightened by the tone of his voice, the woman did as she was told and went to her neighbor's.

A few minutes later, four police cars screeched to a halt in front of her house. The police ran inside her house with their guns drawn. Horrified, the woman went outside to see what was happening.

The vet arrived and explained. When he looked inside her dog's throat, he found two human fingers! He figured the dog had surprised a burglar.

Sure enough, the police found a man in a deep state of shock hiding in the closet and clutching a bloody hand.

(For a complete account of the history of this modern legend and many others like it, see *The Vanishing Hitchhiker* or *The Choking Doberman* by Jan Harold Brunvand, W.W. Norton & Co.)

"The Choking Doberman" is an invisible fiction. The story was even reported as true by several newspapers. Yet no one has come forward with a shred of evidence that it ever really happened. Small details change from place to place (such as the number of fingers the dog bit off, the burglar's race, etc.), but the basic story remains the same. People who hear the tale generally accept the story as true (if not with a grain of salt). Few think of it as an outright piece of fiction, which is what it is.

The real value of this legend is that it evolved with constant retelling until it became *plot perfect*, the same process that perfected the fable, the fairy tale, the riddle, the rhyme and the proverb. The story went through thousands of oral rewrites until it could evolve no further.

"The Choking Doberman" is pure plot. The characters and details that describe place and time take a back seat.

The story has three movements:

The first sets up the story by introducing both drama and mystery, when the woman comes home to find her Doberman choking. She takes her dog to the vet.

The second movement starts when the woman returns home and the phone is ringing. An element of danger is introduced when the vet, very agitated, tells her to get out of the house. We know intuitively that the danger is connected to the mystery of the choking Doberman. But how? We try to guess. The woman flees her house and the unknown danger.

The third movement begins with the arrival of the police, who confirm the magnitude of the danger, and the arrival of the vet, who explains the mystery. The police prove the theory of the dismembered burglar when they capture him.

Now, no one sat around concocting this tale. "Let's see, I need a good hook (*the choking Doberman*), followed by a startling complication (*the phone call*), and a scary climax (*the bleeding intruder*)." The plot evolved according to our expectations of what a story should be. It has the three movements (beginning, middle and end), a protagonist (the woman), an antagonist (the burglar), and plenty of tension and conflict. What happens in "The Choking Doberman" is not that different from what happens in the novels of Agatha Christie or P.D. James. It's only a matter of degree.

Before we begin exploring the nature of plot, I want to make the point that plot isn't an accessory that conveniently organizes your material according to some ritualistic magic. You don't just plug in a plot like a household appliance and expect it to do its job. Plot is organic. It takes hold of the writer and the work from the beginning. Remove the plot from "The Choking Doberman," and there's nothing meaningful left. As readers we're plot-directed. Some writers have tried to write plotless novels (with some limited success), but we're so in love with a good plot that after a few short spasms of rebellion (*angry writer*: "Why must plot be the most important element?") we return to the traditional method of telling stories. I can't say plot is the center of the writer's universe, but it is one of two strong forces — character being the other — that affects everything else in turn.

ON SKELETONS

We've all heard the standard instructional line: *Plot is structure*. Without structure you have nothing. We've been taught to fear plot, because it looms so large over us and so much seems to hinge on it. We've been told a thousand times there are only so many plots and they've all been used and there isn't a story left in the world that hasn't already been told. It's a miracle that any writer escapes being intimidated by the past.

No doubt you've also heard plot described in architectural or mechanical terms. Plot is the skeleton, the scaffold, the super-structure, the chassis, the frame and a dozen other terms. Since we've seen so many buildings under construction, and since we've seen so many biological models of humans and animals over the years, the metaphors are easy to identify with. It seems to make sense, after all. A story should have a plan that helps the writer make the best choices in the process of creating fiction, right?

Let's take the metaphor of the skeleton, since it's one of the more common ones writing instructors use. Plot is a skeleton that holds together your story. All your details hang on the bones of the plot. You can even debone a plot by reducing it to a description of the story. We read these summaries all the time in reviews and critical analyses of fiction. Screenwriters must be able to pitch their plot in about two minutes if they have any hope of selling it. It's the simplistic answer to the simplistic question, "What's your story about?"

Strong metaphors are tough to shake. The visual image of the skeleton is so graphic that we surrender to it. Yes, take out the skeleton and everything falls apart. It seems to make great sense.

The problem with the skeleton metaphor for plot (and all the other architectural and mechanical models) is that it misrepresents what plot is and how it works. Plot isn't a wire hanger that you hang the clothes of a story on. *Plot is diffusive*; it permeates all the atoms of fiction. It can't be deboned. It isn't a series of I-beams that keeps everything from collapsing. It is a force that saturates every page, paragraph and word. Perhaps a better meta-phor for plot would be electromagnetism—the force that draws the atoms of the story together. It correlates images, events and people.

Plot is a process, not an object.

We tend to talk about plots as if they were objects. All of our plot metaphors describe plot as if it were some tangible thing that came in a box. We categorize plots like items in a story inventory. We talk about plot as if it were a dead thing, something static.

This may be the hardest obstacle for you to overcome: thinking of plot as a force, a process, rather than as an object. Once you realize that plot reaches down to the atomic level in your writing, and that every choice you make ultimately affects plot, you will realize its dynamic quality.

Plot is dynamic, not static.

Let's say you'd written "The Choking Doberman." Someone asks you, "What's your story about?" How do you answer?

You answer, "It's about a dog."

Obviously that won't work. Too specific. Anyway, the dog is the subject matter (and then only half of it). So you try something else.

"It's about terror."

Nope. Too vague.

You try another tack. "It's about this woman who comes home and finds her dog choking on something, only to find out it's human fingers!"

Great gory detail, but is it plot?

No.

Your patience is wearing thin. All right, what *is* the plot?

The plot is as old as literature itself. "The Choking Doberman" is a riddle.

The point of a riddle is to solve a puzzle. It comes from the same tradition as Oedipus, who must solve the riddle presented to him by the Sphinx, and the same tradition of Hercules, who had the unenviable task of having to solve twelve tasks, the famous labors, each of which was a riddle to be solved. Fairy tales are chock full of riddles to be solved—children delight in them. So do adults. The riddle is the basis of the mystery, which to this day is arguably the most popular form of literature in the world. Today we think of a riddle as a simple question that has a trick answer. "What has . . . and . . . ?" But a riddle really is any mystifying, misleading or puzzling question that is posed as a problem to be solved or guessed. And that fits "The Choking Doberman."

The story is designed to give you two basic clues. The first clue appears in the first movement: The dog is choking on something. What?

The second clue comes in the second movement, when the vet tells the woman to get out of her house. Why?

To solve the riddle (who?), we must combine clues (what? and why?). We must try to establish a link between the two (cause and effect) and provide the missing piece *before* the end of the story, when the vet and the police explain everything to us. A riddle is a game played between audience and writer. The writer gives clues (preferably clues that make the riddle challenging and therefore fun), and the audience makes a go of it before time is up (in the third movement, when all the explanations come). Take away plot, and all that's left is a jumble of details that add up to nothing.

So before we talk about all the different master plots and how to build them, you should feel comfortable with the concept that plot is a force. It is a force that attracts all the atoms of language (words, sentences, paragraphs) and organizes them according to a certain sense (character, action, location). It is the cumulative effect of plot and character that creates the whole.

So the point of this book isn't so much to give you a rundown of twenty master plots, but to show you how to develop plot in fiction. The book also will show you how to apply whatever plot you choose to your subject matter so you develop plot evenly and effectively.

YOUR PLOT, THE FORCE AND YOU

There's that moment when you begin your work and that huge void of empty pages lies ahead of you. You hesitate. The Chinese proverb that says the longest journey begins with the first step is a little help, but what the proverb doesn't tell you is *which road to take*. The fear always is that you may strike out in the wrong direction, only to have to come back and start all over again. Nothing is more frustrating than to start on something — especially something as ambitious as a novel or a screenplay — and realize halfway through that it isn't right.

What can you do to protect yourself from going off in the wrong direction? The answer is a combination of good news and bad news.

First the bad news.

The bad news is that there are no guarantees. Nothing you can do will guarantee that what you do is right. That shouldn't come as a surprise, but it is a reality.

Now for the good news.

The longest journey begins with the first step, but it helps to know where your journey will take you. This doesn't mean you will know every step of the way, because writing is always full of surprises — twists and turns that the author doesn't expect. That's part of the fun of writing. But most writers I know have a destination in mind. They know where they want to head even if they can't tell you exactly how they intend to get there.

I'm not talking about knowing the ending of the story. That's a different issue. What I'm talking about is understanding the nature of the materials you'll deal with — specifically plot. If you strike out without any idea of destination, you'll wander aimlessly. But if you understand something about the kind of plot you're trying to write, you'll have supplied yourself with a compass that will know when you're wandering and warn you to get back on track.

Even when you get to the end of the work, this compass will guide you through the rewriting, that stage of work that really *makes* what you've written. By having a clear understanding of what your plot is and how the force works in your fiction, you'll have a reliable compass to guide you through the work.

What explorer ever struck out without a direction in mind?

ON DEFINING PLOT

I once heard a Nobel-Prize winning scientist talk about randomness, and something he said has stuck with me: What is randomness? he asked. The chances of something specifically happening at a certain time and place are astronomical, and yet every second of every day is filled with these unlikely events. You drop a dime on the floor. It rolls in a spiral, then twirls to a standstill. What are the odds that could happen exactly the same way again? Millions, maybe trillions, to one. And yet it happened as naturally as if there were no odds against it. Every event in our lives happens as if there were no odds against it.

The scientist argued that randomness does not exist. We have operational definitions, he asserted, definitions that work for a certain series of circumstances and conditions, but we don't have an absolute definition that works in all cases.

The same is true about plot. We have operational definitions of plot, but no grand, irrefutable definition that is absolute. We have only definitions that work for a certain series of circumstances and conditions. Your work is that series of circumstances and conditions, and your work ultimately will provide the proper definition of plot.

It sounds like I'm saying, "Hey, you figure it out, I can't do it for you." That's not what I mean. What I am saying is that each plot is different, but each has its roots in pattern, and this book can help you with those patterns. You will choose a pattern of plot and adapt it to your own specific plot, which is unique for your story.

APPLYING PATTERNS TO YOUR WORK

If you've written much, you know the value of pattern. There's the work pattern: If you sit down every day for so many hours and write, you will produce a lot more than if you write when the fancy strikes you. We rely on patterns as structures.

The same is true inside your own work. By building patterns, you construct a scaffolding for your work. You can build two major patterns in fiction, both of which depend on each other: the pattern of plot and the pattern of character. Once you establish a pattern of plot, you have a dynamic force that will guide you through the action; and once you establish a pattern of character (who acts in the pattern of plot), you have a dynamic force of behavior that will guide you through your character's intent and motivation.

THE EXACT NUMBER OF PLOTS IN THE WORLD

Question: "How many plots are there?"

Answer A: "Who knows? Thousands, tens of thousands, maybe even millions."

Answer B: "Sixty-nine."

Answer C: "There are only thirty-six known plots in the universe."

Answer D: "Two plots, period."

Answer A (Who knows?) is commonly heard in classrooms and found in writing textbooks. Plots have endless possibilities, so there must be endless plots. It is also consistent with what I said about adapting patterns to specific stories.

Answer B (Sixty-nine) was Rudyard Kipling's idea. He felt that only sixty-nine of the countless variations of Answer A were plots. He was talking about patterns.

Answer C (Thirty-six) was the invention of Carlo Gozzi, who catalogued them in a book about plot. He too, was counting patterns. Today when we read that book, about half of the plots are no longer used (because they seem hopelessly out of date), so a revised version of Gozzi might say there are only eighteen plots.

Answer D (Two!) has found favor from Aristotle to modern days, and I'll talk about those two plots in chapter three, because they are so basic that all other stories stem from them. This approach goes one step further than the others in that it categorizes the patterns into two groups. (More on that later.)

All of these answers are right to some degree. Be suspicious of any magic number of plots, because I doubt anyone can completely catalogue the range of human feeling and action in tidy little packages numbered from one to whatever. These people really say the same thing, but in different ways.

Another way to put it might be to say that you can package plot any number of ways, and the way you package it decides what number you'll end up with. There is no magic number, one or one million. This book deals with twenty, but these aren't the only ones in the world. They're twenty of the most basic plots, but any enterprising person can find more, or find another way to package the concept and come out with a different number. Plot is a slippery thing, and no one can hold onto it for long.

In its most basic sense, a plot is a blueprint of human behavior. Thousands of years of human behavior has developed patterns of action and feeling. These patterns are so basic to being human that they haven't changed in the last five thousand years and probably won't change in the next five thousand. On a cosmic scale, five thousand years is a drop in the bucket, but for us mere mortals who eke out lifetimes of about eighty years, five thousand years is a very long time.

In the history of human events it's a long time, too. Some of these patterns of behavior go back even further, to the beginning of humanity and before. We call these behaviors "instincts": the maternal instinct, the instinct to survive, the instinct to defend yourself, and so on. They are primal behaviors, and they are a large part of our own behavior. Remember the story about the mother whose child was trapped beneath an automobile? She was so desperate to save her child she lifted the car with superhuman strength and freed it. We want to protect the ones we love, and sometimes we must go to extremes to do it. This is a basic pattern of behavior that is common to all peoples around the globe, city and jungle alike, at all times in history.

You can probably think of a dozen other such patterns of behavior off the top of your head. But behavior doesn't make plot; it's just the first step toward plot.

First, you must understand the difference between a story and a plot.

THE WHALE HUSBAND MEETS
THE CHOKING DOBERMAN

Before plot there was story. In the days when people lived in makeshift homes that they abandoned daily in search of game, or seasonally as they moved their herds of sheep or yaks, they sat around the fire at night and told stories. Stories about the prowess of the hunter, stories about the swiftness of the gazelle or the slyness of the coyote or the brute strength of the walrus. Story was a narration of events in the sequence that they happened.

Plot was something that grew out of the religious rituals that predated Christ, which developed into the classic drama as we know it. Plot is story that has a pattern of action and reaction.

Among the Indians of the Pacific Northwest, the story of the Whale Husband was once popular:

> A fisherman caught a strange fish, which he gave to his wife to clean. When she finished her task, the wife washed her hands in the sea. Suddenly a Killer Whale rose out of the water and pulled the woman in. The Killer Whale took the fisherman's wife to his home at the bottom of the sea, where she worked as a slave in his house.
>
> With the help of his friend, Shark, the fisherman followed the Killer Whale to his house at the bottom of the sea. Using trickery, Shark snuffed the light in the Killer Whale's house and rescued the wife for the fisherman.

Compare "The Choking Doberman" to "The Whale Husband." The story about the Doberman arouses and directs our expectations, whereas the tale about the Whale Husband does not. "The Choking Doberman" creates a unity of narration so that each event in its sequence connects along the way to make a unified whole. "The Choking Doberman" integrates the questions of who, what and, most important, why. In "The Whale Husband," we have the who and the what, but not the why.

Too many important questions are never answered in "The Whale Husband":

- What does the strange fish have to do with the appearance of the Killer Whale? (We want the events to connect somehow.) We suspect that the Killer Whale took the woman because of the strange fish, but we never find out if that's the case. We can guess that maybe the strange fish was the Killer Whale's wife, so the Killer Whale took revenge. We want the second movement (the Killer Whale stealing the fisherman's wife) to happen *because* of the first movement (the fisherman steals the Killer Whale's wife). But there are no clues, no connections, no apparent *causal relationships*.
- Why does the Killer Whale kidnap the fisherman's wife? Was it for revenge? Or was it just because he was lonely or mean

or perhaps he needed a new housekeeper?
- What was the alliance between Shark and the fisherman? Did Shark have something against the Killer Whale? Where did Shark come from? Why does she help? No answers, no clues.

In all fairness, the story probably has many hidden connotations that are available to the original tellers and listeners, but as it is here it seems to fail our expectations of what a story should be.

Those expectations are what plot is about.

STORY VS. PLOT

Novelist E.M. Forster spent a lot of time thinking about writing. He tried to explain the difference between story and plot in his book *Aspects of the Novel*. "The king died and the queen died." Two events. A simple narration. This is story.

But if you connect the first movement (the death of the king) with the second movement (the death of the queen) and make one action *the result of* the other, we would have a plot. "The king died and then the queen died *of grief.*"

Add a touch of suspense: "The queen died and no one knew why until it was discovered that it was through grief at the death of the king."

Story, then, is a chronicle of events. The listener wants to know what comes next.

Plot is more than just a chronicle of events. The listener asks a different question: *"Why* does this happen?"

Story is a series of events strung like beads on a string. (This happened and then this happened and then. . . .)

Plot is a chain of cause-and-effect relationships that constantly create a pattern of unified action and behavior. Plot involves the reader in the game of "Why?"

Story requires only curiosity to know what will happen next.

Plot requires the ability to remember what has already happened, to figure out the relationships between events and people, and to try to project the outcome.

TWO ENGLISH GENTLEMEN

The following story is from Maugham's notebooks on writing. Maugham said he liked the story but could never figure out how to use it in his own work:

> Two young Englishmen were working on an isolated tea plantation in India. One of the men — we'll call him Clive — got a handful of letters in every post, but the other man — we'll call him Geoffrey — never got any mail.
>
> One day Geoffrey offered five pounds to his friend for one of his letters. (In those days that was lot of money.)
>
> "Of course," Clive replied, and he spread out his mail on a table in front of Geoffrey. "Take your pick."
>
> Geoffrey looked over the mail and then chose a letter.
>
> At dinner that night, Clive casually asked his friend what was in the letter he'd bought.
>
> "None of your business," Geoffrey replied.
>
> "At least tell me who it was from," asked Clive.
>
> Geoffrey refused to tell him.
>
> The two men argued, but Geoffrey wouldn't back down.
>
> A week later, Clive offered to buy the letter back for twice the amount. "Not on your life," said Geoffrey and he walked away.

Maugham's observation about what he saw as the deficiency of this story is interesting:

"I suppose that if I belonged to the modern school of story writers, I should write it just as it is and leave it. It goes against the grain with me. I want a story to have form, and I don't see how you can give it that unless you can bring it to a conclusion that leaves no legitimate room for questioning."

So what happened?

Nobody knows. You invent an ending:

Clive sneaks into Geoffrey's room to steal the letter back, but Geoffrey walks in and surprises Clive going through his things. The men fight, and Clive accidentally kills Geoffrey. He later finds the letter in Geoffrey's effects and reads it . . .

What does it say?

Let's try a couple of different endings.

Ending One

You want to add an ironic twist, the way O. Henry and Guy de Maupassant did in their stories. So you decide the letter is from Clive's haberdasher in London, informing him that his new suits have been finished and are on the way. . . .

The letter turns out to be trivial, hardly worth Geoffrey's death or Clive's torture. Clive became a victim of his own imagination and Geoffrey a victim to his own stubbornness.

But this ending doesn't satisfy us. Why not? We expect more from the letter than a bit of trivial news; we expect the letter to go deeper into the personal lives of the two men. We expect the letter to contain some kind of secret.

Ending Two

The letter is from Geoffrey's girlfriend in London saying that she's making a surprise visit to the plantation, and since Clive was such a good friend, could he please help arrange a surprise reception?

This ending is more ironic because the girlfriend will indeed get a surprise reception, but not the one she anticipates. We also can't help wonder how Clive will explain her boyfriend's death.

This ending also explains why Geoffrey would choose that particular letter (since he would've seen his girlfriend's name and return address on the envelope). And it would explain why Geoffrey would refuse to show the letter to Clive. The letter contains a secret.

Perhaps this version of an ending better fits Maugham's "conclusion that leaves no legitimate room for questioning." Everything's been explained, and we are satisfied.

The difference between "Two English Gentlemen" and "The Whale Husband" is that "Two English Gentlemen" is a story on the verge of a plot. All it needs is a finish to make the story whole.

PAPA ARISTOTLE

Our lives are stories, not plots. Life is often a series of tenuously connected events, coincidences and chance. Real life is too ragged and rarely comes to the kind of conclusion that Maugham preferred, with "no legitimate room for questioning." No wonder life is stranger than fiction.

We prefer order to disorder in fiction. We prefer logic to chaos. Most of all, we prefer unity of purpose, which creates a *whole*. Wouldn't life be great if it contained nothing extraneous or coincidental, if everything that happened to us related to a main purpose? (Or would it? I have grave doubts.) "Two English Gentlemen" fell short of our expectations because the story didn't go "the distance." In other words, the story doesn't seem *whole*. It is a fragment begging a conclusion.

Aristotle, the grandpappy of dramatic theory, proposed some basic common denominators for drama that haven't changed all that much in nearly three thousand years. His concept of *unified action* lies at the heart of plot. Cause and effect. This happens *because* that happened, and so on.

What I'm about to repeat (via Aristotle) may sound so basic to you that it verges on the absurd, but bear with me. It's scary how many people have never grasped this fundamental principle:

A unified action creates a whole made up of a beginning, middle and an end.

We talked about the three movements in each of the three stories so far. The first movement constitutes the beginning, the second constitutes the middle, and the third, of course, constitutes the end.

In the Beginning

The beginning, commonly called the *setup*, is the initial action of the situation, presented to us as a problem that must be solved.

In "The Choking Doberman" it is when the woman comes home and finds her dog choking.

In "The Whale Husband" it is when the husband loses his wife to the Killer Whale (and, we assume, wants her back).

In "Two English Gentlemen" the beginning sets up the situation of two men, one of whom gets mail, while the other doesn't.

The beginning defines your characters and the wants of your major character (or characters). Aristotle says a character wants either happiness or misery. When you ask yourself "What does my character *want*?" you've begun the journey of plot. This want (or need) is called *intent*. In the stories we've looked at, the woman in "The Choking Doberman" wants to save her dog; the fisherman in "The Whale Husband" wants his wife back; and Geoffrey in "Two English Gentlemen" wants mail. Wanting something leads to motivation—why a character does what he does.

In the Middle

Once you've established the intent of your character(s), the story goes into the second phase, which Aristotle called the *rising action*. The character pursues her goal. The woman takes her dog to the vet; the fisherman, with mysterious help from Shark, goes to the Killer Whale's house; and Geoffrey offers to buy a letter from Clive. These actions come directly from intent.

The action clearly grows out of what happened in the beginning. Cause, now effect.

But the protagonist runs into problems that keep her from successfully completing intention. Aristotle called these barriers *reversals*. Reversals cause tension and conflict because they alter the path the protagonist must take to get to her intended goal. In "The Choking Doberman" the reversal comes as the telephone call from the vet. In "Two English Gentlemen" the reversal comes when Clive offers to buy back the letter and Geoffrey refuses. "The Whale Husband," however, doesn't have a reversal in it, and that's where it fails as a plot. The fisherman and the Shark simply complete their intention without resistances. Nothing stops them. No conflict, no tension.

After the reversal, Aristotle suggested something he called *recognition*, which is the point in the story where the relationships between major characters change as a result of the reversal. In "The Choking Doberman" recognition comes when the woman flees her house; in "Two English Gentlemen" it comes when the men fight over the letter.

A reversal is an event, but recognition is the irreversible emotional change within the characters brought about by that event.

Note that both reversal and recognition come from the story being told, not from out of the blue. In "The Whale Husband," help, in the form of Shark, comes from nowhere. In ancient days

this was called *Deus ex Machina*, which is Latin for
the Machine." In the old dramas, the playwright solv
lems of plot by having the gods take care of it. You'd w
ters suffer through their dilemmas, then suddenly soi
god would float out of a hole in the ceiling (attached to a rope that
the audience could see even from the back row), wave his magic
wand, and either solve everyone's problems or put them to death.
We no longer have patience for this kind of contrived ending.
Anything too convenient or too coincidental (sometimes called
idiot plot) turns us off. Mark Twain said it best: "The personages
of a tale shall confine themselves to possibility and *let miracles
alone.*"

In "The Choking Doberman," help comes from the veterinar-
ian, who has already been established in the story.

In screenplays, Hollywood plot structure tends to be formulaic.
The protagonist usually goes through two major reversals (sometimes called *plot points*). Only "Two English Gentlemen" has a
second reversal, one that builds on the heels of the first: when
Clive kills Geoffrey.

In the End

The final stage is the end, which contains the climax, the falling
action and the denouement. The ending is the logical outcome of
all the events in the first two phases. Everything that has happened to this point inevitably leads to a final resolution in which
all is exposed and clarified. We learn about the burglar with the
missing fingers; we discover the contents of the letter. Everything—who, what and where—is explained, and everything
makes sense.

Chapter Two

The Lowest Common Plot Denominators

And much of Madness, and more of Sin, / And Horror the soul of Plot.
— *Edgar Allan Poe*

In one sense, plot seems like a container. It holds everything. Figure out the shape of your story, add all the appropriate details, and somehow it will all set like concrete or Jello.

In another sense, plot is a force of cohesion, as I discussed in the first chapter. Whatever metaphor you choose to represent plot—whether it be a form, a road map or the force—its importance is inescapable. Without it, expect to drift aimlessly, never sure where you are or where you're headed.

Three thousand years of generating plots has given us some common denominators that hold up as a general rule. And like all general rules, they frequently are broken. Pablo Picasso was on target, however, when he said we must first learn the rules to know *how* to break them. So, it is within this spirit I present these common denominators.

LOWEST COMMON DENOMINATOR ONE: MAKE TENSION FUEL YOUR PLOT

Without tension, there is no plot. There is only a very short story and probably a very boring one. Remember the basic plot scenario "Boy Meets Girl"? Without tension (or conflict, if you prefer), the story would go something like this:

Boy meets girl.

Boy asks girl to marry him.

Girl says yes.

End of story.

What's the point? you ask yourself. So the main character's intention (or goal) is to marry the girl. She says yes. So what?

So now add tension.

Boy meets girl.

Boy asks girl to marry him.

Girl says no.

"Why not?" he demands.

"Because you're a drunk," she answers.

The tension comes from her denial. We get an explanation of her refusal. What he does next constitutes effect to the cause (his rejection). Whenever intention is denied, the effect is tension.

LOWEST COMMON DENOMINATOR TWO: CREATE TENSION THROUGH OPPOSITION

The role of the antagonist is to thwart the intention of the protagonist. This opposition can come in many forms. The antagonist may be external in the form of a separate person, place or thing, such as an enemy, a rival or a competitor. Or it may be internal — within the character of the protagonist, who may be trying to overcome some doubt, fear or flaw (such as alcoholism).

In "Boy Meets Girl," her rejection of his marriage proposal sets up a reaction on his part. He can walk away from her (which would be the end of the story) or he can decide to do something to overcome her objection (an effect to the previous cause). The girl's refusal to walk down the aisle is a *local* tension, which means it is the result of a conflict of the moment. Local tension doesn't have much of an effect beyond the immediate circumstances that created the tension. It would take some consummate skill to write an entire novel based on the girl's initial rejection of the marriage proposal (although it might be enough for a short story). A novel or a screenplay is made up of local tensions, but it is also made up of tensions that are more fundamental to the plot itself. If the boy decides he really wants to marry the girl, and realizes he must overcome her objection, that may mean overcoming his alcoholism. The tension of being an alcoholic (wanting to drink as opposed to not wanting to drink) is long-lasting. The immediate tension of the girl's refusal leads us directly to the larger conflict, which is whatever is in the boy's character that drives him to drink. We assume he drinks because of some inner conflict, and we want to know what it is and how he'll deal with it. So, on the one hand, the boy wants to marry his girl, but to do that he must give up drinking, and to give up drinking, he must overcome what is perhaps the real conflict of this story. . . .

LOWEST COMMON DENOMINATOR THREE: MAKE TENSION GROW AS OPPOSITION INCREASES

In our simple story you've seen how the chain of cause and effect builds and how it relates to conflict, which produces the tension you need to keep the story going. But a story requires constant tension. You must increase the tension as you build toward a climax. That means you can't rely on local tension alone; you need a larger conflict that can support the story. Back to our story:

The boy decides to give up drinking. But it's not that easy. (If it were, the story wouldn't be very interesting.) Now we're getting down to fundamental questions of character. Who is this person? What causes him to drink? Will he overcome his dependency? These are the questions the reader will ask and your job as writer is to address them in an interesting and creative way. Notice we've focused on the boy as the main character. His intention is clear: Give up drinking and get the girl. The girl's refusal created local tension and set up the story. The important conflict lies within the boy and whether he can deal with his own demons.

We want to keep our readers engaged in the action—another way of saying that we don't want the story to get stale—so we have the main character encounter along the way a series of barriers, which deepen the opposition. Each conflict gains intensity. Readers feel themselves being thrust toward the cataclysm, the climax, when all hell will break loose and the story will get resolved (for better or for worse). Local tension can't do this by itself, because local tension doesn't build intensity. All local tension does is create a series of equal roadblocks along the way that, after a while, can get boring. The serious conflicts, the ones that are the foundation of plot, are the ones that deal with the characters in fundamental ways.

Our story won't have made much progress if we revise it just to include local tension:

Boy meets girl.

Boy asks girl to marry him.

Girl refuses so long as he's an alcoholic.

Boy goes to Alcoholics Anonymous and gets cured.

Girl agrees to marry boy.

Well, there's a *germ* of something here. We have a story, but we still don't have a plot. The main character has an intention and it is denied, and he must do something to fulfill his intention — but his task doesn't seem all that tough the way it's presented here. He goes to A.A. and boom, he's cured. Anyone who's gone through anything like A.A. knows that isn't true. But at least you can now see the structure of beginning, middle and end:

Beginning: Boy meets girl and he asks her to marry him. Girl turns him down because he's an alcoholic.

Middle: Boy goes to A.A. and is cured.

End: The boy and girl get married and live happily ever after.

So what's the problem? How do you go about fleshing out this story so that you can deepen the opposition?

The conflict in the beginning is local: The girl turns down the boy. But where is the tension in the middle? Where is the tension in the end? There is none. The boy simply solves the problem. The crisis doesn't deepen.

To write a plot that will work here, you must develop the tension not just locally but at the deeper level as you investigate the character of the hero in crisis. It's not enough to have motivating action that gets the story going; you must continually test the character through each phase of dramatic action.

A simple example to study is the film *Fatal Attraction*, directed by Adrian Lyne and starring Michael Douglas and Glenn Close. It's a boy-meets-girl story with a twist. The story is simple enough: Michael Douglas's character has an extramarital one-night stand with a woman who is abnormally fixated on their relationship, and although he does everything he can to distance himself from this unbalanced woman, she reaches into his family with catastrophic effect.

Act I (Setup)

Boy meets girl. Boy is already married (local tension). Boy and girl go to bed together over a weekend while wife is out of town. When boy tries to go home, girl cuts her wrists.

Act II (Complications)

What is interesting about this film in terms of its complications is that they represent a series of escalations. The Glenn Close character begins to interfere with Michael Douglas's life in small ways, such as telephone calls and surprise visits. As Michael Douglas continues to push her away, her actions become increasingly more hostile and desperate. The Michael Douglas character realizes the threat to his marriage and begins to do what he can to cover up. But as the escalation increases and the woman's actions become more and more violent—climaxing in the grotesque killing of the family rabbit—he realizes the threat isn't just to his marriage, but to his family. The color and shape of survival have changed dramatically. The deranged woman then kidnaps their child, and the wife, in a panic, has a bad car accident. Watch the film analytically and notice that every time something happens, the stakes grow larger. The effect of action is to snowball, increasing tension and conflict from the mundane story of a man who's cheated on his wife to one who's battling a psychotic woman who's willing to kill to get her man.

Act III (Resolution)

In the last act the psychotic woman invades their house and tries to kill the wife. They battle it out in a terrifying sequence that includes all the members in this character triangle: wife, husband, mistress. What's interesting is that this film has three different endings, depending on which version you see. The standard ending shows the psychotic woman getting killed, but in the so-called "Director's Edit," which is available for rental, the ending is quite different. In it, the mistress kills herself in such a way that it looks like the husband is guilty of murder. (Reminiscent of Alfred Hitchcock's *Rebecca*, in which the wife does the same thing to her husband.) The husband is then arrested for murder. There is a third ending in which the wife finds evidence to show that the mistress was indeed suicidal, which she takes to the police who are holding her husband.

If we were to look at the structure in the third act, we would find a progression of events in each of the endings shown here:

Step I: The death of the mistress.

Step II: The arrest of the husband for her "murder."

Step III: The wife finds evidence to free her husband from the charge of murder.

Cause and effect. The ending released in theaters, however, only includes the first step. That might have been the best decision, or it might not. My only point here is to show how tension and conflict are carried through the entire story, regenerating in each act and constantly increasing the stakes.

LOWEST COMMON DENOMINATOR FOUR: MAKE CHANGE THE POINT OF YOUR STORY

We expect events to affect the main character in such a way that they force a change in his personality. Your main character should be a different person at the end of the book than at the beginning. If not, your character is static. Meaningful events change people in meaningful ways. In *Fatal Attraction* the change is minimal: We suppose Michael Douglas has learned his lesson and will never cheat on his wife again. The character is flat and static. The story could've been better if we could see the effects of the action as it changes his character. Instead, we must rely on the roller-coaster effect of events to keep us interested. The producers of the movie were more interested in cheap thrills than in exploring how such events affect a family, for the short and the long term.

Let's go back to the basic "Boy Meets Girl." Where are the meaningful events in the story?

There are none. We're supposed to believe that the boy's simple motivation to marry the girl is enough for him to overcome a deep-seated emotional problem. Well, you say, don't you know that love can conquer all? Of course it can, but there's no hint here that the girl does anything to help him through his crisis. We believe in the power of love, but we also know how the real world works, and we want to see opposition—love stacked against, say, his self-destructiveness. That would be a good source of conflict. But our story doesn't give us a clue.

As a result of events in the story, the character should somehow change. The hero of "Boy Meets Girl" may become a better person (provided he can overcome his obstacles), or he may find out that he's a slave to alcoholism and doesn't have the strength or motivation to overcome his affliction. With either ending, the character learns something about himself. He is different at the end than he was at the beginning of the story. This is the true test of events in your story. Ask yourself not only what should happen next, but how it will affect your hero's character.

LOWEST COMMON DENOMINATOR FIVE: WHEN SOMETHING HAPPENS, MAKE SURE IT'S IMPORTANT

On the surface this probably seems obvious. But a lot of writers either forget what it means or they don't really understand it.

As we write, we get swept up in the world we've created. The characters speak. They go places and do things. Part of being a convincing writer has to do with our ability to convince ourselves that the characters we write about are real. As a result of our vicarious participation in this fictional world, we often let the characters "go their own way" and say and do what they please. In a first draft I have no problem with giving characters their head. But unless you're a very disciplined writer, they'll end up going in every which direction. Once characters take on lives of their own, they become difficult to control. They may not share your sense of plot. They may have their own agenda and leave you astounded by their impudence. They defy you. They taunt you. You intended for them to be at a board meeting in New York and suddenly they're at a pig farm in Green Sleeve, Mississippi. They go off on tangents and become involved in situations that have nothing to do with your plot. You're tickled that your characters have such energy and that they drag you along with them, but at the same time you're appalled that they seem bent on ignoring you. Finally you realize you must stop everything and ask yourself, "Who's in charge here?"

To make matters worse, you read over what you've written

and realize it's really *good stuff*. In fact, it may be some of the better writing you've ever done. What should you do?

The answer is simple, and too often painful. It's all right to let yourself go when you write, because you're using the best part of your creative self. But be suspicious of what comes out. Plot is your compass. You should have a general idea of the direction you're headed in, and if you write something that doesn't specifically relate to the advancement of the plot, question it. Ask yourself, "Does this scene (or conversation, or description) contribute in a concrete way to my plot?" If the answer is yes, keep it. If the answer is no, chuck it. Fiction is a lot more economical than life. Whereas life allows in *anything*, fiction is selective. Everything in your writing should relate to your intent. The rest, no matter how brilliantly written, should be taken out.

This is often easier said than done, especially when some of your best writing fails to fulfill the intention of the plot. It's hard, very hard, to muster the courage to say, "This must go."

Novels are more generous than screenplays when it comes to accommodating excesses, and it's true that many master novelists loved their tangents. Laurence Sterne, author of the brilliant novel *Tristram Shandy*, called digressions the "sunshine" of reading. Take them out of a book and "you might as well take the book along with them; — one cold eternal winter would reign in every page of it. . . ." Feodor Dostoevsky claimed he couldn't control his writing. "Whenever I write a novel," he lamented, "I crowd it with a lot of separate stories and episodes; therefore, the whole lacks proportion and harmony. . . . [H]ow frightfully I have always suffered from it, for I have always been aware it was so." All right, you argue, if they can do it, why can't I?

First, you're not a nineteenth-century novelist. The shape of literature has changed in the last hundred years. Books are tighter and leaner. This reflects the age we live in. As readers, we don't want to take the time to wander off in all directions. We demand that the writer get to and stick with the point.

André Gide pointed out that the first condition of art was that it contain nothing unessential; a tight book walks the straight and narrow. Hemingway said write first and then take out all the good stuff and what's left is story. (By "good stuff" Hemingway meant all the material that the author has fallen in love with—not everything that was proper for the story.) Chekhov had the same idea when he said that if you show a shotgun in the first act, it must go off in the third act. Nothing in fiction exists incidentally. The world you create is much more structured and orderly than your own. So if you feel tempted to keep a passage that has a particularly well-written or moving scene but doesn't relate directly to the plot, ask yourself, "Is the writing so strong that the reader won't mind the side trip?" That's the trade-off: The more you make side trips, the more you dilute the effect of tension you've been trying to create, the more you dilute the drama itself. The novel is expansive and can tolerate many such excursions; the screenplay is intolerant and rarely allows any.

The writer, once trained, is intuitively aware of the need to stay close to plot. But no writer worth her salt doesn't occasionally succumb to the charm of her characters and head south.

LOWEST COMMON DENOMINATOR SIX: MAKE THE CAUSAL LOOK CASUAL

The point I've been trying to beat home is that everything in your writing has a reason, a cause that leads to an effect, which in turn becomes the next cause. If you accept the premise that good writing is cause and effect, we progress to the next stage, which says that good writing appears to be casual but in truth is causal.

No writer wants his fiction to be so obvious as to flash a neon sign that says **PLOT!** You don't want your causes to be so obvious that the reader can't fall victim to the charms of the story. You want to write in such a way that what you write about seems just a natural part of the world you've created. In the case of Chekhov's shotgun, we know the gun is important and will prove its importance by the end of the story. We know the shotgun wouldn't be included if it didn't have some relevant purpose to the plot. But that doesn't mean the writer should ram the shotgun down our throat. The writer should be nonchalant, *casual*, about introducing the shotgun to the reader's view. You would introduce it in such a way that the reader almost doesn't notice. *Almost.* But when the shotgun becomes important in a later act, the reader should remember seeing it in the first act.

Shirley Jackson's short story "The Lottery" illustrates the point on a larger scale. The title of the story cues us well. This is a story *about* a lottery. As we read the story we learn that a town holds an annual lottery and has been doing so since time immemorial. We focus on the mechanics of the lottery and the people involved. The lottery is the subject of the story, and we have no reason to be suspicious of it until the end of the story when we learn, to our surprise, that the winner of the lottery will be stoned to death by the other townspeople. Jackson's feat as a writer was similar to sleight of hand. She made us look one way when we should have been looking the other. As we read, we're more concerned about the mechanics of the lottery than what that lottery actually represents. We are caught off guard at the end and stunned when we learn the truth.

Ford Madox Ford, author of *The Good Soldier*, explained the concept clearly. He said the first thing the writer had to consider was the story. If you get away from story you will produce what Ford called a "longeur" which was, he said, "a patch over which the mind will progress heavily." You may have a great scene from your own life that you want to put into the story and, what the heck, the novel is big and forgiving and you figure you can put anything you want into it without really hurting the book. As long as it's *good*, right? Wrong, said Ford. If it doesn't push the story forward, it doesn't belong. Don't distract the reader with asides. What you are doing is *diluting* the dramatic effect. "A good novel needs all the attention the reader can give it," said Ford. Focus, focus, focus.

Of course you can *appear* to digress. What looks like an aside (the casual vs. the causal) is in truth important to the story. "That is," Ford said, "the art which conceals your Art." Ford believed the author insulted the reader by demanding attention, and if you gave your reader an excuse to walk away from the book, he would. Other delights always beckon us. So you should provide the reader with what appear to be, but aren't really, digressions. All pieces fit, all pieces are important. "Not one single thread must ever escape your purpose," warned Ford.

Ford's key concepts are that you should appear to digress (that is, make the causal seem casual), and in so doing, let the reader relax. But as the writer, you are always building your story, advancing your plot, with the reader unawares.

Let me explain it in cinematic terms. We've placed the props on the set of the first act. The shotgun is on the back wall. Depending on the director's shot, he can make the shotgun obvious, with a close-up of it, or he can camouflage the shotgun among the other objects in the room with a medium shot. The close-up calls attention to the shotgun, and anyone who's ever seen at least one murder mystery knows exactly what's afoot. But if the director is coy and doesn't make the shotgun obvious, it will appear unimportant. Only later, when the shotgun makes its next appearance, will the viewer realize how important it was.

This same rule applies for conversations and characters. By making the causal world appear casual, the reader accepts the convention that fiction is very much like life.

Only writers know it just ain't so.

LOWEST COMMON DENOMINATOR SEVEN: MAKE SURE YOU LEAVE LADY LUCK AND CHANCE TO THE LOTTERY

From time to time I hear a writer crowing, "I love being a writer. It's like being God. You create a world and you can do anything you want in it."

Here's where life and art stop imitating each other.

Life is chaos punctuated by short periods of order. From day to day we don't have the vaguest notion of what will happen. We may have plans, we may have schedules that say we should be at lunch at 12:30 with our sister-in-law at the Western Cafe, but, to paraphrase Robert Burns, there's many a slip between the cup and the lip. These are our guesses about how our day will go, but the truth is, as anyone can attest, life is always a gamble. Anything can intrude at any time. "Expect the Unexpected" should be our motto. If there is a chain of cause-and-effect relationships in our lives, it's under constant modification to consider current circumstances. And Lord only knows what current circumstances are from moment to moment. We live our lives provisionally, always adapting to what comes at us. Life is filled with long shots and unbelievable coincidences. The chances of anyone winning Lotto

America are about a zillion to one, but someone does win it. In life we expect things to happen out of the blue.

In fiction, we won't tolerate it.

This is the "hand of God" paradox. If you're God, you can do anything, at least in the world you create, right? Well ... not exactly. You must work under a load of restrictions. The first restriction states that you must create a world that has its own set of rules. Call it the rules of the game, if you want, but those rules must be consistent from beginning to end. Even the world Alice enters through the looking glass has its rules, and once we understand how they work, they make sense in their own way.

The second restriction states that when something happens in this world, it must happen for a reason. You can argue, of course, that everything in our own world happens for a reason, but if we can't make out what that reason is, we attribute it to chance, luck, coincidence. But fiction leaves no room for chance. The reason something happens must always be evident at some point in the story. Readers won't tolerate the unknown in fiction.

So you're not much of a god, after all. You still must play by the rules, even if they are your own rules. You've set up the game, so you're stuck with it. No out-of-the-blue solutions. (Remember Mark Twain's admonition to leave miracles alone?) Your readers won't let you concoct what they will perceive as ridiculous solutions. Avoid the easy way out, where the character just happens to be in the right spot at the right time.

The well-read person jumps out at this point and says, "Ha! What about Shakespeare! And Dickens, he's the worst offender of them all! How come they get away with it and we can't?"

It's true, the characters in both Shakespeare and Dickens are always in the right spot at the right time. They overhear conversations; they find evidence; they see things either at the most opportune or inopportune times. That's okay, because we understand these are devices to make the plot work, and we're more interested in the characters than in the plots themselves. After all, these are works about human character (note the titles: *Othello, King Lear, Hamlet, David Copperfield* and *Martin Chuzzelwit*). Such conventions were accepted at the time anyway, and that's not the case now. We demand more from fiction. We don't want plot contrivances.

LOWEST COMMON DENOMINATOR EIGHT: MAKE SURE YOUR CENTRAL CHARACTER PERFORMS THE CENTRAL ACTION OF THE CLIMAX

It is the essence of plot to ask a question. In *Hamlet*, for instance, the question is whether Hamlet will kill the king once he knows Claudius is responsible for his father's death. In *Othello*, the question is whether the Moor will regain his lost love for Desdemona. In *Cyrano de Bergerac*—whether the original version or Steve Martin's—the question is the same: Will he ever succeed in telling Roxane he loves her? In *Romeo and Juliet*, we wonder if Romeo can find happiness in his marriage to Juliet. And so on. Plot asks a question, and the climax answers it—oftentimes simply with a yes or no. In the case of Hamlet and Cyrano: Yes. In the case of Othello and Romeo: No.

Climax is the point of no return. The question is posed in Act I, and everything that happens between Acts I and III leads to the resulting action, the climax.

When you write the climax, however, don't forget the first rule: Your main character must perform the central action. Keep the main character in center stage of the action, and don't let her be overwhelmed by events to the extent that the events themselves act on her. Too often main characters disappear at the end, caught up in circumstances and events that diminish the purpose of the plot.

And don't let your antagonist or a secondary character perform the main action of the climax, either. Your main character should act, not be acted upon. Romeo kills Tybalt; Hamlet kills Polonius; Othello believes that Desdemona really gave Iago his handkerchief; and Cyrano checkmates de Guiche. These events lead directly to the final events: the deaths of Romeo, Juliet, Hamlet and Desdemona; and the winning of Roxane.

These, then, are some of the basic common denominators of plot. Now let's get down to the types of plots themselves—all two of them.

Chapter Three

The Strong Force

There are only two or three human stories, and they go on repeating themselves as fiercely as if they had never happened before.
— *Willa Cather*

In the course of researching this book, I read anyone who had anything to say about plot. After a while, I felt like I was reading cookbooks, with each author offering a recipe for success.

I'm not knocking other writers, because the best often have something valuable to say. In fact you'll find many of their comments scattered through this book.

What all writers have in common is a method. Once they get the method down, some of them then write a book about it. Those books should be titled "This Is What Works for Me," because readers who respect certain writers too often take their methods as gospel. These methods may be tried and true for those writers, but there's the mistaken assumption floating around that if it works for one person, it must work for everyone else, too.

Not so.

There's a method for each of us. The writer must know how he works *and* thinks in order to discover which method works best. Somebody like Vladimir Nabokov, who was meticulous and structured, laid out his work on index cards from beginning to end before writing the first word. Other writers, such as Toni Morrison and Katherine Anne Porter, began at the end. "If I didn't know the ending of a story, I wouldn't begin," wrote Porter. "I always write my last line, my last paragraphs, my last page first."

Other writers think that's a terrible idea. But then Anthony Burgess, the author of *A Clockwork Orange*, probably said it best when he described his method: "I start at the beginning, go on to the end, and then stop."

I don't bring this up to confuse you, but to make you think about your own work habits and the value of what other writers have to offer by way of advice. But remember what Somerset Maugham said the next time you come across something some great writer said: "There are three rules for writing a novel. Unfortunately no one knows what they are."

The trick for any author is to find out what works for him, and then do it. The same is true when it comes to plot.

How many plots are there? The real question is, "Does it really matter how many plots there are?"

Not really.

What matters is your understanding of the story and how to create a pattern of plot that works for it.

TO HELL AND BACK

The best place to start a discussion about plots is to trace their bloodlines to the beginning. By doing this, you should be able to understand the evolutionary tree from which all plots developed. It's not like studying some fossilized prehistoric ancestor that no longer walks the earth; on the contrary, the two basic plots from which all other plots flow are still the foundation of all literature. If you understand the essence of your plot, you will understand better how to go about writing it.

In Dante's *Inferno* there are only two basic sins in all the levels of Hell. One is called *forza*, crimes of violence and force. The other basic sin is called *forda*, which is Italian for fraud. Force and fraud. The damned who have been sent to Hell for crimes of violence weren't at the lowest circles of Hell; those were reserved for people who committed fraud, or sins of the mind. In Dante's mind, anyway, crimes of the mind were far worse than crimes of physical violence.

Dante understood human character. These two sins come from two basic functions of human beings. Force is power, strength, physicality. Fraud comes from wit, cleverness, mentality. The

Body and The Mind. If we look at plots, then, we should divide them into these two categories: plots of the body, and plots of the mind.

A clear representation of this duality is in Aesop's fables. The lion, a universal symbol of strength, represents force, power, physical strength. No one ever portrayed the lion as being particularly bright. Being strong was enough.

The fox, on the other hand, is portrayed as clever, witty and devious. His strength isn't physical, it's mental. We seem to take particular delight in those fables in which the physically weaker animal outwits the physically superior animal. In fairy tales, we take equal delight when the harmless child outwits the threatening ogre. We put a lot of stock in mental skills — more than we put in physical skills.

The Greek masks of tragedy and comedy embody the same idea. The frowning mask represents tragedy, which is the theater of force. The laughing mask represents comedy, which is the theater of fraud. The foundation of comedy is deception: mistaken identities, double meanings, confusion. Federico Garcia Lorca confirmed this when he said life is a tragedy for those who feel and a comedy for those who think.

Shakespeare's comedies verify this. Comedy often depends on language to be understood, so it is a form of *forda*. This was the genius of the Marx Brothers; they brought anarchy to language and turned the world of logic upside down.

Chico: "Pick a number between one and ten."

Groucho: "Eleven."

Chico (dismayed): "Right."

It makes no sense. But in the world of the Marx Brothers, somehow the number eleven can be found between one and ten. (Notice how jokes are never funny when you try to explain them?) This kind of shtick is completely mental — as were many of the Marx Brothers' funniest routines. Of course, they performed physical comedy brilliantly too, but there is a mentality operating even at the physical level. That was the genius of Charlie Chaplin, too. We understood the deeper pathos, the intellectual implications of his comedy, and understanding that made it sadly funny.

We have two plots then: *forza*, plots of the body, and *forda*, plots of the mind.

THE ACTION PLOT

You're at the beginning of the awesome task of starting your work. You have nothing but blank pages in front of you. You have an idea that may be completely sketched out in your head in what Nabokov called "a clear preview," or you may have a vague feeling of what you want to write and start with what Isak Dinesen called "a tingle." Aldous Huxley said he only had a dim idea of what he was going to write, and William Faulkner said all he had to start with was a memory or mental picture. Fine. Either you know everything or you know nothing. No help there.

What you should do based on your "clear preview" or your "tingle" is ask yourself which of the two plots most closely fits your idea. Is it an action story, an adventure that relies on doing? Or does your story deal more with the inner workings of character and human nature?

Most novels and films for the mass market fall into the first category. The public has a ravenous appetite for adventure stories, whether they're about Matt Helm and James Bond or Indiana Jones and Luke Skywalker. The racks of B. Dalton and Waldenbooks sag with these books. We love a good thriller for airports and the beach, whether it be by Tom Clancy, Robert Ludlum, Michael Crichton or any of a hundred others. We're addicted to movies series like *Alien*, *Lethal Weapon* and *Terminator* because of the sheer physical energy they exude. The motion is fast and furious, and we love the roller coaster ride. The primary focus of these books and films is *action*. Our main concern as readers or viewers is "What happens next?" The role of character and thought in these works is reduced pretty much to the bare necessities — enough so they can advance the action. That doesn't mean there can't be any character development at all; it just means that if you had to describe the book as either an action story or a character story, you would choose action because it dominates character by some degree.

With the action plot we don't really get involved with any great moral or intellectual questions. And at the end, the main character probably doesn't change all that much, which is convenient for a sequel. The action plot is a puzzle plot; we're challenged to solve some sort of mystery. Our rewards are suspense, surprise and expectation. Science fiction, Westerns, romances and detective novels usually — but not always — fall into this category. The great writers in these forms — Stanislaw Lem, Ray Bradbury, Arthur Conan Doyle and Robert Louis Stevenson, for instance — write more for the mind than for the gut.

PLOTS OF THE MIND

The author who is more concerned in plots of the mind delves inward, into human nature and the relationships between people (and the events that surround them). These are interior journeys that examine beliefs and attitudes. The plot of the mind is about ideas. The characters are almost always searching for some kind of meaning.

Obviously, serious literature favors this kind of plot over action plots. The plot of the mind examines life instead of just portraying it in some unrealistic way. Again, this doesn't mean that you can't include action in a plot of the mind. But in weighing the mental against the physical, interior against exterior, the mental and interior will dominate to some degree.

THE MEANING OF LIFE AND THE THREE STOOGES

Earlier I made the distinction between tragedy and comedy by saying tragedy is a plot of the body and comedy is a plot of the mind. Those were the original Greek distinctions, but things have changed in the last three thousand years. Now tragedy can be either plot. Comedy, however, seems firmly rooted in the Greek tradition.

A great comedic writer once said "Dying is easy; comedy is hard." Writing high drama is easy by comparison. No doubt about it, being funny is tough. The funniest line in the world can come off totally flat if told incorrectly. *Timing*, we've heard a thousand times, *is everything*.

Freud made the mistake of trying to analyze humor, and I won't make the same mistake here. But the reason comedy is so tough is that it appeals so much to the mind. Comedy is anarchy; it takes the existing order and stands it on its head. The whole concept of a double entendre is that it plays on another concept that the reader/viewer must already know to understand the humor.

Sure there's slapstick, a purely physical humor. The Three Stooges, for instance, seem anything but intellectual. But their comedy, however physical, lampoons society and its institutions. It's not just that they're throwing pies; it's whom they're throwing pies at: the prim and proper matron, the mortgage banker, all those stiff-shirted characters we live with daily. Their routines let us act out our own fantasies. A good comedic writer must make all these connections for us and give us emotional release, because we really want to throw those pies, too. However physical comedy gets, it has a strong undercurrent of the mind.

The true comic novel, Anthony Burgess pointed out, was the one that had to do with people's recognition of their unimportance in the universe.

Heady stuff for the Three Stooges.

DECIDING ON A PLOT

Once you've made the decision to write a novel or a screenplay, your next decision should be to decide which of the two plots your story will follow, because that shapes everything else you do.

Will your story be plot driven? If so, the mechanism of the story is more important than the specific characters themselves. The characters are there to make the plot happen. The novels of Agatha Christie are plot driven. So are the novels of Mickey Spillane and Dashiell Hammett, although their styles are entirely different. Each of those authors knew *going in* what kind of book they would write.

If your story is character driven, the mechanism of the plot is less important than the people themselves. Films such as *Driving Miss Daisy* and *Fried Green Tomatoes* are about people, and while they certainly have plots, those plots aren't center stage front. We're more intrigued by the characters. We're more intrigued by Kafka's Gregor Samsa than the unexplained reason he turns into a noxious bug. We're more interested in Anna Karenina and Emma Bovary and Huckleberry Finn and Jay Gatsby than we are in the plots behind them.

Know from the beginning where your focus will be. Will it be on the action? Or the people? Once you decide, you'll know what the *strong force* in your book will be. You'll eventually form a balance between the action and character, but you'll have a focus that will keep you from flip-flopping around. If you choose a plot of action, that will be your strong force; the aspects of your work that fall under the category of the mind will be your *weak force*. And vice versa: A plot of the mind can be the strong force, and its subsidiary qualities that deal with action will be the weak force. It can work either way, in any proportion you see fit, with one force dominating.

By choosing your strong and weak forces, your story will have proportion and consistency. You'll achieve *proportion* by establishing the relationship of one force to the other, and you'll achieve *consistency* by maintaining that relationship through the entire work.

Decide, and you'll have a starting place.

Chapter Four

Deep Structure

There are no dull subjects. / There are only dull writers.

> —H.L. Mencken

Y ou have made two major decisions to this point. You have an idea (sort of), and you've picked the strong force of your plot. What do you do next?

Before you try to figure out which plot pattern best suits your story, you must develop the idea for your story so that you can develop the deep structure.

Deep structure, like the strong force, guides development of your idea.

The central concept of deep structure is morality. Now don't freak out and think I'm saying that writing should somehow reflect the Ten Commandments or the precepts of Jesus or good, clean living. My use of the word *morality* here is much more basic than the meanings that first come to mind in our society.

Every piece of literature and every film ever made carries within it a moral system. It doesn't matter how artistic or rotten that work is, it contains a moral structure that gives us a sense of the world and how it ought to be. Either directly or indirectly, fiction tells us how to behave and how not to behave, what is right and what is wrong. It tells us what is acceptable behavior and what is unacceptable. This moral system holds only for the world created within that fiction. A work of fiction may reflect the same moral standards most of us share, or it may suggest that it's all right and maybe even desirable to cheat, lie, steal and sleep with your neighbor. The criminal isn't punished; in fact, she's rewarded.

It may be that the author is sloppy or lazy and doesn't understand or develop that moral system. It gets included by default and may be muddled, but it's there nonetheless. In bad works of writing we don't take these moral systems seriously; we dismiss them at face. In more serious works, in which the author is concerned with the implications of his moral system, it becomes serious food for thought; it becomes part of the message of the work itself. It doesn't matter if you're writing a romance, a mystery or the sequel to *Finnegan's Wake*. There's a world of difference between Albert Camus, whose works include a sophisticated system of morality, and a romance from Harlequin or Silhouette, which includes a simplistic moral system.

Your work, at least by implication, asks the question, "How should I act in these given circumstances?" Since every writer takes sides (a point of view), you tell your readers what's correct and incorrect behavior.

Take the book and film *Shane*.

Shane is a morality play. At the beginning, Shane comes out of the hills from nowhere (and back to nowhere at the end), which has had critics compare him to a frontier Jesus Christ, the Greek god Apollo, Hercules and a knight errant. Shane is a mysterious man, but he has a strong code of behavior. He brings his strength to the homesteaders, which gives them strength to fight the greedy, cruel cattlemen. Even when Shane is tempted by the homesteader's wife, Marion, he remains at all times dedicated to his moral system. We are left with nuances, moments of electricity between her and Shane, but he doesn't waver. Shane is a moral standard. He brings faith to the valley and the wicked are destroyed.

The morality of *Shane* parallels our Judeo-Christian ethics. We recognize proper behavior. Other works might suggest behavior that runs contrary to what we've been taught. The wicked aren't always destroyed. Sometimes they come out on top. Crime *does* pay.

As writers, we have the right to choose whatever moral system we want to portray and draw whatever conclusions we want from that system. But if we really want to reach someone, we must be *convincing*.

Easier said than done.

Most of what we read isn't very convincing when it gets down to the core morality of the work. If you write a serious book, you want to create an argument for this kind of behavior that is so powerful it will affect the reader in her own life. A tough task. If you write a book for entertainment only, however, your goal is simpler: You want to create an argument that works in the world of the book. It doesn't have to carry over into the world and change lives. Only the greatest of works and most talented of writers have the genius to affect our lives in large ways. I suspect good works (as opposed to great works) affect us in small ways. Even bad works affect us.

What is this argument? How do you make it convincing? The argument is the heart of your deep structure, and you must know how to fashion that argument so it's convincing.

A WORD ABOUT TWO-TIMING

Our way of dealing with the complications of the world is to simplify them into either/or arguments. We divide the world into opposites. We try, in vain, to make everything black and white.

We know the world isn't that simple, that most of life is in the gray range. But our way of thinking is so dedicated to opposites that it's impossible to escape them. Everything is good or bad, ugly or beautiful, light or dark, up or down, rich or poor, weak or strong, happy or sad, protagonist or antagonist. We divide the world to better comprehend it. We divide to simplify. Instead of an infinite number of states, we pretend there are only two.

It doesn't take much to realize this perception won't do if we're trying to get serious about the true nature of love, happiness or whatever. You must give up black-and-white thinking and examine the grays. The trouble with grays, however, is that there are no easy solutions.

Therein lies the key.

Easy solutions are . . . easy. They represent clichéd thinking. Good vs. bad. One character is kind-hearted, brave, sincere and on a mission, but the other character is dark-hearted, cowardly, insincere and intent on stopping the good character from reaching his goal. We know this pattern inside out — so well, in fact that we don't have to read the rest of the story. We know who's supposed to win and who's supposed to lose, and we know *why*. There won't be many surprises here. White hats vs. black hats. And because the readers know they're supposed to root for the good guy and despise the bad guy, the writer really can't put any twists in the story. Unless the reader is in a really perverse mood, she's been pulling for the good guy all along — and then he doesn't make it? Definitely a Hollywood taboo.

There's no challenge here. As a writer, you may dazzle us with your fancy footwork (the action), but underneath it all is nothing. Sure, no one cares about the moral universe of Indiana Jones or James Bond. They're good guys, and good guys fight evil, period. Strip away the action, and there's nothing left.

The author's task is to move into the world of grays, where there are no obvious or even right answers. Into a world where decisions are always risky because you aren't sure if they're the right decisions. The author who takes a simplistic point of view isn't interested in understanding the complex human dynamics of life or the difficulty of decisions we must make.

The deep tension (as opposed to local tension) I talked about in the earlier chapter comes from impossible situations, situations where there is no clear right or wrong, no clear winner or loser, no clear yes or no. *Put your main character between a rock and a hard place.* That's the true source of tension in fiction.

HOW TO GET BETWEEN A ROCK AND A HARD PLACE

We each have our prejudices, rooted in our own moral system. If you were a god and could fashion any world you wanted, your fiction would reflect that world. In your world, crime would never go unpunished. Or ex-wives or husbands. Or politicians. In your world, the Chicago Cubs might win the World Series; the Indianapolis Colts might win the Super Bowl. The mind boggles at the opportunities for you to set things straight — at least on paper. You're a god, remember? You can do what you want.

If you still entertain any delusions of grandeur about being all-powerful, this is the time to lose them. The writer is a slave, not a god. You're a slave to your characters and to the premise of your story. If you must find a model to represent the status of the author, it would be not as a god but as a referee.

Conflict depends on conflicting forces. In the one corner you have a force (let's say the protagonist), and the force has an objective: to win, to solve, to free . . . always an infinitive. In the other corner you have an opposing force (the antagonist), and this force has an objective too: to block the protagonist. That's important to plot, and it's been drilled into you since you were old enough to read. Little Red Riding Hood's objective is to reach Grandmother's house. The wolf's objective is to eat Little Red Riding Hood. And so on.

The same concept of opposing forces applies to ideas as well. *Writing a story without presenting a meaningful opposing force is propaganda.*

Let me explain. As a writer you have your point of view—your prejudices, if you will. Let's say you were a battered wife for twelve years, the victim of a controlling and abusive husband. When you go to write about it, the story unfolds as it happened:

He storms in from work at night, throws his jacket down on the sofa and demands, "What's for dinner?"

"I made you a lovely duck à l'orange, dear." The table is set with their best china and crystal; the candles are lit. She's obviously gone to a lot of trouble for him.

"Duck! You know I hate duck. *Can't you ever do anything right?* Make me a sandwich."

A tear collects in the corner of her eye, but she accepts his abuse stoically. "What kind of sandwich?"

"I don't care," he says abruptly. "And get me a beer."

He turns on the television and is gone.

Enough.

I don't have to go on. You know the score and you know the story. The characters are already defined as types. She is the silent-suffering, kind-hearted, devoted wife; he is the loud, obnoxious, cruel husband. You can't wait for him to get his comeuppance. You hope he suffers.

But this is propaganda.

Propaganda?

The author's point of view here is obvious and one-sided. I've sided with the wife and have exaggerated her just as I've exaggerated the husband beyond belief. They're *types*. "Begin with an individual and you find that you have created a type," wrote F. Scott Fitzgerald, "begin with a type and you find that you have created — nothing." The author is trying to settle a personal score. The fiction may be therapeutic and help the writer work out hostility, but that's not the purpose of fiction if you intend to show it to someone else. The purpose of fiction is to tell a story, not to get even or to work out your own personal problems.

You can always tell propaganda because the writer has a cause. The writer is on a soapbox lecturing, telling us who is good and who is bad and what is right and what is wrong. Lord knows we get lectured to enough in the real world; we don't read or go to the movies so someone else can lecture to us some more. If you use your characters to say what *you* want them to say, you're writing propaganda. If your characters say what *they* want to say, you're writing fiction. Isaac Bashevis Singer claimed characters had their own lives and their own logic, and that the writer had to act accordingly. You manipulate characters in the sense that you make them conform to the basic requirements of your plot. You don't let them run roughshod over you. In a sense, you build a corral for your characters to run around in. The fence keeps them confined to the limitations of the plot. But where they run *inside* the corral is a function of each character's freedom to be what or who he/she wants *within the confines of the plot itself.*

Jorge Luis Borges said it best: "Many of my characters are fools and they're always playing tricks on me and treating me badly."

More of a slave than a god.

How, then, do you avoid writing propaganda? First start with your attitude. If you have a score to settle or a point to make, or if you're intent on making the world see things *your* way, go write an essay. If you're interested in telling a story, a story that grabs us and fascinates us, a story that captures the paradoxes of living in this upside-down world, write fiction.

Start with a premise, not a conclusion. Start with a *situation*.

Let's go back to our married couple. She was the saint and he was Satan. Not very interesting. Why not? Too one-sided. The story can't go anywhere. We'll side with the saint because we have no sympathy for or understanding of Satan. Our emotional response is just as stock as the characters: "Poor dear, why does she put up with it? C'mon, honey, *fight back!*" And to him we say, "You dumb, cruel S.O.B. Boy, are you going to get it!" That story is on autopilot; it doesn't need a writer or a reader.

The fatal flaw in the story is its blatant one-sidedness. She's too good, and he's too bad. Life doesn't work that way. As human beings, we all contain a light and a dark side, and real characterizations capture that without prejudice. What is the dark side of the wife? In what way is she responsible for this horrible state of affairs? And what about him? Yes, he's cruel and abusive, but how did he get that way? In his own way, he's as much a victim as she is. When you stop taking sides and start thinking about these two as *people*, you begin to understand why they act as they do. The difference is that the author is interested in writing about the *situation* and writing about it fairly. Let the characters duke it out if they want, but you're the referee, and you must make sure that the situation is the prime concern. Don't let a character take control of the situation to the extent that it becomes one-sided. Make sure they stay in the ring together, and give them equal time. John Cheever made the point: "The legend that characters run away from their authors — taking up drugs, having sex operations and becoming president — implies that the writer is a fool with no knowledge or mastery of his craft. The idea of authors running around helplessly behind their cretinous inventions is contemptible." The referee, not the characters, controls the situation.

A good example to study of the husband-wife story that shows two real people struggling to put their lives in order is Robert Benton's film, *Kramer vs. Kramer* (1979), with Dustin Hoffman and Meryl Streep. It's a moving story because there is no villain. Both characters are caught between a rock and a hard place. There are no clear and "right" decisions. Joanna Kramer "abandons" her son and her marriage, but we understand what drove her to that extreme, and when she comes back later to fight for her son, we understand why she's come back. We feel for both parties and we feel their mutual agony. Nothing is easy here. There's no one to root for, no villain we can point our finger at and say, *"You!"*

What we get in *Kramer vs. Kramer* are opposing views: the wife's point of view *and* the husband's point of view. The two points of view clash. The clash gives us conflict. Opposing views means you're responsible for giving not just one argument, but two separate arguments, each of which opposes the other. This is the essence of being between a rock and a hard place.

Tolstoy captured this idea perfectly: "The best stories don't come from 'good vs. bad' but from 'good vs. good.' "

Kramer vs. Kramer is a story of "good vs. good." And the trick to capturing "good versus good" is in the quality of the opposing arguments.

HOW TO CREATE OPPOSING ARGUMENTS

Opposing arguments are the result of irreconcilability. They grow when there is no definitive answer to a problem; there are only temporary, operational solutions that may work in a certain place on a certain day but not in all places on all days. Most of the great issues of our day are irreconcilable: abortion, euthanasia, capital punishment, divorce, custody, homosexuality, revenge, temptation — to name a few. The hottest irreconcilable argument today in the United States is that of abortion. There are two arguments, one for each side of the issue. Either abortion is wrong because it is murder of an unborn child, or it's not wrong because an unviable fetus cannot be considered a living thing. This is a simple rendition of the arguments, which are much more complex, of course, but the point is that the issue is seen from completely different points of view, from opposite sides of the fence. There is no absolute solution, only temporary ones, which come in the form of Supreme Court decisions such as *Roe vs. Wade*, and even then, those decisions are subject to review and reversal. Sure, we have our own personal belief: Abortion is wrong or not, and we subscribe to one or the other argument. We take sides. But is it the author's role to take sides when writing fiction? If you think it is, you're writing propaganda: Your characters are in service to the idea *you* want to get across. If you think it's the author's responsibility to tell the best story possible and not preach, you have little choice but to present a situation that includes *both* sides of the argument sympathetically. Only then is your character between a rock and a hard place.

Both arguments should be logical. If you're serious about presenting both sides of an issue and capturing your character in the middle, it's important that both sides of the issue be valid. Don't put all your energy into the solution you prefer and then create a weak argument that represents the opposite view in a token way. That's cheating. For every point you make on one side of the argument, show an equally powerful point on the other side of the argument. If you don't, the reader will see through you, and you'll lose the source of your conflict.

Both arguments should be valid. By *valid* I mean well-founded. We should recognize the arguments as being truly possible arguments in our world. Let's return to the irreconcilability of the topic of abortion and create a woman who is caught unmercilessly between both arguments. Her name is Sandy and she's a deeply religious woman. A Catholic. Her religion has told her all her life that abortion is a mortal sin. She believes what her church has taught her and in her soul she believes abortion is wrong.

Then Sandy's raped. The violence shakes her emotionally.

Then she finds out she's pregnant.

The law says she's entitled to an abortion on demand. Sandy hates the fetus growing inside her; every day she is reminded of the awful crime against her. The thought of having her rapist's child is more than she can take. The child would always be a reminder. But her religion says she will be damned if she has the abortion.

Damned in this life if she doesn't have an abortion and damned in the next life if she does. Classic irreconcilability. Both arguments are logical, and they're both valid. How can she save herself? Or should she sacrifice herself to bear the child? She could give the child up for adoption — but then, the child is half *hers* too. The more she seeks a solution, the less chance there seems to be in finding one. This is the true source of conflict.

Both arguments should be compelling. *Logical* and *valid* are not enough in and of themselves. They are intellectual aspects. For an argument to be compelling, it should appeal to us emotionally as well. As a writer, you aren't concerned with teaching your reader the "right" thing to do under these circumstances. You're concerned with putting the reader in the shoes of your protagonist, making the reader "feel" for Sandy and understand the complexity of her dilemma, so the reader understands that there are no easy solutions and that someone, anyone, who has the misfortune to have this happen would suffer terribly.

That is the essence of a compelling argument.

There you have it. To develop deep structure, you must develop an irreconcilable argument that has two mutually exclusive sides, both of which are equally logical, valid and compelling.

SOMETIMES DOING THE RIGHT THING IS WRONG AND SOMETIMES DOING THE WRONG THING IS RIGHT

Let's take a closer look at the whole question of good and evil.

There are two worlds. One is the "oughta be" world and the other is the "as is, where is" world. The "oughta be" world is the one we'd like to live in. In this world, good is good and evil is evil and the division between the two is as large as the part in the Red Sea. When situations occur, the decisions are obvious, the results clear. However . . .

The world we live in has few clear decisions and probably even fewer clear results. The water is rarely, if ever, clear. The black-and-white world of "oughta be" gives way to a hundred shades of gray in the "as is, where is" world. We know how we should act in different situations, but when those situations come up in our lives, *it's never that clear or easy.*

Sometimes situations force us to reexamine what is right and what is wrong. We've all been in situations where doing the right thing was obviously the wrong thing to do, and in situations where doing the wrong thing was obviously right. It may start with something simple, such as telling a little white lie to spare someone's feelings. Or it may end up with a decision to do something of catastrophic proportions. That's when the phrases *the end justifies the means* and *rules are made to be broken* come in handy.

If the morality in your work deals with traditional concepts of right and wrong and the basic moral dilemmas that we are all faced with at some point in our lives, take a closer look at those dilemmas. Forget easy solutions. They don't help and they rarely work. Worse, they're of little comfort for the character who must suffer through a complicated moral issue when all he has are a bunch of clichés at hand. We live in the "as is, where is" world, and the issues that plague us (and our characters) most are the ones that defy simple solutions.

Gray areas allow irreconcilability, where action is neither wrong nor right. In the absence of absolute solutions ("this is *always* the right thing to do"), there must be artificial or operational ones, ones that work for your character in those specific circumstances. What is "right" in our society is often decided arbitrarily by artificial means (by the courts or by social consensus, for instance), but life constantly throws situations at us in which abiding by the law is wrong. Effect? Moral dilemma. Do you obey the law? Or do you break the law for what you consider a greater good? Where do you draw the line? *How* do you draw the line?

These are the real issues that confront us every day.

Whatever approach you take to your story, and whatever kind of moral system is at work, try to develop your idea so that you create the dynamic tension of irreconcilability. Be consistent and be fair to both sides of the issue.

Chapter Five

Triangles

What is character but the determination of incident? / What is incident but the illustration of character?

—*Henry James*

This chapter is about the relationship between character and plot. It's strange, in a way, to separate the discussion of character from the other elements—it's like talking about each part of a car engine individually and not how the parts all work together—but some considerations of character as they relate to plot bear discussion. The previous chapters included discussion about characters to some degree because I wanted you to see how the primary elements relate and depend on each other. You don't separate these elements when you write. Everything comes to bear all at once. I don't know of any writer who sits down at the word processor and says, "Okay, this morning I'm going to write character." And yet that's how most books treat the subject: "Okay, now we're going to talk about character." Henry James is right: When a character *does* something, he becomes that character, and it's the character's act of doing that becomes your plot. The two depend on each other.

First let's look at the dynamics of character in plot.

People relate to each other. When Alfred (A) walks into a room and sees Beatrice (B) for the first time, he falls in love. Alfred asks Beatrice out but she tells him to get lost. The story is under way.

The character dynamic here is two. That doesn't mean it's two because there are two people, but because there are a maximum of two character and emotional interactions possible: A's relationship to B, and B's relationship to A.

Add a third major character, Chuck (C). Beatrice loves Chuck, not Alfred. The character dynamic in this case is not three, but *six*, because there are six possible emotional interactions:

- A's relationship to B;
- B's relationship to A;
- A's relationship to C;
- B's relationship to C;
- C's relationship to A;
- C's relationship to B.

Now add a fourth major character, Dana (D). Chuck loves Dana, not Beatrice or Alfred. The character dynamic is now *twelve*, with twelve emotional interactions possible:

- A's relationship to B, and B's to A;
- A's relationship to C, and C's to A;
- A's relationship to D, and D's to A;
- B's relationship to C, and C's to B;
- B's relationship to D, and D's to B;
- C's relationship to D, and D's to C.

As a writer, you certainly aren't obliged to cover *every* angle of all the possible relationships. But you'll find that the more characters you add to the mixture, the more difficult it will become to keep up with all of them and to keep them in the action. If you include too many characters, you may "lose" them from time to time—in effect, forget about them—and when you try to bring them back into the action it will seem forced and artificial. Pick the number of characters that you feel comfortable with. That number should allow maximum interaction between characters to keep the reader interested, but not so many that you feel like you're in the middle of an endless juggling act.

Don't even think of adding a fifth major character. If you did, the character dynamic would be *twenty*. (Sounds like a nineteenth-century Russian novel, doesn't it?)

Obviously it would be hard if not impossible to keep up with the emotional relationships and interactions with a dynamic of twenty. Think of the incredible burden on the writer trying to juggle twenty character interactions simultaneously. Juggling twelve is possible, but it takes great skill: You'd have major characters going in and out of phase constantly, with usually no more than three majors in a scene at any one time, except for big confrontation scenes and the climax.

Now let's go to the other extreme and look at the original scenario of two major characters with a dynamic of two. We're confined to seeing how Alfred acts in the presence of Beatrice and how Beatrice acts in the presence of Alfred. The situation doesn't offer us the flexibility we need to be comfortable developing their characters. Of course it's been done, and done well, particularly on the stage. But having just two major characters limits what you can do with those characters, and you'll need to be a strong, inventive writer to overcome the handicap.

This brings us to the Rule of Three. If you pay attention to the structure — whether it's the classic fable or fairy tale or folktale, or a B-movie on television — you'll notice that the number three holds strong sway. Character *triangles* make the strongest character combination and are the most common in stories. Events also tend to happen in threes. The hero tries three times to overcome an obstacle. He fails the first two times and succeeds the third.

This isn't a secret numerology thing. There's actually a rather obvious reason for it: balance. If the hero tries to do something the first time and actually does it, there's no tension. If the hero tries to do it twice and succeeds the second time, there is some tension, but not enough to build on. The third time is the charm. Four times and it gets boring.

The same is true with characters. One person isn't enough to get full interaction. Two is possible, but it doesn't have a wild card to make things interesting. Three is just right. Things can be unpredictable but not too complicated. As a writer, think about the virtues of the number three. Not too simple, not too complicated — just right.

Which brings us to the classic triangle: three major characters with a dynamic of six. Now you'll have room to move. The romantic comedy *Ghost*, with Patrick Swayze, Whoopi Goldberg and Demi Moore, gives us a clear model. In the story Swayze and

Moore's characters are in love; he's killed during a mugging. He becomes a ghost but can't communicate with her.

Enter Goldberg, a fake psychic, who learns (to her surprise more than anyone's) that she really *can* communicate with the dead (Swayze). This is more than she can take, and she wants no part of it. But Swayze convinces her she must talk to Moore because she's in danger (from the man who had him killed).

If the story had been set up that Swayze's character could talk directly to Moore's from the beyond, the story wouldn't have any real tension to it. But since he must talk through a third and thoroughly unlikely person (we find out she's got a record for being a con artist), the plot suddenly takes on greater depth and comic possibilities:

1. Swayze must convince Goldberg that he's a ghost and is talking to her from the great beyond, then

2. Goldberg must convince Moore that she really can talk to her dead boyfriend.

All six character interactions take place in the story:

- Moore relates directly to Goldberg and indirectly (through Whoopi) to her dead boyfriend;
- Swayze relates directly to Goldberg and indirectly (again through Whoopi) to his living girlfriend;
- And Goldberg (as the medium) relates directly to both Swayze and Moore.

The character triangle looks like this:

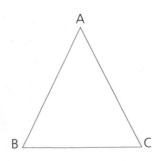

It's a tight package with a twist that works well.

Or take another ghost story, the Gothic romance *Rebecca* by Daphne du Maurier (later made into a film by Alfred Hitchcock).

The setup is simple: Dark, brooding and mysterious Maxim de Winter brings back a naive, head-over-heels-in-love bride to his estate, where the memory of his dead wife Rebecca still looms very large, especially through the character of the housekeeper, a sinister woman who was (and still is) entirely dedicated to the dead woman. De Winter is haunted by his beautiful, dead wife and cannot return the love his new wife lavishes on him.

In *Rebecca*, the ghost of the dead wife doesn't literally stalk the halls of the mansion, but she does figuratively. Reminders of her are everywhere. The new wife (who curiously never has a name in the film) cannot overcome the presence of the old wife. To make matters worse, the housekeeper plots the new wife's destruction.

All three points of the triangle are developed:

- Maxim de Winter's relationships to the housekeeper and his new wife (both of which are affected by Rebecca);
- The housekeeper's relationships to de Winter and his new wife (again both affected by Rebecca); and
- The new wife's relationships with her husband and the housekeeper (you guessed it, all affected by Rebecca).

Rebecca, whom we never see in flashback or ghostly vision, affects everyone and everything in this story. So the triangle looks different because all three major characters are affected by a fourth character *who never appears*. The triangle then, would look like this:

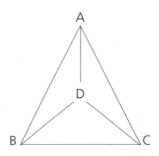

In terms of sophistication of plot, *Rebecca* is the better story. *Ghost* is simple and straightforward and clever, but it lacks depth of character. We enjoy it mainly because of its cleverness, which is manifested through humor. *Rebecca*, on the other hand, even with its Gothic coloring (cliffs and storms and huge, hollow castles) deals more with people.

So when you develop your opposing forces in your deep structure, decide which level of character dynamic you want in your book. Ask yourself how many major characters best suits your story: two? three? four? And understand the consequences of having two, three or four major characters.

THE DYNAMIC DUO

Plot and character. They work together and are inseparable. As you develop your story, remember that the reader wants to understand why your major characters do what they do. That is their motivation. To understand why a character makes one particular choice as opposed to another, there must be a logical connection (action/reaction). And yet you shouldn't have the character behave predictably, because then your story will be predictable (a nice way of saying *boring*).

At times the character's behavior should surprise us ("Why did she do *that*?"), but then, upon examining the action, we should understand why it happened. Just because there's a logical connection between cause and effect doesn't mean it has to be obvious.

Aristotle felt that characters became happy or miserable as a result of their actions. The process of becoming happy or miserable is plot itself. The events that happen to the protagonist change her. That change will probably leave her happier or sadder (and perhaps wiser). Aristotle put plot before character. Today we don't agree that must be the case. But it is true that we understand *who* a person is by what he *does*. Action equals character. What a character says about himself isn't that important. Paddy Chayefsky, the author of such films as *Network* and *Hospital*, said that the writer is first obligated to create a set of incidents. Once you've established those incidents (plot beats), you should create characters who can make those incidents happen. "The characters take shape in order to make the story true," said Chayefsky.

Your character will come to life by doing, not by sitting around and telling us what she feels about life or about the crisis of the moment. *Do*, don't just *say*. Then your major characters will develop in relation to the other characters in your story.

There's a short scene in *Lawrence of Arabia* that gives insight into the main character. The point of the scene is to show that Lawrence is determined to achieve his goal, whatever the personal cost. He harbors an almost pathological fear that he's too weak to accomplish his goal of uniting a fractured Arabia. He's not your typical macho type out to conquer the world; in fact, Lawrence is afraid of any kind of pain. It would be easy for him to sit around with some of his buddies and say, "Gee, fellas, I'm not sure I'm really up to this task." Talk is cheap.

The scene in the film is far more intense and doesn't have a single word of dialogue. Pure action. Alone, Lawrence lights a match and holds it between his fingers until the flame burns him. In the context of the story this isn't bravado. We know Lawrence is afraid of pain, so we understand when he tries to overcome that fear by letting the match burn his fingers. This scene becomes important later in the film, when Lawrence is captured and tortured by the Turks.

Plot, then, is a function of character, and character is a function of plot. The two can't be divided in any meaningful way. Action is their common ground. Without action there is no character, and without action there is no plot.

A final note: Later in this book I divide plots into action-based and character-based plots. You might ask yourself how I can make those distinctions when I've just said that character and action can't be divided. Well, obviously they can be. The division is based on your focus. If you as a writer are more interested in writing a story about events (action) and create your characters to make the action happen, you're writing an action-based plot. Your focus isn't on people but on events. If, on the other hand, you write a story in which characters are the most important element, you have a character-based plot.

Chapter Six

Twenty Master Plots: Prologue

Adam was the only man who, when he said a good thing, knew that nobody had said it before him.

—*Mark Twain*

The rest of this book is dedicated to twenty master plots and how they are constructed. That may sound odd after my telling you there are only two master plots, as if they had somehow mutated and increased their power by ten. The truth still holds about plots of the mind and plots of the body, and in these twenty are examples of both categories. Beyond the basic two plots, it doesn't matter which number you come up with, whether it's Gozzi's thirty-six plots or Kipling's sixty-nine, or whatever. As I said before, it's only a matter of packaging. I present these twenty basic plots as a way of showing the different types of patterns that emerge from *forda* (stories of the mind) and *forza* (stories of action).

The key word is *pattern*: patterns of action (plot) and patterns of behavior (character), which integrate to make a whole. The master plots that follow are general categories such as revenge, temptation, maturation and love; and from these categories an infinite number of stories can flow. But my primary concern in presenting these plots is to give you a sense of the pattern, not to give you a template so you can trace the design (although you could if you wanted to). As contemporary writers, we are all under a terrific strain to be original, to make the big breakthrough, though no one has any idea what that means. These plot patterns are as old as the hills and in some cases older. But that doesn't mean they've lost their effectiveness; rather, time proves their worthiness, their importance to us. We use the same plots today that were used in the world's oldest literature. Plot is one of the few aspects in all of art that isn't subject to fashion. We may favor certain types of plots over others during a particular historical period, but the plots themselves don't change.

THE QUEST BEGINS

So what does this quest for originality mean? Find a new plot that no one has used before? Obviously not, because plots are based on common human experience. If you found a plot that had never been used before, you're into an area that is outside the realm of shared human behavior. Originality doesn't apply to the plots themselves but to how we present those plots.

Each plot seems to have its own character, its own flavor. If you're serious about becoming a writer, you must learn from what others have done before you. That's why I give a lot of examples in each of these chapters about master plots. The more you read, the more you'll understand the nature of the pattern. You'll understand where you can bend and shape the plot and where you can't. You'll understand what the reader expects and what the reader rejects. You'll learn the "rules" for each plot, and then learn how to break those rules to put a new spin on the plot. I've never come across a writer, no matter how great (that is, "original"), who didn't admit to getting his ideas from others. Lionel Trilling made it clear: "Immature artists imitate. Mature artists steal." (That's odd, because T.S. Eliot said, "The immature poet steals; the mature poet plagiarizes." Who stole from the other?)

Everyone steals to some degree. If Shakespeare, Chaucer and Milton were alive today, they'd spend half their time in court trying to explain where they got their stories. (In those days it was okay to steal another person's story, as long as you made it *better*.) We all have our sources, and we rely heavily on them.

Proceed, then, with confidence. Plots are in the public domain. Use and abuse them at will. Find the plot that most closely fits your story. Don't be afraid to tailor a plot to your specific idea. Don't hold rigid to the ideas. Mold, shape, form. Don't lose sight of the general rhythm that these plots have created over time, however. What are the basic movements in the plot? If you start to cut out movements, you may do more damage than good. These plots have taken centuries to evolve.

The trick in learning how to use plot is not copying but adapting it to the needs of your story. As you read over the master plots, try to match your idea with the basic concepts that these plots employ. It might very well be that your idea fits two, three or even more of these plots.

That means you need to shape your idea more than you already have. This is the first major decision you must make, and it will affect everything else that you do. So ask yourself as you read the outline of each of these major plots, "Does this plot offer me what I need in terms of story and character? How well does my idea fit with the plot?" If it doesn't fit exactly, don't let that bother you; the plots as I've described them are more or less "middle of the road," and they are very flexible. But each plot does have a basic thrust to it, which is the force that will guide your story-telling. Make sure you're comfortable with it. If not, read the others and then decide which fits your idea the best.

Shaping ideas is a constant process for most writers. They don't have everything mapped out absolutely before they begin writing. A writer's blueprint doesn't have to look like an architect's blueprint. You should have an idea and a sense of what you want to do with that idea (plot). But that sense may change one time, a dozen times or a thousand times during the course of the writing. Don't let that unnerve you. If you feel you need a guide to follow, use the master plot outlines in this book to give you a sense of what you need to accomplish in each of the plot's major movements. Say to yourself, "All right, in the first movement, some event should happen that forces my protagonist to start her life over. What should that event be? How can I be convincing?" This book will give you the guidelines; use them and adapt them, but don't get boxed in by them.

Don't feel bad about adapting the plot to your needs. What these plots will show you are their basic patterns. As you write, you'll embellish the pattern—that's a natural part of the process.

Chapter Seven

Master Plot #1: Quest

While many things are too strange to be believed, nothing is too strange to have happened.

— *Thomas Hardy*

The quest plot, as the name implies, is the protagonist's search for a person, place or thing, tangible or intangible. It may be the Holy Grail, Valhalla, immortality, Atlantis or The Middle Kingdom. The main character is specifically (as opposed to incidentally) looking for something that she hopes or expects to find that will significantly change her life.

The historical range of this plot is enormous, starting from *Gilgamesh*, the great Babylonian epic, written about four thousand years ago, on to *Don Quixote* and then to *The Grapes of Wrath*. This plot is one of the world's most enduring.

You might be tempted to say that *Raiders of the Lost Ark* and *Indiana Jones and the Last Crusade* are also quest plots because Indiana Jones is searching for the Ark of the Covenant and the Holy Grail (or whatever the artifact of the day is). Wrong.

Alfred Hitchcock used to talk about the MacGuffin in his films. The MacGuffin is an object that seems to be important to the characters but is of little importance to the director (and consequently of no importance to the viewer). In *North by Northwest* the MacGuffin was the pre-Columbian statue with the microfilm hidden in it; in *Psycho* the MacGuffin was the stolen money; in *Notorious* it was the uranium in the wine bottles. The MacGuffin in *Raiders of the Lost Ark* is the Ark itself, and in *Indiana Jones and the Last Crusade* it is the Holy Grail. In the quest plot, the object of the search is everything to the protagonist, not simply an excuse for the action. The character is shaped by his quest and his success or failure at obtaining the object of the search. In Spielberg's film, Indiana Jones is neither better nor worse for wear after his trials and tribulations. His quest has no effect on him as a human being (as much as it can be said he is one). Therefore, *Indiana Jones* isn't a true quest plot.

The quest plot, while very physical, relies heavily on its protagonist. You must have a fleshed-out figure as your main character. Indiana Jones, however enjoyable he is to watch as he gets out of scrape after scrape, lacks any real depth as a human being.

The object of the protagonist's search reflects heavily on his character and usually alters it in some way, thus affecting the character change, which is important by the end. Gilgamesh sets out to find immortality, and what he discovers along the way changes him in fundamental ways; Don Quixote sets out as a madman knight errant to redress the wrongs of the entire world and to find his lady Dulcinea tel Toboso; Dorothy's quest in *The Wizard of Oz* is simpler: she wants to find home; the Joads in *The Grapes of Wrath* are looking for a new life in California; the title character in *Lord Jim* seeks his lost honor; Conway searches for his Shangri-La in *Lost Horizon*; and Jason, of course, wants the Golden Fleece. Take out the object of their quest, and the story falls apart. In every case the hero is much different at the end of the story than at the beginning.

In *Treasure of the Sierra Madre*, Fred C. Dobbs, the character played by Humphrey Bogart, seeks gold in the remote hills of Mexico. Here the quest is obvious: gold. What's not obvious is how his quest changes his character because of his greed.

A hallmark of quest plots is that the action moves around a lot; the protagonists are always on the move, seeking, searching. Gilgamesh not only roams the cedar forests of Babylon but ends up in the underworld; Don Quixote travels all over Spain; Dorothy starts out in Kansas but ends up in Oz; the Joads travel from Oklahoma to the Promised Land of California; Jim of *Lord Jim* goes to sea and wanders from Bombay to Calcutta; and no one knows exactly where Jason went.

In this kind of plot, the protagonist starts at home and often ends at home. Gilgamesh, Don Quixote, Dorothy and Jason all find their way home; the Joads and Jim do not, probably because they don't have a home to which they can return.

The object of this journey, other than the quest, is wisdom. All the characters in these stories learn something about the world and about themselves. Sometimes they return heroes, wiser for their journey; sometimes they return disillusioned and sick. Jason gets the Golden Fleece *and* the girl, and Dorothy and Toto get back to Kansas. But Don Quixote, abused for all his troubles, gives up and goes home, repudiating everything. Gilgamesh learns to his dismay that death is a bummer after all. The reality of California doesn't exactly please the Joads, either. But in each case there is a lesson to be learned, a lesson that shapes the protagonist.

These stories, by nature, are episodic. The protagonist may start at home, but she'll go from place to place in search of the object of her desire, encountering a variety of events along the way. These events should relate in some way to accomplishing the final goal. The protagonist must ask directions, find and solve clues and pay dues before getting the price of admission.

A major part of the quest is the search itself and the wisdom the main character accumulates along the way. She must be psychologically ready to receive the wisdom, and therefore the search becomes a series of successive classes. She should graduate one class before moving on to the next.

STRUCTURE OF THE QUEST PLOT

Act One

In Act One (setup), the hero is at the point of origination, usually home. A force moves him to act, either out of necessity or by desire.

In *Jason and the Golden Fleece*, Jason, who has been living a blissful existence on a mountaintop with a centaur (half-man, half-horse), finds out that his uncle, the evil king, has stolen the crown that is rightfully his. So Jason goes off to demand his throne.

Gilgamesh, on the other hand, is busy at the beginning of the story building the Great Wall of Babylon. He's not actually building the wall himself; he's got the city's inhabitants working double overtime to get it done. The people are so exhausted (and under-paid) that they petition the gods to send someone to stop the madman. One of the gods figures it's time to teach the king a lesson and creates a warrior out of clay to fight the king.

Don Quixote starts out at home, too. He's been reading too many romances about chivalry and suddenly fancies himself a knight. He dons his grandfather's armor, gets on his rickety old horse, and sets out on his first adventure.

Dorothy, too, is unhappy with her state of affairs. An orphan, she wants to run away from the farm where she lives with her Aunt Em and Uncle Henry, whom she accuses of being "unappre-ciative." She also wants to get away from her nasty neighbor, Miss Gulch, who's been threatening to kill her dog.

In each case, something spurs the protagonist to action: Jason's desire to become king; Gilgamesh's need to defend himself against the clay warrior from Hell; Don Quixote's desire to be-come a knight and make a difference in an indifferent world; and Dorothy's decision to run away from home. The authors don't spend a lot of time telling us who the hero is, why the hero is unhappy and what the hero intends to do about it. In each case, the quest starts with immediate decisions to act.

Then the story enters a transitional phase. The decision to act leads directly to the first major event away from home.

Jason shows up at the king's palace. In those days it was com-mon to have an oracle warn you to watch out for a man with only one shoe, and when Jason shows up with only one sandal, the king knows who he is and pretends to welcome him — while trying to figure out how to kill him. They have a great feast and the king tells the story about the Golden Fleece.

To the king's surprise, Jason pledges to get the fleece back. The king thinks it's a great idea and, to give Jason the proper incentive, he offers to give Jason his throne back if he's success-ful. (He figures Jason has no chance to pull it off, so what the hey.) Jason puts together a crew that is a cross between *The Magnificent Seven* and *The Dirty Dozen* and sets off to find the Golden Fleece.

Don Quixote goes through a similar trial. His first encounter on the road is with some traveling salesmen who beat him up when he challenges them to a passage at arms. It's his first test as a knight, and he flunks it miserably. He must go home to recover from his lumps and bruises. Meanwhile, Don Q's friends, fearing for his mental health, burn all his books. Of course this convinces Don Quixote that his books are being held hostage by an evil wizard. So it's back on the road for Don Q.

Gilgamesh has other problems. A goddess sends down a clay man named Enkidu to teach him a lesson he won't forget for abusing his people. Enkidu shows up at the temple playing the role of bouncer. He refuses to let Gilgamesh into the temple. Gilgamesh, who isn't used to hearing no for an answer, challenges Enkidu to a Babylonian version of a duel.

The pair duke it out. But it's a draw. Enkidu is impressed; so is Gilgamesh. The pair become solid friends. They go off together to fight the dreadful giant Humbuba.

Dorothy's initial adventure is no less bizarre. She's run away to the carnival, but Professor Marvel, the carny showman, convinces her to go back to her family. Before she can make it back, a Kansas "twister" snatches her—house, dog and all.

When the house finally touches down, Dorothy finds herself in the brilliant, garish, Technicolor world of Oz. The first thing she sees are the Munchkins, who are happily singing "Ding dong, the wicked witch is dead." Dorothy's house, it seems, has landed on top of the witch.

In each case, the first incident, the *motivating incident*, prompts the hero to leave home. It isn't enough for him simply to want to go; something must spur him on. There may be doubt in the hero's mind about leaving (as with Don Quixote and Dorothy), but the motivating incident turns the tide. It establishes the hero, the hero's "home base," and the reason for leaving.

The motivating incident also serves as a bridge between the first and second acts.

As you sketch the action for your adaptation of this plot, show your character moving from one state to another. All of the characters we've discussed here start out in a kind of innocent or naive state. They don't fully understand what lies ahead of them. They think they know what they want, but experience teaches them something else.

Your character should clearly identify what she is searching for. Maybe it's a desire to get away from home and find a new life—a plot often used with teenagers who feel stifled by their parents and their school. In any case, invest your character with a strong desire to go somewhere, to do something. Your character should have a strong mental image (which may be accurate or totally off base) of what she wants to achieve, and a strong desire to achieve it. She also should be strongly motivated, with forces at work that make her action imperative. Make sure you give your character the proper motivation to go on the quest.

The intent of the character—to find whatever goal he has set for himself—is different from the motivation. Intent is what the character wants to achieve; motivation is his reason for wanting to achieve it.

We should learn a lot about the main character in the first act. We want to understand why he's motivated to go on the quest. The experience is almost certain to change everything—but for now at least we know where the character is "coming from."

The Buddy Concept. The main character rarely travels alone. Gilgamesh has Enkidu; Don Quixote has Sancho Panza; Jason has his Argonauts; Dorothy has the Tin Woodman, the Lion and the Scarecrow. The buddies are usually picked up late in the first act (as a result of the motivating incident). In none of the previous examples does the hero begin with all his or her buddies; they are acquired along the way. This gives us time to focus on the protagonist without complicating issues with a supporting cast.

The majority of these stories also have a helpful character, someone or something that helps the protagonist achieve her quest. It may be Lancelot's Lady of the Lake in *Le Morte d'Arthur* or the good witch Glinda in *The Wizard of Oz*. In fairy tales, it is usually an animal—anything from a toad to a dove—that helps the main character find what she's seeking. The protagonist isn't a loner; she relies on the help of others.

If you plan to use a helpful friend or animal, the best place to introduce this character is in the first act. Otherwise you may be accused of contriving the story by bringing on a character at just the right time to help your hero out of a tight spot. Lay your groundwork in Act One, and follow through in Act Two.

Act Two

As basic as it sounds, the middle connects the beginning and the end. Act One asks the question, and Act Three gives the answer. All Act Two does is make the story interesting.

Act One of *The Wizard of Oz* asks the question: Will Dorothy find her way back home? Act Three answers the question: Yes.

Will Jason find the Golden Fleece (and get his kingdom back)? Yes.

Will Gilgamesh find the secret of life? Yes, but it doesn't do him any good.

Will Don Quixote find his lady Dulcinea del Toboso (who's really a chesty farm girl with a great talent for salting pork)? Yes.

(Notice the word *find* in each case? This is the bottom-line description of a quest plot.)

So Act One provides the question, and Act Three provides the answer. That leaves Act Two. In literature, the shortest distance between two points is not a straight line.

Act Two is the flavoring, the spice. If we know the answer as soon as Act Two, the story will be boring. The idea is to keep the reader wondering. A roller coaster ride would be no fun without a middle. If, just as your car got started, you pulled in at the end, you'd feel cheated. It's the ride, the going up and down, the unexpected turns, the bursts of speed and the topsy-turvy feeling of uncertainty that we love most.

The same is true for a story. The journey is as important as the end: As with a roller coaster, there's a specific path that connects the start to the finish. Once connected, the entire journey makes sense, each step of the way contributes to understanding either character or the object of the quest.

Dorothy doesn't go to an all-night diner and pick up some bikers from Oakland. Nor does Jason enter his chariot in the Athens 500. Those events have nothing to do with their stories. They might make great scenes, *but*—you know the drill.

Jason and his Argonauts head out for the Golden Fleece, but before they get there, they must prove to the gods (and to the reader) that they are worthy men, and that Jason possesses both the strength and wisdom to be king. These aren't lessons that ever come easily.

Gilgamesh has a tough task ahead, too. In the second act, after the dynamic duo slay the giant Humbuba as their first test of strength together, Enkidu starts to have nightmares about death. The two get tangled up with the gods, who don't like the way things are going, and Enkidu dies. Gilgamesh is heartbroken. He decides to find Utnapishtim, the man who holds the secret of life, so he can bring back his pal.

Don Quixote is a loosely constructed book. Cervantes was a satirist, and he took time to poke fun at all the literary and social conventions of the day. Don Quixote seems to wander in all directions, as if Cervantes barely had a handle on his topic. But the book is a panoramic view of the people and the times. We follow the crazy old man because of what each of these episodes teaches us: about the clash between idealism and materialism; about the nature of the Spanish character; about the foibles of madness and inspiration; and about the basic nature of character. (Even though Don Quixote goes from adventure to adventure as a knight errant intent on saving the world, his real quest is for his lady Dulcinea, even though she exists only in his fevered mind.)

Dorothy's quest is similar to Don Quixote's in many ways. It's not hard to see the parallels between the great knight of La Mancha and the brainless Scarecrow, the heartless Tin Woodman and the Cowardly Lion. Although their adventures have a different spin on them, the effect is the same. (We don't share Don Quixote's hallucinations with him — we see them from a distance — but we share Dorothy's hallucinations with her as if they were real.)

Each of Dorothy's buddies has his own quest — the Scarecrow, his brain; the Tin Woodman, his heart; and the Cowardly Lion, his courage. Together they survive the various scourges of the Wicked Witch, including winged monkeys, ferocious talking trees and sleep-inducing flowers. (All this may sound fantastic, but it's no more bizarre than what the Argonauts encounter on their trip.)

As you begin your Act Two, try to imagine what difficulties would make the most interesting and challenging obstacles for your main character. The skill in making obstacles is not just presenting hurdles for your character to run over, but hurdles that somehow alter your character. These are life experiences that *teach* your character something about his quest and something about himself. Any quest, such as with Fred C. Dobbs's search for gold in *Treasure of the Sierra Madre*, is ultimately a journey about self. Fred Dobbs isn't the person he thought he was. Life tests him, and he fails.

You also need to keep the challenges interesting. If your character climbs a mountain, the obstacles he encounters may be obvious: a piton gives way, a snowstorm settles in, a landslide blocks his path. But these obstacles in themselves are only physical. It's how these obstacles *affect* the character that counts. Does he give up? Does he fall into a deep depression? Does he decide to take a desperate chance? The mountain should teach the character each step of the way.

The true relationship between character and event depends on your ability to bring the two of them together.

Act Three

Plot is a game of connect-the-dots. Each scene you write is a dot. If you're a good writer, the reader will understand the relationships between any two dots and connect them. When it's all over, the reader has the completed picture before her.

In the first and second acts (or dramatic phases, if you prefer the term), the reader shouldn't be able to project the picture properly. You've given clues, perhaps (some of them might even be red herrings to throw the reader off the track), but you don't want to get caught early on in your story. If you are, your audience will abandon you or give you a curt, "I thought so."

The final movement of your fiction includes the revelation. In the quest plot, the revelation occurs once the protagonist obtains (or is denied) the object of her search.

It isn't unusual in this type of plot for there to be additional complications *as a result of obtaining the goal*. Things aren't what the hero expected them to be, and it could be that what the hero was searching for all this time wasn't what she really wanted. But there is the moment of *realization*, which is an insight made by the hero about the nature and meaning of the quest itself.

Jason, through his bravery and cleverness (with a little help from his friends on Mount Olympus), kills the dragon that guards the Golden Fleece. Okay, that means he goes home and collects his crown, right?

Not exactly.

Jason returns to the evil king and throws the fleece at his feet and demands the king turn over the keys to the kingdom. Only the fleece is no longer golden. The king welshes on the bet. Jason points out there was nothing in the bet about the fleece having to stay golden, only that he would find and retrieve it.

Still the king refuses.

Jason has to take matters into his own hands. That night, while everyone is asleep, Jason kills the king.

Now he has everything: his rightful kingdom, the enchanted Medea, and the not-so-Golden Fleece.

You might ask yourself, "Why didn't Jason just kill the king up front and save himself a lot of grief?" He could've, of course, but then he wouldn't have been a hero. It is Jason's trials that make him a king, not the crown.

This tale isn't that different from dozens of fairy tales that circulated throughout Europe during the Middle Ages. We know the tales: they're always about a young boy or girl who must go out in the world to find something. It is their contact with the outside world, the world away from home, that teaches them the lessons they need to mature into adults. Jason learns the lessons he needs to mature into a king.

Dorothy matures, too. She isn't on her way to becoming a queen, but she is on her way to becoming an adult, just as her friends are on their way to becoming integrated human beings by finding their potpourri of brains, heart and nerve.

After Dorothy's triumph against the Wicked Witch of the West, she and her friends confront the great wizard, who in spite of his promises to help everyone turns out to be a bumbling old humbug. But the wizard, who looks suspiciously like Professor Marvel from the carnival, is clever enough to point out that everybody already has what they want, having proven themselves by rescuing Dorothy from the clutches of the witch.

Everyone but Dorothy, that is, who's still hung up in Oz and can't get home.

The wizard promises to take her home in his hot air balloon, but that plan goes awry when the balloon sails off without her. Dorothy finally gets home with the help of the good witch Glinda. All she has to do is say, "There's no place like home," and bang, she's back in her own bed in Kansas along with Aunt Em and Uncle Henry. Dorothy's realization that true happiness can be found in her own backyard depends on her verbal acknowledgement. As soon as she says it out loud and with feeling, she's home.

Gilgamesh, in his search for immortality for his friend Enkidu, ends up going to the underworld in search of the secrets of life. He meets the Babylonian version of Noah, who tells him about the Great Flood. The old man is a terrible fatalist and tells Gilgamesh that nothing lasts forever and that life is brief, and death is part of the process. He also tells Gilgamesh that the secret of life is a rose that grows at the bottom of the waters of death. Gilgamesh tries to get the rose, but an evil serpent eats it first.

Gilgamesh goes home disillusioned, alone and defeated. He makes a final plea to the gods, one of whom takes sympathy on him and arranges a meeting with his dead pal. Enkidu tells Gilgamesh what life after death is like: full of worms, neglect and disrespect. Gilgamesh accepts his lot because he must, and he returns to his kingdom feeling mortal for the first time.

Don Quixote goes home just as disillusioned. Like Gilgamesh, he doesn't find the object of his quest, and he gives in to the harsh world around him.

As you bring your main character to the climax of your story, and as you make him confront the realities that have presented themselves during the course of your story, you have either created a character who rejects the lessons he's learned (and goes back to point zero) or one who learns from them by accepting them. This plot, more than many others, points out the change in your character from beginning to end.

CHECKLIST

As you write your story, keep these points in mind:

1. A quest plot should be about a search for a person, place or thing; develop a close parallel between your protagonist's intent and motivation and the object he's trying to find.

2. Your plot should move around a lot, visiting many people and places. But don't just move your character around as the wind blows. Movement should be orchestrated according to your plan of cause and effect. (You can make the journey *seem* like there's nothing guiding it—making it seem casual—but in fact it is causal.)

3. Consider bringing your plot full circle geographically. The protagonist frequently ends up in the same place where she started.

4. Make your character substantially different at the end of the story as a result of her quest. This plot is about the character who makes the search, not about the object of the search itself. Your character is in the process of changing during the course of the story. What or who is she becoming?

5. The object of the journey is wisdom, which takes the form of self-realization for the hero. Oftentimes this is the process of maturation. It may be about a child who learns the lessons of adulthood, but it also may be about an adult who learns the lessons of life.

6. Your first act should include a motivating incident, which initiates your hero's actual search. Don't just launch into a quest; make sure your readers understand *why* your character wants to go on the quest.

7. Your hero should have at least one traveling companion. He must have interactions with other characters to keep the story from becoming too abstract or too interior. Your hero needs someone to bounce ideas off of, someone to argue with.

8. Consider including a helpful character.

9. Your last act should include your character's revelation, which occurs either after giving up the search or after successfully concluding it.

10. What your character discovers is usually different from what he originally sought.

Chapter Eight

Master Plot #2: Adventure

Who is original? Everything that we are doing, everything that we think, exists already, and we are only intermediaries, that's all, who make use of what is in the air.

—Henry Miller

The adventure plot resembles the quest plot in many ways, but there are some profound differences between them. The quest plot is a character plot; it is a plot of the mind. The adventure plot, on the other hand, is an action plot; it is a plot of the body.

The difference lies mainly in the focus. In the quest plot, the focus from beginning to end is the person making the journey; in the adventure plot, the focus is the journey itself.

The world loves a good adventure story. For the hero, it is a going out into the world; for the readers, it is a vicarious adventure to places they've never been, like Fez and Novosibirsk and Tierra del Fuego. It is eating dinner in a small restaurant on the Left Bank or eating Mongolian barbecue outside a yurt with a flock of sheep and goats at your side. Adventure is love in strange places. It is whatever is exotic and strange. Adventure is doing things we'll probably never do, going to the brink of danger and returning safely.

The protagonist goes in search of fortune, and according to the dictates of adventure, fortune is never found at home, but somewhere over the rainbow.

Since the purpose of the adventure is the journey, it's not important that the hero change in any appreciable way. This isn't a psychological story like the quest plot. What's important is the moment at hand and the one following it. What's important is a sense of breathlessness.

We don't get lectures about the meaning of life and we don't get characters who suffer from post-Modernist angst. The protagonist is perfectly fitted for the adventure: she is swept up in the event because the event is always larger than the character. The character may prevail through skill or daring but is defined by the event. Indiana Jones and Luke Skywalker and James Bond are defined by their actions in their stories.

Going into the world can mean different things. Consider Jules Verne's *Twenty Thousand Leagues Under the Sea* or Jack London's *The Sea Wolf* or even Daniel Defoe's *Robinson Crusoe*. In these stories the world is defined variously as the bottom of the ocean; aboard the sailing ship *Ghost* with a tyrannical captain; or marooned on an island off the coast of South America. The world can take many forms. What's important about the locations is that they are anything but the mundane world we inhabit. Readers enjoy adventures as much for the places they get to go as for the action that involves the character.

The world may also be an invention such as another planet, a sunken continent or the interior of the planet; or it can be pure imagination, such as the lands of *Gulliver's Travels*.

Bruno Bettelheim, the Freudian analyst who interprets fairy tales, talks at great length about the child's fear of leaving Mother's lap and going into the world. Many fairy tales are about just that: venturing into the unknown. The adventure story for adults is nothing more than an extension of the child's fairy tale.

ONCE UPON A TIME . . .

When it comes to studying the structure of the adventure, the fairy tale is the best place to begin. People tend to underestimate the value and technical skill of fairy tales. They aren't simplistic tales for grade-school minds; they're exquisitely fashioned fictions that are precise, economical and rich with meaning and symbolism. And yet they appeal to the young mind, which doesn't get tangled up with all kinds of heavy moralizing or complicated plots.

Fairy tales use a relatively limited number of plots, but one of the most common is the adventure plot. "The Three Languages" as collected by the Brothers Grimm is the prototypical adventure. The story begins with an aged Swiss count with a son who, according to the count, is stupid. The count orders his son to leave the castle to be educated. Adventures usually begin at home, but once a reason has been established for leaving, the hero departs immediately.

As is typical with fairy tales, the story begins with the first line, a lesson a lot of us could learn. While the child may be reluctant to leave home, the adult is usually eager to get out. In either case, there should be some kind of motivating incident that forces the hero to move. In the case of "The Three Languages," the motivating force comes in the second line, when the father throws his son out of the house. The son has no choice; he must leave. Simpler reasons for the leaving (out of curiosity, for example) aren't enough; the act should *impel* the character. Oftentimes the character has no choice but to act. Ned Land in *Twenty Thousand Leagues Under the Sea* leaves to investigate a giant sea monster that has been sinking merchant ships. Robin Hood begins his journey as the prince of thieves only after he shoots one of the king's stags on a bet and must go on the lam. Lemuel Gulliver gets shipwrecked, as does Robinson Crusoe, as does Humphrey Van Weyden in Jack London's *The Sea Wolf*, who has the misfortune of being picked up by the brutish sea captain Wolf Larsen. Same with Kipling's *Captains Courageous*. Even Mole in Kenneth Grahame's *The Wind in the Willows* gets spring fever and leaves his hole in the ground to stroll in the meadow, where he meets Water Rat, who takes him for a trip down the river.

THREE STRIKES . . . YOU'RE OUT

Meanwhile, back at the castle, the count has kicked his son out and told him he must study with a celebrated master. The boy obeys and spends a year with the master. At the end of the year he comes home and the count asks him what he's learned. "I have learnt what the dogs say when they bark," the boy replies.

The count isn't exactly thrilled and sends his son to a second master for a year, at the end of which the boy comes back. Again the count asks his son what he's learned. "I have learnt what the birds say," the son answers.

This time the count is furious. "Oh, you lost man, you have spent the precious time and learnt nothing; are you not ashamed to appear before my eyes?" He sends his son to a third master with the warning that if he doesn't learn anything useful this time, he shouldn't bother coming home.

A year later the boy shows up at the castle gate. (Are you projecting the pattern?)

The father asks what he's learned this time. "Dear father, I have this year learnt what the frogs croak."

That's the last straw for the count. He disinherits his son and orders him taken into the woods and killed. The servants haul him off but feel sorry for the boy and let him go.

The boy is now alone in the forest and can't go back; he must go forth into the unknown and fend for himself.

All of this action constitutes the first movement of the plot. Its elements are basic: a father who wants his "stupid" son to learn something; a son who obeys the orders of his father but doesn't learn what his father thinks he should learn; and the father's disinheritance of his son, which allows for no going back (since his father assumes his son is dead).

There are five events in the first act; they are pure cause and effect, and you can follow them easily: the initial impetus for movement ("get an education"), the three journeys to celebrated masters (each resulting in failure), and the final rejection and sentence of death. Each scene stems directly from the one preceding it. That's the beauty and economy of the fairy tale.

The boy in "The Three Languages" does go forth into the world, but he returns each time, suggesting he really doesn't want to go; he's only doing so because his father wants him to. Finally his father throws him out (both literally and figuratively). No longer guided by the demands of his father, *he must act on his own now*. This distinguishes the first from the second act: The boy's motivation is different.

As you develop your own idea for this plot, keep in mind that you should develop a series of events and locations that are colorful and exciting, but that also mesh for the sake of the plot. In the case of "The Three Languages," we are entranced by the dark, mysterious mood of the places the boy visits. There is also a good reason for the boy to go to each place. We don't understand that until the end of the story, but looking back it's clear that each step of his education has come into play.

Don't just move your character through a series of unrelated stops. Try to tell a story. You're free from the restraints of the quest plot, in which each event challenges the hero in some meaningful way and affects his character. In the adventure plot, the character can simply enjoy the events for their worth. But don't abandon cause and effect. Your hero is still an important figure in the book, and the reader always looks to find some correlation between place and event with the hero.

Now let's begin the second movement.

The boy (let's call him Hans) comes to a great castle and asks for a night's lodging. The lord of the castle, who isn't a great host, says he can sleep in the ruins of an old tower nearby but to watch out for the wild dogs who might kill him.

Hans goes down to the tower and, having learned the language of dogs, eavesdrops on them. He finds out that the dogs are crazy because they're under a curse that forces them to guard a great treasure in the tower. He tells the lord that he knows how to get the treasure and release the dogs from the curse that keeps them there. The lord is impressed, promising to adopt Hans if he can get the treasure. Hans delivers the treasure and finds a new father.

End of second movement.

Notice how the author *goes back* to the material in the first movement and builds on it in the second? Lay the groundwork for the journey in the first movement, then actually make the journey in the second movement. As you develop a series of events (and difficulties for your hero), remember to keep the reader challenged. Description of exotic places and people can be interesting, but you still must deliver the goods when it comes to some kind of story. Otherwise you have the equivalent of a pile of adjectives with no nouns. Put your characters into interesting situations, but make sure those situations relate to some kind of intent on behalf of the hero. It may be something as simple as a young man who goes out into the world to find a wife. It may be the story of a woman who goes into the world to find her lost father. This is the core of the story; don't be sidetracked from it. The rest is just window dressing. It may be exciting and colorful, but it's still just window dressing.

The actions of the second movement depend on the action of the first movement. In "The Three Languages," we understand how Hans happens to know dogspeak. For the first time, Hans thinks and acts on his own, and he uses his education effectively. Notice also the insight into Hans' character: He doesn't keep the treasure for himself. Instead, he turns it over to the lord of the castle, who repays him with adoption. Hans has replaced an ungrateful father with a grateful one.

The focus isn't on Hans, however. The focus is on the adventure. For the sake of summarizing the story I've left out the details of Hans' encounter with the dogs, but it has elements of fear, terror, fascination and revelation (the treasure). It is from these details the adventure takes its color and power. The plot is continuous, and Hans doesn't go off chasing a woman or fighting an ogre guarding a bridge. Such scenes would serve no purpose to the plot. Hans does only what he must to advance the plot.

THE CRYSTAL BALL

But where is this story headed? Two elements should be obvious. Hans learned three things from the celebrated masters: the speech of dogs, frogs and birds. The second act included an episode that dealt with dogs. Therefore, the third act must include episodes that deal with frogs and birds.

Having gotten a taste of the world, Hans decides to visit Rome. He leaves home willingly and with the blessing of his father (as opposed to his violent ejection in Act One).

On his way he passes a marsh where frogs are croaking. Hans listens in ". . . and when he became aware of what they were saying, he grew very thoughtful and sad."

He continues his journey, and when he gets to Rome he finds out the pope has just died. The cardinals are deadlocked about whom they should appoint as his successor. They decide to wait for a sign from God.

They don't have long to wait. As soon as the young count enters the church, two snow-white doves fly down and land on his shoulders. The cardinals, who know a sign when they see one, ask Hans on the spot if he would be the next pope. Hans doesn't believe he's worthy enough to be pope, but the doves counsel him to accept.

He does and is anointed and consecrated. This is what the frogs in the marsh had told him: that he would be the next pope.

The third act fulfills the promises of the first two acts. Hans moves through successive states of being. He starts out as dumb Hans (Act One), develops into the young adopted count (Act Two) and ends up as the pope (Act Three). Each stage depends on the previous one. He also moves through three fathers. Hans starts out with the irresponsible and intolerant father of Act One, graduates to an understanding and giving father in Act Two, and graduates again to be the figurative son of God.

Heroes in adventures don't usually change much during the course of the story. The reader is basically concerned with the chain of events and with what happens next. Yes, Hans becomes the pope, but we don't see any evidence of a changed Hans. He can't even speak Latin; when he gives Mass, the doves have to prompt him. He's still pretty much the same person, although he's become more self-reliant (which is the point of the story). We don't see a high level of spiritual consciousness or insight that elevates his character. If it weren't for the birds . . .

Frequently, an adventure includes a romance. There's no romance in "The Three Languages" because it wouldn't be fitting for a pope-to-be to have a girlfriend, but in many other fairy tales (and adult adventures) the hero encounters a member of the opposite sex along the way. Kings and princes must have their queens and princesses (and vice versa).

What does Act Three accomplish in the adventure plot? As is true with most plots, the question that you raise in your first act is answered in your third. Will Hans make his way in the world? Yes. But it is the journey to the "yes" that intrigues us most. In fact, the "yes" may not even be that important to the reader. The adventure plot is a process plot: We enjoy the journey at least as much as (if not more than) the resolution at the end of the story.

If you decide to use this plot, do your homework. Since a large part of your success depends on sounding convincing—this person really knows what she's talking about—you either should have firsthand knowledge of the events, and the places in which they happen, or you need to spend time in the library gleaning those details that add authenticity. It's details that convince—not just knowing the names of places, but knowing those little details that collectively give a sense of the look, smell and taste of the place. Immerse yourself in the location. Flood yourself in details. You never know what you need until you need it, so *take careful notes*. Nothing is more frustrating than reading a detail you didn't think was important and then realizing as you write that it's the perfect detail—but you have no idea which book it was in. If you take careful notes (including the name of the book and the author), you can always go back.

You can't take shortcuts around details. Without them, you'll be giving broad sketches, which aren't convincing. The next time you read an adventure book, notice what a large role those details play in creating a time and a place, and notice how naturally a good author weaves the two together so they seem inseparable.

CHECKLIST

As you write, keep these points in mind:

1. The focus of your story should be on the journey more than on the person making the journey.

2. Your story should concern a foray into the world, to new and strange places and events.

3. Your hero goes in search of fortune; it is never found at home.

4. Your hero should be motivated by someone or something to begin the adventure.

5. The events in each of your acts depend on the same chain of cause-and-effect relationships that motivates your hero at the beginning.

6. Your hero doesn't necessarily have to change in any meaningful way by the end of the story.

7. Adventures often include romance.

Chapter Nine

Master Plot #3: Pursuit

The English country gentleman galloping after a fox — the unspeakable in full pursuit of the uneatable.

— *Oscar Wilde*

Two games never seem to fail to capture the imagination of children: hide-and-seek and tag. Try to remember the excitement of being on the hunt and finding where everyone was hiding. Or if you were the hunted, the excitement of eluding capture. It was a test of cleverness (how well you could hide) and nerve.

Tag is like that, too. Chasing and being chased, always trying to outwit the other person. We never lose our appetite for the game. For children as well as adults, there's something fundamentally exciting in finding what has been hidden. As we grow older, we grow more sophisticated about how we play the game, but the thrill at the heart of it never changes. It is pure exhilaration.

The pursuit plot is the literary version of hide-and-seek.

The basic premise of the plot is simple: One person chases another. All you need is a cast of two: the pursuer and the pursued. Since this is a physical plot, the chase is more important than the people who take part in it.

Structurally, this is one of the simplest plots. In the first dramatic phase, the situation is quickly established as the guidelines for the race are set up. *Runners on your mark . . .* We must know who the bad guy is and who the good guy is, and why one will be chasing the other. (The good guy doesn't always chase the bad guy; it's often the other way around.) It's in this phase that you establish the stakes of the race (death, imprisonment, marriage, etc.). *Get set* . . . You also need a motivating incident to get the chase going. *Go!*

The second dramatic phase is pure chase. Here we rely on a variety of twists, turns and reversals, perhaps more than in any other plot. Keep your reader involved in the chase by using all the tricks in your bag of surprises.

The third dramatic phase resolves the chase. Either the pursuer escapes permanently or is caught permanently. (Or at least it has the illusion of being permanent. Many movie sequels depend on jump-starting the same chase again and again.)

Hollywood has a long-standing affair with the pursuit plot, probably because it translates well to the screen. Steven Spielberg got his start with this plot. His first film (made for television) was *Duel*, in which Dennis Weaver is chased mercilessly by — a truck. We never see or find out who's driving the truck, so it takes on a demonic personality as if motivated out of sheer meanness. There's no rhyme or reason for it, nor does there have to be: We like the excitement of the semi trying to run down Weaver's character, and we like seeing how Weaver escapes his pursuer.

Then there were the *Smokey and the Bandit* movies with Burt Reynolds and Jackie Gleason. For years the American public delighted in their improbable antics. Even Spielberg's first feature film, *Sugarland Express*, was a pursuit film. Those films made no pretense at anything serious other than the chase. Speeding (on film anyway) isn't exciting unless there's the prospect of getting caught. Gleason's steadfast character and his dimwit nephew follow the bandits halfway across the country in a vain attempt to bring them to justice. Getting caught accomplishes nothing in these comedies, because with no chase, there's only a vacuum.

Inspector Javert relentlessly pursues Jean Valjean in *Les Miserables*, and Sherlock Holmes relentlessly pursues Dr. Moriarity throughout the tales. If you're the pursuer, you want to catch the pursued; if you're the pursued, you want to elude capture. The task for the writer is to be clever enough to sustain the chase without letting the reader get bored. Both sides live for the chase and are defined by it. As readers, we expect a great deal of physical action, a variety of clever dodges and ruses that come into play just when it seems the pursuer has cornered the pursued.

The pursued can't get too far ahead of the pursuer, either, because the tension of the chase comes from the proximity of the two characters. Think back to the game of tag. You're running down someone who's doing everything she can to get away from you. You close in. The tension increases as you get closer. She tries to give you the slip; you stay with her. *The tension is greatest at the moment just before it seems capture is inevitable.* Then *wham*, something happens, and the inevitable is foiled, either by the cleverness of the pursued or by some interference.

The classic example of this is the relationship between Wile E. Coyote and the Roadrunner. Both live for the chase. It is obvious to everyone except Wile E. Coyote that the Roadrunner can outwit and outrun him at any given moment. Yet Wile E. Coyote keeps trying, hoping in his heart that sooner or later Providence will side with him. The Roadrunner taunts his opponent and lets him get *so close*, but at the last possible second, he jets off in a cloud of dust. This is the basic relationship between pursuer and pursued.

Think of some of the other pursuit films you've seen: *Jaws* (man vs. beast), *The French Connection, Night of the Living Dead, Terminator, Alien, Midnight Run, Narrow Margin, Romancing the Stone*, and just about any of the slasher flicks, such as *Friday the Thirteenth, Halloween* and *Nightmare on Elm Street*. Then there are the cartoon characters (of both page and screen) who exist solely for the chase: Batman and Superman, in particular.

There are also classic films in this category, such as *Bonnie and Clyde* and *Moby Dick*. I include the film version of *Moby Dick* in this category because it's concerned mostly with Ahab's obsession with chasing the whale. That obsession overshadows everything else. Unlike the book, which delves into the psychologies of the crew members, the film is more concerned with the chase.

Then there's one of the best pursuit films ever made, *Butch Cassidy and the Sundance Kid*. From the start of the story, Butch and Sundance are on the run. Known as "The Hole in the Wall Gang," the pair have made a career of holding up the Union Pacific Railroad. They've become so good at it, in fact, that the railroad president has personally made it his business to have the two men hunted down. Butch and Sundance have come up with the clever idea of robbing a single train twice: once on its way in and again on its way out. Who would anticipate that the robbers would be so daring?

They hold up the incoming train. Butch celebrates in a whorehouse, while Sundance visits his renegade schoolteacher girlfriend. Then they hold up the outgoing train.

The plan backfires. A posse is waiting for them in a back-up train, and the chase begins and doesn't stop until the end of the story.

PURSUING THE PURSUIT PLOT

The elements of a pursuit plot are fairly standard: Someone runs, someone chases. It is a simple (but powerful) physical motion that evokes simple (and equally powerful) emotions. It doesn't matter if the pursuit is a standard chase by a posse or a submarine chase, as in *The Hunt for Red October*. What distinguishes one story from another is the quality of the chase itself. If you resort to standard clichés, the chase won't have the excitement your reader demands. If the territory is too familiar, you'll have a harder time getting the reader involved.

Your key to keeping the chase exciting is to make it unpredictable. If you recall our earlier discussion about patterns, you will remember how important they are in developing plot. But in a plot like this one, you don't want the patterns to be obvious. You want to develop exciting series of twists and turns so that the reader stays off balance. Don't cater to expectation. If you lure the reader into thinking a certain event is going to happen, play off that expectation. The event should fit the pattern you've been building but still be something of a surprise. It's a case of the reader being right and wrong at the same time. He expected a certain event to occur (and it did) but not in the way he expected. This means originality, which is the greatest task of the writer. Find a new way of doing it, or put a new twist on an old way. Freshen up your ideas. Every hand should have a wild card in it.

Of course, the pure physicality of the chase can draw us in. The car chase scene in *Bullitt* is one of the best ever filmed: You can feel yourself lurch in your seat as the cars fly over the streets of San Francisco. Equally powerful is the car chase scene in Bensonhurst, Brooklyn, in *The French Connection*, in which "Popeye" Doyle chases a train under the El. These scenes draw us in physically, not mentally.

But a car chase is a car chase. It's a stock in trade device now. So what must you do to make your pursuit plot unique? If you're familiar with the works of Ed McBain or Elmore Leonard, you know how taut writing can make simple movement suspenseful. They make any movement unpredictable because the reader isn't sure what the consequences of that movement will be. Their characters can't do anything without something threatening the precarious balance of sanity or the law. Leonard's *Fifty-two Pickup* is a fine example of this kind of writing.

Aristotle said action defined character. True. What a person does reflects who she is. But Aristotle didn't know about Hollywood.

There comes a point where action no longer defines character, where action is solely for the sake of action. For all the action in a Steven Spielberg or George Lucas film, very little of it reveals anything important about the principal characters. Nor do we care. What we *do* care is that the action be *stimulating, engaging and unique*. This means trying to avoid the standard clichés. It means tension must hum like a taut wire through your story. This isn't just for movie scripts; it's true for writing pursuit novels, too. In many ways this plot relies on old clichés, so it's important for you to find the new spin to put on old stories to make them engaging for us again.

Butch Cassidy and the Sundance Kid works because it turns the traditional Western inside out. The bad guys are good guys; they're fun-loving and likeable. They don't have a five-day beard, stink, spit, and stomp on defenseless men, women and children. *They go against type.* (The same is true for the lead characters in *Bonnie and Clyde*.) Butch is a romantic, an optimist, who puts a positive spin on everything; Sundance is more practical, a realist, but nonetheless engaging and appealing. The two men are well-meaning social misfits. Their action stimulates us, their comic notions engage us, and the situations they get involved in are unique. Remember the scene in which the pair are chased to the top of a bluff and there's no escape except by jumping off a cliff into the raging torrent below? In its basic form we've seen this scene before. The desperadoes, living up to their name, make the desperate leap.

But William Goldman brings a twist to the scene that makes it unforgettable: Sundance, we find out at the last possible moment, can't swim. The scene is tense but funny. We don't learn anything important about the character, for his inability to swim is a device that suits the scene only. But it works because the dialogue is funny and the situation has an angle that we haven't seen before.

Which brings up a final trademark of the pursuit plot: *confinement*. To heighten tension during the chase, it is inevitable at some point that the pursued become trapped or confined. As in the scene with Butch and Sundance at the top of the bluff, they've got their backs to the cliff and their fronts to the posse. *The closer the quarters, the greater the tension.* Some films, such as the *Alien* series, have done spectacularly well using this principle. The main character, Ripley, is always at close quarters, whether it's on a spaceship or on a hostile planet. She's given *no place to run*. The same is true with *Outland*, which takes place on a space station, and *Narrow Margin*, which takes place on a train. Confine your action, even to the point of claustrophobia, and you will increase the tension of your story.

A final word about using confined spaces: While it is true that limiting the characters' range of movement raises tension, it is also true that too much confinement sometimes makes movement and action difficult. For example, Agatha Christie uses the train in *Murder on the Orient Express* to its fullest advantage. The characters can't leave the train, yet they have enough places to move and hide and perform the action. If you were to try to confine the action even further to, say, one car on the train, you might deny your characters the freedom they need to move around. Other good examples come from film. *Die Hard* uses an entire office building and Steven Seagall's *Under Siege* uses a battleship, both of which work well. But *Passenger 57*, with Wesley Snipes, uses a hijacked airplane, which proves to be too small to contain the story. There just aren't enough places to go or things to do on an airplane.

CHECKLIST

As you write, keep these points in mind:

1. In the pursuit plot, the chase is more important than the people who take part in it.

2. Make sure there's a real danger of the pursued getting caught.

3. Your pursuer should have a reasonable chance of catching the pursued; he may even capture the pursued momentarily.

4. Rely heavily on physical action.

5. Your story and your characters should be stimulating, engaging and unique.

6. Develop your characters and situations against type in order to avoid clichés.

7. Keep your situations as geographically confined as possible; the smaller the area for the chase, the greater the tension.

8. The first dramatic phase should have three stages: a) establish the ground rules for the chase, b) establish the stakes and c) start the race with a motivating incident.

Chapter Ten

Master Plot #4: Rescue

Rescue my soul from their destructions, my darling from the lions.
— *Psalms 35:17*

Like the adventure plot, the hero of the rescue plot must go forth into the world. Like the quest plot, the hero of the rescue plot searches for someone or something. And like the pursuit plot, the hero ordinarily chases the antagonist. The rescue plot, like the others, is a physical plot: It depends on action more than it depends on the psychological subtleties of character. But the similarities end there. The rescue plot is the first we've looked at that relies heavily on the third arm of the triangle: the antagonist.

The story depends on the dynamic among the three characters—the protagonist, the victim and the antagonist—each of whom serves a specific function. The characters serve the plot (as opposed to the plot serving the characters), which is a condition of a physical plot. As readers, we care more about the action as it involves the three majors than we care about them as unique human beings. The conflict is a result of the search and the hero's attempts to gain back what he has lost.

Before we look at the role of each of the major characters, let's look at the role of the plot itself.

The moral argument at the heart of this plot is most commonly clear-cut: The antagonist is wrong, and the hero is right. The reader tends to enjoy the chase more than anything else and seems satisfied with the shallow morality that lies at the foundation of the story. Under these conditions it's difficult to develop an argument that has two equally valid, compelling and logical sides to it.

Let me give you an example. As a writer for television, I keep my eye on the kinds of stories that networks like to produce—not the movies they get from theaters, but the films they produce themselves, often called Movies of the Week. These films often are topical; the news story of the day is almost certain to end up as a television drama. Several television films have been made about child abductions. One estranged parent, having been denied custody of his child by the courts, kidnaps the child and disappears. The character triangle is the father, the mother and the child. The primary conflict takes place between the father and the mother; the child is the victim.

All of the Movies of the Week I've seen have treated the subject in the traditional way: one hero (the good parent), one villain (the evil parent) and one victim (the child). The most common scenario has been about a psychologically disturbed and abusive father who kidnaps his child once the court denies him custody. Claiming the rights of fatherhood (his moral platform), he disappears after abducting his child either from the home or schoolyard. The mother (who has her own moral platform) spends the rest of the film finding and retrieving her child. Sound familiar?

You might remember from an earlier chapter when I (and Tolstoy) said the best stories don't come from good vs. bad but from good vs. good. What would happen if you eliminated the villain, the evil parent who defies the court order and cruelly kidnaps the child? The story I find interesting—the story I have yet to see on television—is when both parents have an equal moral claim on the child. What happens then? That's what I mean when I talk about being between a rock and a hard place.

But in rescue plots, the concept of rescue seems to imply right vs. wrong. It's inherent in the word "rescue." To be rescued is to be delivered from confinement, danger, violence or evil. The more interesting story, it seems to me, lacks these elements, and therefore no rescue is possible. You can see how this plot in some ways doesn't allow the kind of character development that you would need to make an interesting story *except* as an action plot, where the chase and the rescue are the main focus.

Now let's look at the role of each of the three major characters.

THE PROTAGONIST

The action of the plot tends to focus on the protagonist because she is the character who does all the searching. The situation is straightforward. The protagonist has some kind of attachment to the person who's the object of the search. This attachment provides the motivation for conducting the search.

The strongest and most common attachment is love. The prince wants to rescue the princess. The husband wants to rescue his wife. A mother wants to rescue her children. The attachment can be for reasons much less ideal, as in the case of mercenaries who've been hired to find someone, but almost always some idealistic notion surfaces in their motivation. Even in a case such as *The Magnificent Seven* (based on the Akira Kurosawa's *The Seven Samurai*), the battle-hardened hired guns who agree to rescue the small, meaningless village in Mexico from bandits do so out of a sense of justice. Whatever the motivation, it is a strong moral urge to right a wrong.

The hero often must go to the end of the world to find what he's looking for. It may be literal, in the sense of princes who must travel to the evil kingdom, or it may be figurative, in the sense that the hero must go to a place that's alien to him (another city, for instance). The point is that the protagonist goes to a place he's unfamiliar with, which puts him at a disadvantage. He must overcome that disadvantage to affect the rescue. It's a sign of greater strength for the hero to fight his battles on the villain's turf and win than for the hero to fight on familiar ground. It's also a source of greater tension. The protagonist's emotional focus in these situations is usually fixed more on his opponent than on the person or thing he's lost, making the plot seem like a contest or duel between him and the antagonist.

Alexander Pushkin wrote a poem called "Ruslan and Lyudmila," which was later turned into an opera by the same name by Mikhail Glinka. The story begins with the marriage of Lyudmila, the daughter of Vladimir, grand prince of Kiev, to Ruslan. It's a grand wedding. After the wedding feast the newlyweds go to their nuptial chamber to consummate the marriage. But before the couple can become as one, there's a burst of thunder and light, and the evil magician Chernomor steals Lyudmila from Ruslan's arms!

The grand prince is so outraged by the crime that he promises his daughter to any person who can bring her back. Ruslan must now go into the world, confront the dark wizard and rescue his beloved, proving his worthiness.

The story is Ruslan's more than it is Lyudmila's or Chernomor's. He is the hero and must perform the tasks necessary to retrieve his lost love.

THE ANTAGONIST

The majority of the literature that deals with rescue deals with kidnapping. We know the pattern well. The evil magician kidnaps the beautiful princess and takes her to his castle for himself. This model hasn't changed much in five thousand years. The evil magician takes many disguises in modern literature, but he's not hard to spot. He may have lost all his powers of magic, but the evil part of his character remains intact.

The antagonist plays backseat to the protagonist, of course. Since it's the protagonist who must do the searching, and since we generally follow the protagonist and not the antagonist, we only encounter the antagonist from time to time as a reminder of his powers and what the protagonist must overcome to succeed. The more powerful the opponent, the more meaningful the victory. Therefore, the villain must interfere constantly with the protagonist's attempt at rescue. The pair interact to create the story's tension. It doesn't matter whether it's the title character in the play *Madame Ranevskaya* trying to rescue her cherry orchard from Lopakhin, or John Wayne trying to rescue Natalie Wood from the Comanchero Scar in *The Rescuers*.

That doesn't mean the villain is an incidental character, because the times the hero encounters him are crucial. (I'll discuss these interactions later in the chapter.) *The antagonist is a device whose purpose is to deprive the protagonist of what she believes rightfully belongs to her.* He is often clever (devious), which allows him to consistently outwit his opponent until the third act.

THE VICTIM

The conflict in the rescue plot lies between the protagonist and the antagonist. The victim is the least part of the triangle. Without the victim, of course, there is no story, but the victim is, in fact, incidental to the plot. Rarely is the victim more than a shadowy embodiment of that which the hero seeks. In William Goldman's *The Princess Bride* it's the princess who must be saved, and all we need to know is that she's beautiful and pure. In a way, the victim is like Hitchcock's MacGuffin: She is the character everyone looks for and no one really cares about. We don't care much about how she feels and even less about what she thinks. In this sense, the victim is more object than human. We know Rapunzel for her beautiful, long hair, but what else do we know about her? We only know she's been made a prisoner by a witch for the sins of her parents. We don't know if she graduated high school, has any brothers or sisters, is ambitious, etc. What's important is that she's there so the king's son can try to rescue her. (He fails.)

Of the three majors in the triangle, the victim is the least important.

STRUCTURE

In an adventure plot, the protagonist may encounter a variety of events that only loosely relate to the plot. But in a rescue plot, although the protagonist goes forth into world, she is tightly focused on a task (that of rescuing someone). The point of the adventure plot is for the hero to learn, but the point of the rescue plot is to save someone or something.

The rescue plot has three dramatic phases, which correspond to the three-act structure.

The first act is separation. The protagonist is separated from the victim by the antagonist, which is the motivating incident. The first act establishes the hero and the victim, as well as their relationship, so we can understand why they should not be denied each other's company. The abduction takes place toward the end of the first act (as the first reversal). Chernomor snatches Lyudmila from the marriage bed. King Kong snatches Ann Redman (Fay Wray).

The second act is pursuit. The protagonist, denied, pursues

the antagonist. What the protagonist does and where she goes is defined primarily by the actions of the antagonist. If the antagonist lives in the Dark Kingdom, the protagonist must journey there. If the antagonist hides in a corn field in the middle of Kansas, it behooves the protagonist to follow. The obstacles the protagonist meets along the way are usually the products of the antagonist. Traps, tricks, diversions, red herrings and the like. The true hero perseveres and overcomes the obstacles, but not without difficulty. The adventure hero rarely suffers any meaningful disability. If she is wounded, it's not bad enough to force her to discontinue; there is no obstacle she can't overcome in the pursuit of the antagonist. Since the reader knows, at least intuitively, the outcome of the chase, it's important for the writer to make the chase as entertaining as possible. The traps, tricks and turns should be clever and surprising. If they are predictable, you have precious little left to offer the reader.

Eddie Murphy, the Chosen One in *The Golden Child*, must rescue the Tibetan *wunderkind* who is born once every thousand generations; his task is to overcome the forces of evil that have stolen the child. Eddie Murphy's character is unlikely as the Chosen One, but a variety of tasks prove his worthiness and his inner righteousness. The task often elevates the common person to heroic proportion. Only then can he take on the awesome powers of the Chosen One.

The third act is the inevitable confrontation between the protagonist and the antagonist. Usually it's an action-packed clash between the forces of good and evil. You know the type. As in the second act, since the reader pretty much knows how this will turn out, the writer must provide the surprises in another form: the confrontation scenes themselves. They should be entertaining and filled with surprises. When Luke Skywalker finally faces Darth Vader, we *know* how it will turn out. After all, Darth Vader is wearing a black hat. The surprise? The duel is between father and son.

There are other ways of surprising the reader/viewer. In *The Searchers*, we find out the woman everyone's been trying to rescue doesn't want to be rescued. She wasn't kidnapped; she took off to get away from her husband. You may want to pull the rug out from under the reader by having the hero fail. That would be a surprise for sure, but be careful. Don't disappoint the reader. You'll need a damn convincing rationale for doing something like that. The reader has certain expectations, and unless you've been building a foundation all along for such an ending, the reader will probably reject it out of hand.

The rescue plot is perhaps more formulaic than most of the other plots. It has standard characters and situations. But don't underestimate its immense appeal. Like the revenge and temptation plots, it is one of the most satisfying emotionally. It confirms the moral order of the universe by overcoming evil; it restores order in a chaotic world; and it reaffirms the power of love.

CHECKLIST

As you write, keep these points in mind:

1. The rescue plot relies more on action than on the development of characterization.

2. Your character triangle should consist of a hero, a villain and a victim. The hero should rescue the victim from the villain.

3. The moral argument of the rescue plot tends to be black and white.

4. The focus of your story should be on the hero's pursuit of the villain.

5. Your hero should go out into the world to pursue the villain, and usually must contend with the villain on the villain's turf.

6. Your hero should be defined by her relationship to the villain.

7. Use your antagonist as a device whose purpose is to deprive the hero of what he believes is rightfully his.

8. Make sure the antagonist constantly interferes with the hero's progress.

9. The victim is generally the weakest of the three characters and serves mainly as a mechanism to force the hero to confront the antagonist.

10. Develop the three dramatic phases of separation, pursuit, and confrontation and reunion.

Chapter Eleven

Master Plot #5: Escape

Oh, that I had wings like a dove: For then I would fly away, and be at rest.
— *Psalms 55:6*

T he previous two plots (pursuit and rescue) have much in common with the escape plot. The escape plot is physical, and as such, concentrates its energy on the mechanics of capture and escape. That would eliminate stories about characters who try to escape a personal demon (such as addictions, phobias and dependencies). Those are character plots (plots of the mind). Escape in this plot is literal: The protagonist is confined against her will and wants to escape.

Literature is ripe with examples such as *The Prisoner of Zenda* by Sir Anthony Hope Hawkins, *Typee* by Herman Melville, "The Ransom of Red Chief" by O. Henry, *Midnight Express* by William Hayes and William Hofer (made into a film by Alan Parker), "Occurrence at Owl Creek Bridge" by Ambrose Bierce, and films such as *Papillon, The Invasion of the Body Snatchers, The Great Escape* and *Stalag 17*. It is also a familiar theme of fairy tales: the child who is being held prisoner by a witch or an ogre.

The thrust of this plot is in many ways the flip side of the rescue plot. In the rescue plot the reader follows the rescuer, and the victim waits patiently to be saved. In the escape plot, however, the victim frees herself.

The moral argument of this plot tends to be black and white: The hero is unjustly imprisoned. But not always. Sometimes the essence of the escape plot is nothing more than a test of wills between two strong personalities: the jailor and the jailed. They devote themselves to the task at hand: the warden to keeping his charge imprisoned, and the ward to escaping imprisonment. John Carpenter's *Escape From New York* has no meaningful moral structure, not even the basic reaffirmation of right over wrong, but in terms of an escape adventure, it's fun to watch.

By comparison, read Hayes and Hofer's *Midnight Express*, whose title is prison jargon for "escape." It deals realistically with the horror of imprisonment in Turkey and the character's need to escape in order to survive. In it, Billy Hayes is caught trying to smuggle hashish out of Turkey. He tries to make his first escape when he shows the authorities where he bought the hashish, but he's unsuccessful and is sent to prison, which is a Hell on earth. His sentence is four years and two months, which, according to his lawyer, is a light sentence. Hayes is determined to serve his time and get out, even though he must witness homosexual crimes, knifings, even the torturing of children. At first he hopes his lawyer will get an appeal, but nothing happens. Finally, two months before his release date, Hayes gets a summons. Hoping for an early release, he finds out to his horror the court intends to make an example of him and is going to retry him as a smuggler. He's given a thirty-year sentence — a virtual death sentence — and sent back to prison.

Hayes now knows there's no way out except escape.

The rest of the story details Hayes' attempts at escape. He makes plans to escape through an underground tunnel system beneath the prison but is thwarted when the tunnel dead-ends. Through a series of incidents that take him to the depths of Hell, he finally gets his chance to escape and takes it.

ESCAPE PLOT—PHASE ONE

The story typifies the three dramatic phases of the escape plot. In the first phase, the protagonist is imprisoned. The crime may be real or imagined (the protagonist accordingly guilty or innocent). In the case of *Midnight Express*, the punishment doesn't fit the crime, so as readers we are offended by the excess and side with Billy Hayes, who's a decent human being among animals.

In "An Occurrence at Owl Creek Bridge," Peyton Farquhar stands on a railroad bridge in northern Alabama looking down at the swift waters below. His hands are tied behind his back, and there's a noose around his neck. He's about to be hung by Union soldiers. This situation, compared to the five-year ordeal of Billy Hayes, takes place in a few minutes. Either Farquhar will be hung or he'll escape through some miracle. The conflict is clear and the tension immediate.

In Melville's *Typee*, Toby and Tom jump ship at one of the Marquesas Islands, only to end up the "guests" of a tribe of cannibals, who are fascinated with the Englishmen. The cannibals defer having their guests for dinner, but they will not let them leave, either.

In O. Henry's "The Ransom of Red Chief," Sam and Bill kidnap the only child of a wealthy man and take him to a cave. The situation seems straightforward: If the father wants his boy back, he must pay a ransom.

ESCAPE PLOT — PHASE TWO

The second phase of the escape plot deals with imprisonment and plans for escape. There may be an attempted escape during the first dramatic phase, but it always fails. Either the escape is foiled or, if it succeeds, the protagonist is recaptured and returned to prison.

The plot question is a simple one: Will the protagonist escape? The third dramatic phase contains the answer, but in most cases the reader will be able to guess correctly well in advance what the outcome will be. This is a result of the simple moral structure. If the forces are clearly drawn between good and evil, we don't expect evil to prevail. It's dissatisfying for the reader to be rooting for the protagonist only to see him fail at the end. Readers prefer an upbeat ending, a triumph rather than a defeat. We expect Billy Hayes to escape; we expect Farquhar will somehow escape hanging; we expect Toby and Tom to escape the cookpot; and we expect that Johnny's father will pay the ransom for the return of his son (although with O. Henry, we also expect the unexpected; we would be disappointed if the end didn't have some twist to it).

In "An Occurrence at Owl Creek Bridge," the sergeant in charge of the execution steps off the board that is keeping Farquhar up. Farquhar falls, the noose tight around his neck. On his way down, the author relates his crime: As a staunch supporter of the South he had tried to burn down the Owl Creek Bridge before the Union troops arrived. But he was captured and sentenced to death. Farquhar dreams of throwing off the noose, diving into the water and returning to his wife and family, who await him at home.

Toby and Tom attempt their own escapes, but the Typee cannibals obviously have other plans for them. Tom comes down with a disease that swells his leg; Toby convinces the Typees to let him get help for his friend, but on his way out hostile warriors from another tribe attack him, forcing him back to the Typees.

"The Ransom of Red Chief," on the other hand, begins working in a strange direction by the second phase. After Sam and Bill kidnap Johnny, Sam leaves to return a horse and buggy while Bill watches the boy. When Sam comes back, however, he finds Bill and Johnny have been playing a game of trappers and Indians. Johnny, who announces himself as "Red Chief," now has his poor battered captor tied up! Red Chief then declares that in the morning he will scalp Bill and burn Sam at the stake.

The ironic twist is already evident. Johnny is the captor and Bill and Sam are the captives. He terrorizes the two men by keeping them from sleeping and threatening them with their morning executions. He attacks them with a hot potato and then with a rock. The two men have no chance against him.

ESCAPE PLOT—PHASE THREE

The third phase consists of the escape itself. Usually the well-laid plans of the second dramatic phase fall apart. (If they didn't, the action would be too predictable.) Wild cards come into play. Enter the unexpected. All hell breaks loose. To this point the situation has been tightly controlled by the antagonist, but suddenly the situation becomes fluid, out of control either by gratuitous circumstance or by design of the hero. The hero, who has been at a distinct disadvantage, finally gets the upper hand, and if there's a moral score to settle, the time has come for settling it.

The third dramatic phase is usually the most active of phases. Since the second phase consists of escape plans, the third phase is the realization of the escape itself, even though most often it's under circumstances different from those planned in the second phase.

Peyton Farquhar drops from the bridge, and then, ". . . all at once, with terrible suddenness, the light about him shot upward with the noise of a loud splash; a frightful roaring was in his ears, and all was cold and dark. . . . He knew that the rope had broken and he had fallen into the stream." He struggles to escape to free his hands as he rises to the surface. But the Union soldiers open fire on him, forcing him back under the water.

The swift current takes Farquhar downstream and out of range. Exhausted, he starts the walk home with only the thought of his wife on his mind. He reaches his house, barely able to stand, and there is his wife, waiting for him. He reaches out to embrace her.

Then comes the final line of the story: "Peyton Farquhar was dead; his body, with a broken neck, swung gently from side to side beneath the timbers of the Owl Creek Bridge."

The escape, it turns out, was no escape at all. Or perhaps it was, since in Farquhar's mind he had escaped. Bierce can get away with this kind of ending because the short story was written for the effect of the last line. We don't get to know Peyton Farquhar, so we don't care that much about him. His life, or death, is immaterial to the plot, which is successful only because of its radical turn at the end.

O. Henry uses a similar strategy in "The Ransom of Red Chief." We can see where the story is going as we see Red Chief take over his captors. The difference between the stories is that "The Ransom of Red Chief" is played for comic rather than dramatic effect. The journey of Peyton Farquhar is prosaic. We go along for the ride to see where it's going. In the case of O. Henry's story, we go along for the ride because we enjoy the ride. The notion of a ten-year-old boy turning the table on two kidnappers and terrorizing them as they meant to do to him is amusing.

To add insult to injury, Johnny has such a good time torturing his captors that he doesn't want to go home.

Sam finally mails the ransom note. The father's reply: He will take back his son—provided the kidnappers pay *him* $250!

Meanwhile, the kidnappers have been trying in vain to free themselves of Johnny. Finally, out of exasperation, they pay the ransom of $250 just to get rid of the kid. The plot reversal works as comedy.

Your responsibility as writer is to keep the reader off-balance by constantly shifting the terms of the escape. Nothing goes as planned; something always goes wrong. And that's the joy of it.

CHECKLIST

As you write, keep these points in mind:

1. Escape is always literal. Your hero should be confined against his will (often unjustly) and wants to escape.

2. The moral argument of your plot should be black and white.

3. Your hero should be the victim (as opposed to the rescue plot, in which the hero saves the victim).

4. Your first dramatic phase deals with the hero's imprisonment and any initial attempts at escape, which fail.

5. Your second dramatic phase deals with the hero's plans for escape. These plans are almost always thwarted.

6. Your third dramatic phase deals with the actual escape.

7. The antagonist has control of the hero during the first two dramatic phases; the hero gains control in the last dramatic phase.

Chapter Twelve

Master Plot #6: Revenge

If you prick us, do we not bleed? If you tickle us, do we not laugh? If you poison us, do we not die? And if you wrong us, shall we not revenge?

    —Shakespeare, The Merchant of Venice, III, i

Francis Bacon called revenge a wild justice. In literature the dominant motive for this plot is loud and clear: retaliation by the protagonist against the antagonist for real or imagined injury. It's a visceral plot, which means it reaches into us at a deep emotional level. We bristle against injustice and we want to see it corrected. And almost always, the retaliation is outside the limits of the law. This is the wild justice that Bacon spoke about. There are times when the law cannot properly dispense justice, so we take the matter into our own hands. We have a Biblical precedent that we've heard quoted so many times that we can recite it in our sleep: "An eye for an eye, tooth for tooth; hand for hand, foot for foot" (Exodus 21:24). In the throes of righteousness it's easy to overlook Jesus' response: "If any one strikes you on the right cheek, turn to him the other also; and if any one would sue you and take your coat, let him have your cloak as well; and if any one forces you to go one mile, go with him two miles." Fine sentiments, but obviously not human nature. If you hit me, I will hit you back. (There have been some fine stories about people who cling to their faith when tempted by revenge, but they're better people than most of us are.)

Revenge is vigilante justice, which has as much power today as it had a thousand years ago.

The theme of revenge was a favorite among the Greeks, but it reached its highest expression in seventeenth-century Elizabethan and Jacobean tragedy.

Thomas Kyd's *The Spanish Tragedy*, written about 1590, is about Hieronimo, who wavers on the verge of madness after his son is murdered. Between his spells of madness, he discovers who has killed his son and why, and he plots revenge. Sound familiar?

Not yet? Then two more clues. The ghost of the murdered son calls for his father to carry out the revenge. Hieronimo then stages a play in which the murderers are killed. Figure it out yet?

Antonio's Revenge, you say? In this play by John Marston, Antonio's murdered father appears as a ghost and begs his son to avenge his murder, which he does during a court ball.

Or maybe you thought of George Chapman's *The Revenge of Bussy d'Amboise*, when Bussy's ghost begs his brother to avenge his murder? Or was it Henry Chettle's *Tragedy of Hoffman*? Or Cyril Tourneur's *The Revengers Tragedie*?

Most likely it was Shakespeare's *Hamlet*, which is probably the most famous revenge story ever told. (Remember what I said earlier about Shakespeare's originality?) Sure, others told the same story, but none told it so well. The talking ghost crying out for revenge, the feigned madness, the play-within-the-play and the carnage at the end were all stock devices used in the revenge tragedy.

Most of our contemporary revenge stories don't have the range of character and feeling that Shakespeare brought to *Hamlet*. Still, the pattern of the revenge plot hasn't changed in the last three thousand years. At the heart of the story is the protagonist, who is generally a good person forced to take vengeance into her own hands when the law won't give satisfaction. Then there's the antagonist, the person who has committed the crime, who for some quirk in the natural progress of events has escaped punishment for his crime. Last, there's the victim, the person whom the protagonist must avenge. As a character, the victim obviously is expendable; his purpose is to arouse our sympathies, for him and for the protagonist (who has been denied love, companionship or the like). Sometimes the victim is the protagonist himself. The more heinous the crime (rape, murder, incest), the more the protagonist is justified in seeking vengeance. We don't expect the character to go on a campaign of revenge for someone having shoplifted a quart of beer out of her store or for claiming an undeserved deduction on his income tax form.

The first rule of revenge is that the punishment must equal the crime—thus the concept of "getting even." The Bible's warrant doesn't allow us to exceed that which has been received. "An eye for an eye; a tooth for a tooth. . . ." And with our primitive sense of justice, we are content to exact that same punishment. No more, and no less.

The basic dramatic structure of the plot has changed very little over time. Its three dramatic phases remain consistent from early Greek tragedy to modern Hollywood melodrama.

THE FIRST DRAMATIC PHASE—THE CRIME

The first dramatic phase consists primarily of the crime. The hero and his loved ones are established when suddenly an awful crime intrudes, terminating the hero's happiness. The hero is unable to defend against the crime. Either he's not present or he's restrained (and forced to watch, which adds to the horror).

In some stories, such as the older ones I've cited, a murder has been committed before the story begins. Hamlet's father is already murdered. Generally it's good advice for any writer to start a scene late and get out early; that is, don't drag your reader through every detail leading up to the action, and don't "hang around" after it. Confine your writing to the core of the scene. But I don't recommend cutting the scenes so tightly that the audience doesn't witness the crime, because it may be an important element for the reader to experience emotionally. If someone commits a wrongdoing against me or my family, and I want others to share in my outrage, the most effective way for me to gain your empathy is to make you witness the crime. These scenes are not only powerful because of their content, but because they create a strong bond between the audience and the victim. We feel for the victim. We are as outraged as she is, and we want justice as badly as she does. If the crime occurs before your readers enter the story, they are less inclined to feel empathetic. Sympathetic, maybe, but not empathetic. One of your primary goals in this plot is to build a strong emotional bridge between your readers and your main character.

The hero may rely on justice from other sources, such as the police, but that almost never gives satisfaction. He then realizes that if there is any justice to be had, he must dispense it himself.

THE SECOND DRAMATIC PHASE—REVENGE

The second dramatic phase starts as the hero makes his plans for revenge. He prepares for action. If the vengeance involves a single antagonist, the second phase may deal with pursuit (finding) as well as preparation for revenge. In the case of serial revenge, in which several people must pay for the crime, the hero may start dispensing justice in this phase. There is often a third party (to complete the triangle), who tries to stop the hero from achieving his intention. In *Death Wish* it's the police officer investigating the case. In *Sudden Impact* it's Harry Calahan investigating the case. In both cases, the police are sympathetic to the hero's cause and end up helping in some way. In *The Outlaw Josey Wales*, the third arm of the triangle is an old Indian, who adds both a comic touch and historical proportion, since he too has been a victim.

THE THIRD DRAMATIC PHASE—CONFRONTATION

The third dramatic phase deals with the confrontation. In the case of serial revenge, the final criminal to get his due is the most important: Either he's the ringleader, or the most psychopathic, or whatever. This is the moment of triumph for the protagonist. Her motivation has been single-minded all along. She either succeeds or fails. In the case of *Utu*, the powerful revenge film from New Zealand, the hero is a Maori man who finds his entire village massacred by the British army. He swears "utu"—traditional revenge—and wages his own war against the British. One man against an army. His serial revenge is successful until the third phase, when he's captured. He's executed, but his death is heroic. In popular literature, however, the protagonist is almost always successful, and once the vengeance is accomplished, she can return to "normal" life.

Revenge is an emotionally powerful motivation; it tends to almost possess the hero. The drama has hard edges and can make some readers uncomfortable with the violence that it entails. Although violence isn't a prerequisite of this plot, classical revenge usually involves violence, and an informal survey of stories in this category will show violence is a common motif.

But revenge can take nonviolent forms as well. What happens, for instance, when you want to write a comedy in this form? As with plots that incorporate violence, the punishment in a comedy must fit the crime. There are lesser crimes, crimes that don't require violence to settle the score; for example, it would be appropriate for a con man to be conned in return, such as in the "sting" story. Not all sting stories are revenge plots, but many are. The Pulitzer-Prize winning dramatist David Mamet is famous for his stories about stings and con artists. However, the best example of the sting as a revenge plot is the 1973 film by the same name starring Paul Newman and Robert Redford. Sting stories get their energy and appeal from elaborate cons that take a long time to set up (and usually don't go as planned). These intricate inventions developed in the second dramatic phase delight us; they are complicated, unwieldy and seemingly impossible.

Unfortunately, well-crafted revenge stories are the exception rather than the rule. Edgar Allan Poe's short story "The Cask of Amontillado" is a wonderful exception. The story has only two characters, Montressor and Fortunato. Because it's a short story, Poe had the flexibility to bend the basic formula.

Fortunato commits the crime. Montressor is the victim. The crime? An insult. Montressor tells the story, and we never find out what the insult was. He tells us, "The thousand injuries of Fortunato I had borne as I best could, but when he ventured upon insult I vowed revenge." We suspect the man has a screw loose.

Montressor plans his revenge. It must be perfect, one in which his victim will know exactly what is happening to him. During a carnival, a time of "supreme madness," Montressor lures Fortunato into his wine cellar to taste some amontillado. He chains Fortunato to a wall and then entombs him behind a wall of stone, where he will wait for his death in darkness, repenting for his crime.

Fortunato, of course, is as much in the dark as we are. This revenge is for an imaginary insult or an insult so blown out of proportion that the punishment also is blown out of proportion.

One reason the tale works so well is that it's told in the first person. Montressor assumes we will condone his actions and share in the grotesque perfection of revenge. Although he sounds sane for most of the story, he reveals his true self at the end, when Fortunato starts to scream from behind the wall that Montressor is building. He unsheathes his sword, thrusts it about in the air and starts to scream himself, drowning out the screams of his victim.

It's a sketch of madness, little more. Diabolical, chilling and clever. But we can't sympathize with Montressor; we quickly despise him. It would have been next to impossible to pull off this story as a novel. Poe's four pages is about as far as he could go.

Euripides went further with *Medea*.

Master Plot #18, "Wretched Excess," arguably could be the logical place for Medea because the title character takes revenge to all-time extremes. But the plot is still revenge, and therefore I keep it in this category.

If Hell hath no fury like a woman scorned, Medea is the personification of the scorned woman. When her husband deserts her for another woman, she swears revenge. But like Montressor, she has no sense of proportion, and she violates the first rule of revenge: She punishes her husband (and herself) far more than the crime would allow. Medea pays the price for her severity, but even so, she never becomes a sympathetic character. *Medea* is a cautionary tale that warns against excess of emotion and decries the price of bitterness.

Medea's plan is to murder her husband, Jason; his new wife, Glauce; and Glauce's father. But, like Montressor, she wants Jason to suffer for his crime against her. Killing him would be too easy. So she decides to kill Glauce, Glauce's father, and her own children, thereby denying Jason everyone he loves.

Medea apologizes to Jason for her earlier outburst and asks if she can send her children with gifts for his new wife as a sign of her repentance. Jason is pleased, of course, and agrees.

Medea's gift to Glauce is a beautiful golden robe, a present from her grandfather, Helios, god of the sun. But before she gives the robe to her children to give to Glauce, she douses it with a deadly drug.

When Glauce tries on the robe the drug sears her flesh and she dies in agony. Her father tries to save her and is himself contaminated and dies the same death.

Meanwhile, Medea's children return to her. She has second thoughts about killing them, as her maternal instincts momentarily interfere with her plan of revenge. But, as Euripides points out, Medea isn't a Greek—she is a barbarian—and she takes a sword and slaughters her children.

Jason is insane with grief and, as he pounds on the doors to Medea's house, she appears at the balcony holding the bodies of her dead children. Medea escapes in a chariot sent by Helios, and as she carries away the bodies of the children, she taunts Jason with the loneliness and grief that await him. Even though she must suffer the same fate, it will always be tempered by the sweetness of her revenge.

The examples of Poe and Euripides are atypical of the revenge plot. The protagonists in both cases claim the rights of justice, but in excess to their due. They're tragic, pathetic characters, but they don't have, nor do they deserve, our sympathies. Their revenges are outrages in themselves.

In 1974 Paramount released a film starring Charles Bronson that created an uproar of protest. Social and political leaders denounced the film as neo-Fascist; the Catholic church slapped the picture with a "C" rating (condemned). And yet people from every race, age, sex and economic class around the world lined up in droves to see it.

The film was *Death Wish*, film's version of the ultimate revenge fantasy, that of the ordinary man seeking revenge as a one-man vigilante committee. The film was remade twice more with virtually no change in the plot, and still it continued to make big money at the box office.

Paul Kersey (Charles Bronson) is a successful, big-city architect. He's an upper-middle-class liberal with a beautiful wife and a beautiful home. Three out-and-out crazy punks upset his world when they break into his apartment, kill his wife and rape his daughter, who spends the rest of the film catatonic. The police can do nothing.

Furious with the incompetence of the police, Kersey takes matters into his own hands. He starts haunting the cesspools of New York, inviting muggers to take a shot at him. And when they take him up on his offer, he takes a shot at them—literally. The press dubs him the New York Vigilante. He is a media hero; crime in the city drops while he stalks the streets.

The police capture him but instead of arresting him tell him to leave town. (Sounds a lot like a stock Western plot: The hired sheriff cleans up the town, but the townspeople get fed up with all the violence associated with the clean-up and ask him to leave.) Kersey leaves New York for Los Angeles, where he takes up his crusade in *Death Wish II* when his Mexican maid and teenaged daughter are raped and killed. (Don't ask where the daughter came from.)

As an action melodrama, the *Death Wish* series manipulates our emotions expertly. We're fed up with crime in the streets; we hate the vermin that inhabit our cities, and we keep waiting for some knight in shining armor to emerge and clean up the town the way Marshalls Earp and Dillon did in their day. We're also frustrated with a system that either has too much red tape or is just incompetent.

Along comes Kersey. Give him a justified cause (he loses his family to scum), give him a gun, and let him loose to do his own thing. And then let us participate vicariously in his victories. When I saw *Death Wish* in the theater, the audience applauded and cheered when the bad guys got it. I also saw it in a video club in Moscow, and the Russians loved it. For a moment, Bronson's character was our defending champion. We immediately side with Kersey's anger and frustration; it's *our* anger and frustration. And as Kersey scours the streets, *we feel cleansed*. This is the heart of catharsis, of cleansing.

Critics were concerned the movie would spawn copycat vigilantes. It didn't happen, of course. It did, however, spawn copycat versions of the film worldwide, proving its appeal to a wide audience and the power and depth of the emotions we bring to it.

Interestingly enough, the author of the novel *Death Wish* wrote a sequel called *Death Sentence*, in which he proposed alternative solutions to vigilantism. To date no one has optioned the book for a film.

Paul Kersey and Hamlet are both bent on revenge. But the similarities stop there. Paul Kersey is a sketch of a man, a type. In the beginning of his story he detests violence, a typically liberal attitude, but by the end of the story he is addicted to it. He does change as a character, but the change is without any real depth or soul-searching. He just goes with the flow.

Hamlet struggles from the beginning of the play to the end. When the ghost of his father tells him he didn't die accidentally but was murdered by Hamlet's uncle, Claudius, Hamlet doesn't go storming off to dispense justice. He is a thinking person. Is the ghost real? Is it a demon sent to torment him? He doesn't know whether to believe the ghost. He needs proof.

Hamlet becomes depressed. He isn't a violent man, and the thought of running a sword through his uncle turns his stomach. Unlike manipulative plots like *Death Wish*, in which characters enter into the notion of revenge easily once given a provocation, Hamlet suffers tremendously. He doubts the ghost. He doubts himself. He wants to do the right thing, but he truly doesn't know what it is.

When a troupe of actors arrive, Hamlet comes up with a plan to find out if Claudius is guilty. He has the actors play out the scenario of his father's murder as the ghost related to him, and he watches Claudius for his reaction.

Claudius gives himself away. He's so unnerved that he must leave the performance. Hamlet now is certain the ghost is his dead father, and that Claudius had murdered him. The task of vengeance now falls squarely on him.

And yet when he comes upon Claudius while he's praying, Hamlet can't kill him. He rationalizes, believing if he kills Claudius while he's praying, Claudius will be in a state of grace.

Claudius is no fool. He thinks Hamlet is plotting to take the crown away from him and so hatches his own plan to kill Hamlet. But the plan backfires.

Hamlet wavers between sanity and madness, destroying the people around him. This has become a true disaster in the making, involving the entire court. He kills the old man Polonius (thinking he was killing Claudius), which causes his son, Laertes, to swear to avenge *his* father's death. Claudius seizes the opportunity and sets up a duel, betting on his nephew, but poisoning the tip of Laertes' sword so that even a scratch would be fatal to Hamlet. Then, to hedge his bets, Claudius also puts a cup of poison near Hamlet in case he should get thirsty during the duel.

But Hamlet's mother drinks from the cup and dies.

Laertes wounds Hamlet, poisoning him.

Hamlet runs Laertes through. But before he dies, he tells Hamlet that Claudius was responsible for poisoning the sword.

Hamlet runs Claudius through, and then, in the true tradition of the revenge tragedy, Hamlet dies.

End of story, a total wipeout. (You can see that Shakespeare was still influenced by the Greek version of the revenge tragedy, such as *Medea*.)

Although revenge tragedies are still as bloody as they were during the Greek era, the hero now survives the ordeal. The point of the old revenge tragedies is that there's a heavy price to pay for revenge. Innocent people get swept up in it and die, and the hero almost always pays the price for revenge with her own death. There was never any satisfaction at having accomplished vengeance.

Today, however, the hero seems to bask in self-righteousness. She feels justified and liberated by the act of vengeance. She walks away at the end, somehow a better person, and if there's a price to pay, it's small in comparison to the suffering the old heroes went through.

Revenge is an emotionally powerful (and one might say dangerous) plot to work with. You manipulate powerful emotions in your reader by creating a situation that cries for justice. We respond at a deep level when someone violates us or anyone else who doesn't deserve violation. In many cases, victims are like Everyman. It's as if you say to the reader, "If it could happen to this person, it could happen to you, too." Chilling. And to protect ourselves from that kind of outrage (murder, rape, mayhem, etc.) we demand swift and complete justice. You put yourself in a strong moral position as you write this plot. You say what is proper and what is improper behavior. Be careful. What you recommend may be wild justice, but that too may have its price.

Now let's say you want to write a story about a bookkeeper who cheats on the books. As readers, we may not feel offended by the crime. The call for revenge wouldn't seem justified. What would you do, turn him in to the I.R.S.? You certainly wouldn't cut off his head. Limit your revenge story to a grievous crime — one that does major physical or mental damage to your hero. Even in *The Sting*, Redford is avenging the death of his close friend.

This brings us back to the discussion about motivation and intent. Revenge is the intent of your hero. But what is your hero's motivation for wanting to get revenge? Be careful how you develop this aspect of your protagonist. Do you want the reader to remain sympathetic, or do you want to show how seeking revenge distorts the values of the character? Understand both the cause (the crime) and the effect (how the crime affects the victim or someone close to the victim who wants revenge).

This plot examines the dark side of human nature. Don't lose your character amidst the turmoil of the action.

CHECKLIST

Keep in mind the following points as you develop this plot:

1. Your protagonist seeks retaliation against the antagonist for a real or imagined injury.

2. Most (but not all) revenge plots focus more on the act of the revenge than on a meaningful examination of the character's motives.

3. The hero's justice is "wild," vigilante justice that usually goes outside the limits of the law.

4. Revenge plots tend to manipulate the feelings of the reader by avenging the injustices of the world by a man or woman of action who is forced to act by events when the institutions that normally deal with these problems prove inadequate.

5. Your hero should have moral justification for vengeance.

6. Your hero's vengeance may equal but may not exceed the offense perpetrated against the hero (the punishment must fit the crime).

7. Your hero first should try to deal with the offense in traditional ways, such as relying on the police — an effort that usually fails.

8. The first dramatic phase establishes the hero's normal life; then the antagonist interferes with it by committing a crime. Make the audience understand the full impact of the crime against the hero, and what it costs both physically and emotionally.

Your hero then gets no satisfaction by going through official channels and realizes he must pursue his own cause if he wants to avenge the crime.

9. The second dramatic phase includes your hero making plans for revenge and then pursuing the antagonist.

Your antagonist may elude the hero's vengeance either by chance or design. This act usually pits the two opposing characters against each other.

10. The last dramatic phase includes the confrontation between your hero and antagonist. Often the hero's plans go awry, forcing him to improvise. Either the hero succeeds or fails in his attempts. In contemporary revenge plots, the hero usually doesn't pay much of an emotional price for the revenge. This allows the action to become cathartic for the audience.

Chapter Thirteen

Master Plot #7: The Riddle

The mystery story is really two stories in one: the story of what happened and the story of what appeared to happen.

— *Mary Roberts Rinehart*

W hat child doesn't love riddles? What adult doesn't like the puzzle to solve, the brain teaser to ponder, the conundrum to untangle? They delight us because they challenge and entertain us.

A riddle is a deliberately enigmatic or ambiguous question. The answer requires understanding the subtleties of meaning within the words themselves, which are clues to another meaning. "What's black and white and red all over?" goes one well-known children's riddle. Answer: "A newspaper." Why? Because we take the word *red* to mean *read* and *all over* to mean *everywhere*. The words of the riddle suggest a hidden meaning, and you must search the words for clues that provide the solution, in addition to some insight on your part. The object of the riddle, which is its subject, is usually described in an enigmatic way:

What runs all day and lies under the bed at night?

A dog.

That's an acceptable answer, but it doesn't satisfy. Why not? Because it lacks the element of surprise and cleverness. The answer is prosaic, *obvious*.

What runs all day and lies under the bed at night?

A shoe.

Maybe not a great riddle, but the answer is more satisfying than "a dog." The riddle implies something alive (because it runs and lies), and the answer is inanimate, but still meets the conditions of the riddle. A riddle is a guessing game, often with a twist. It's usually witty and shrewd, and sometimes insightful.

Children's riddles are simpler; adult riddles are more sophisticated and require greater thinking skills. Take this old English rhyming riddle, for example:

> *Little Nancy Etticoat*
> *In a white petticoat*
> *And a red nose;*
> *The longer she stands*
> *The shorter she grows.*

This riddle, like most riddles, follows a simple structure based on two elements. The first element is general (Little Nancy Etticoat / In a white petticoat / And a red nose) and is understood generally and metaphorically. The second element is specific (The longer she stands / The shorter she grows) and is understood literally. The second element is also a paradox. How is it possible for someone to grow shorter the longer she stands?

The clues are in the first element. If we take Little Nancy Etticoat to be a thing personified rather than a person, we know two things about her/it: it is "dressed" in white and has a red "nose."

Rephrase the question: What is it that is white and has a red "nose" that grows shorter the longer it stands?

At this point you must make a leap of understanding. Since this riddle is old (that is, before the days of electricity), it no longer is current. But you'll understand the answer as soon as you hear it (if you haven't figured it out already).

Answer: a candle. The red "nose" is its flame. The longer a candle burns ("stands"), the shorter it becomes ("grows").

Most cultures have had the riddle as part of their folklore since ancient times. We are familiar with the literary riddles in *Through the Looking Glass* ("Humpty Dumpty") and in fairy tales in which the hero must answer a riddle before he can be granted the hand of the princess in marriage.

This test of cleverness (wit as opposed to strength; mentality as opposed to physicality) is considered the ultimate test. Hercules must perform tremendous physical feats, but cleaning out the Augean stables is nothing compared to the test of the riddle.

The most famous riddle in all of literature is the one the Sphinx asks Oedipus. The Sphinx apparently had nothing better to do with her life than ask young men passing by a riddle she'd made up. No harm. Except that if you didn't answer the riddle correctly, she'd eat you.

Try your luck:

What has one voice and walks on four legs in the morning, on two at midday, and on three legs in the evening? (Remember, you're barbecue if you can't come up with the right answer.)

When Oedipus gave the right answer to the Sphinx, she got so depressed she killed herself. And the happy people of the kingdom made Oedipus their king. Not bad for a day's work.

Oedipus' answer: "A man, who crawls on all fours as a baby, walks on two feet when grown, and leans on a cane when aged."

The riddle in higher cultures is an important part of the literature. In early literature they're generally the realm of gods, ogres and beasts, and it's up to the hero to answer the riddle correctly if he wants to pass or win the freedom of a captive princess. But as we became more sophisticated and took gods out of the equation, the riddle evolved into much more sophisticated forms. Rather than one-liners, they became part of the weave of stories themselves.

Today the riddle has metamorphosized into the mystery. The short text of the riddle has become the longer text of the short story and the novel. But the focus is the same: It is a challenge to the reader to solve the problem.

Your mystery should have at its heart a paradox that begs a solution. The plot itself is physical, because it focuses on events (who, what, where, when and why) that must be evaluated and interpreted (the same as the riddle must be interpreted). Things are not what they seem on the surface. Clues lie within the words. The answer is not obvious (which wouldn't satisfy), but the answer *is* there. And in the best tradition of the mystery, the answer is in plain view.

Don't kid yourself about developing a mystery. It requires a lot of cleverness and the ability to deceive the reader. If you remember the parlor game of charades, you have a rough idea of what it's like to write this kind of story. The goal of charades is to convey to the audience through a series of clues the "title" of a person, place or thing. This title is the "solution" to your story — reality as opposed to appearance. But for the audience to solve the puzzle, it must work with a series of cumulative clues — which are often ambiguous — and then try to sort through those clues to understand the true relationship among them. The clues in charades aren't always clear (except when you look back and understand the rationale that created them). The audience understands that things aren't always what they seem to be, but that a clue is a clue. All the audience must do is interpret the clue *correctly*.

Easier said than done. You want to create clues that don't have obvious, absolute solutions. You want to create clues that could mean one thing as well as another, and only a person who's been attentive and understands the interconnection among clues will piece them together to make sense of them. Readers tend to get angry with writers who throw in red herrings; that is, clues that aren't real clues at all, but are added for the sole purpose of throwing the reader off the track. Let the reader throw herself off track by misinterpreting ambiguous clues. Don't toss in clues that don't add up. Don't give clues that are throw-aways. Concentrate on clues that must be understood *correctly*, clues that can be misunderstood. This is the heart of the author's cleverness. Readers don't mind making wrong turns if they feel they read the road sign incorrectly. They *do* mind if you set up a false road sign. Remember, this is a game, and you must play fairly. Give the reader a chance.

That doesn't mean you should make it easy. Try to find a nice tension between figuring out the solution too easily and making it impossible to figure out. If you're too coy, you'll lose your readers. Give them *something*. But put the burden on the reader to interpret that something correctly.

Herman Melville wrote a mystery called *Benito Cereno*. The story seems simple, but that's the trick of the mystery writer: Things are rarely what they seem. The captain of one slave ship visits the captain of another slave ship. The visiting captain guides us through the story. We see everything through his eyes. Only he's not terribly bright. He sees clues all around him, but he fails to make sense of them. But we do. As the captain of the ship gives him the tour, he sees slaves sharpening axes. Strange, the visiting captain thinks to himself, slaves shouldn't be allowed to have weapons. *Exactly.* The appearance is that Benito Cereno is running a lax slave ship. The reality is that the slaves have taken over the ship and are just pretending that they're still slaves because they don't want the visiting captain to know. The visiting captain is too dim-witted to interpret the clues. Melville challenges the reader: Can you figure it out? Mysteries rely heavily on the rule about making the causal look casual. The best place to hide a clue is in plain view.

Edgar Allan Poe is credited with being the first American short story writer, and one of his most famous stories is "The Purloined Letter." Many consider this to be the first "mystery" story as we know it, with a detective seeking a solution to a riddle/problem.

The detective is C. Auguste Dupin, who spawned a whole generation of detectives, from Hercule Poirot by Agatha Christie to Inspector Maigret by Georges Simenon. Unlike the man of action, Dupin is thoughtful, acting as the surrogate thinker for the reader, exploring, uncovering, explaining. The challenge for the reader is to solve the riddle before the protagonist does, which makes the riddle a contest. If the protagonist figures out the riddle before you do, you lose; if you figure it before the protagonist, you win.

"The Purloined Letter" presents the riddle from the start. The prefect of the Parisian police bursts into Dupin's apartment to tell him that a certain minister of the court has stolen a compromising letter from the Queen. We never learn what's in the letter, but whatever it is, it's political dynamite, and the prefect has been charged with getting back the letter. He's searched the minister's apartment from top to bottom but can't find the letter. He wants Dupin's advice.

Dupin asks some questions about the physical appearance of the letter and the prefect's method of searching the minister's apartments. He suggests the prefect search the apartment again.

A month later, the letter is still missing. When Dupin learns that the Queen is willing to pay 50,000 francs for the return of the letter, he produces it instantly, to everyone's amazement.

Based on the evidence given, how did Dupin know where to look?

Dupin explains. The trick was understanding the mind of the minister. A clever man himself, the minister would expect the police to conduct a careful search of his apartment for the letter, so it would be stupid for him to hide the letter under a chair or some out-of-the-way place where it would certainly be found. From this Dupin surmises that the best place to hide the letter would be in plain sight; that is, not to hide the letter.

On a visit to the minister's apartment, he sees a letter hanging from a ribbon over the mantle. Sure enough, it turns out to be the missing letter.

"The Purloined Letter" is a riddle, and it presents the same challenges to the reader as the one-liners above. The game is more sophisticated, more challenging, but it's still the same game.

WHODUNIT?

Frank R. Stockton is not exactly a household name, but he did write one story in 1882 that everyone called "The Lady or the Tiger?"

This story is an example of the unresolved paradox. In a past era, a barbaric king had developed his own system of justice. He put men who offended him into an arena with two doors and told them to choose a door (something like an ancient Monty Hall). Behind one door was a ferocious tiger that would instantly devour the hapless man, and behind the other door was a ravishing princess who instantly became his wife.

A young man of lowly station fell in love with the king's daughter (and she with him), and when the king found out about it, he made the young man face the test in the arena. What would it be, the princess or the tiger?

Except the princess wasn't the king's daughter; it was some other young woman. The king's daughter, who loved the young man, did some snooping on her own and found out what was behind the doors. When the young man looked up at her, she signaled for him to choose the right door.

Therein lies the dilemma. If she saves her lover, he'll belong to another woman. And since these people are barbarians, they lack civilities such as selflessness, so it wouldn't be beyond the princess to prefer death for her lover than to let him have another woman. The young man is faced with a dilemma: What is behind the right door, the princess or the tiger?

When asked for the solution, Stockton wisely said, "If you decide which it was—the lady or the tiger—you find out what kind of person you are yourself." The decision, if there is one, belongs to the reader and how he views the world and human nature.

But a story like this can't go far. It presents the paradox and let us savor it momentarily. The characters are purely stock (king, princess, commoner), and the situation and the action play over everything else. In short, it's a gimmick.

In the last hundred years we've developed the riddle/mystery into its own form, with stories that are much more sophisticated than Poe's or Stockton's. Agatha Christie, Raymond Chandler, Dashiell Hammett, P.D. James, Georges Simenon, Mickey Spillane, Arthur Conan Doyle, H.P. Lovecraft, Dorothy Sayers, Ambrose Bierce, Guy de Maupassant . . . the list is impossibly long, containing a number of the world's brightest writers (and many not so bright). For some it's an art form; for others, it's a business. The latter churn out books one after another, working with formulas that have proven successful in the past. (Mickey Spillane once said, "I have no fans. You know what I got? Customers.")

The form developed its own conventions. One such hallmark is the intrusion of the dark, cruel criminal underworld into everyday life. These two extremes create an imbalance between good and bad, dark and light, right and wrong, safety and danger. This instability creates what critic Daniel Einstein calls "painful insecurity, rampant cynicism, and violent, unforeseen death."

Most of us at one point or another have read a mystery novel or watched 1940s *film noire* adaptations, such as Raymond Chandler's *The Blue Dahlia*, Dashiell Hammett's *The Maltese Falcon* or Agatha Christie's *And Then There Were None*. A 1931 German film, titled *Der Mann, Der Seiner Morder Sucht* (*A Man Searches for His Murderer*), was remade in the United States as *D.O.A.* in 1949 starring Edmond O'Brien (and remade again in the late

1980s starring Dennis Quaid). Structurally, it follows the same format as the riddle, opening with the general and moving to the specific.

THE FIRST DRAMATIC PHASE

D.O.A. begins with the protagonist, Frank Bigelow, entering a police station to report a homicide. When the police ask him who was murdered, he answers, "I was."

Flashback to the setup: Bigelow is a small-town accountant. He's about to leave for San Francisco. His secretary, who's also his fiancee, characterizes him for us: "You're just like any other man only a little more so. You have a feeling of being trapped, hemmed in, and you don't know whether or not you like it."

He leaves for the bright lights of the big city.

On the first night of his stay he goes to a jazz bar. Enter hot blonde. The place is undulating with sexual tension and a life that's much different from the staid life Bigelow's been living back home. He makes a pass at the blonde; she accepts. While they're having a drink together, a sinister man switches drinks on Bigelow while he's distracted by the blonde. The drink is bitter and he orders another.

Bigelow pays the price for "straying" the same way Michael Douglas' character does in *Fatal Attraction*, even though Bigelow only talks to her. He returns to his hotel room, has second thoughts about the blonde, and tears up her telephone number.

He wakes up sick. At first he thinks he's hung over, but he keeps getting sicker. He goes to the hospital. The doctors examine him and tell him that he's been poisoned and has three days to live.

The twist here is that the detective is also the victim. He must solve his own murder. His time frame is specific, since he'll be dead in three days. Like the riddle of little Nancy Etticoat, the first part of the riddle introduces the general. We meet the victim; we witness the crime; we meet the detective who will try to solve the crime (in this case the same person as the victim). The riddle is presented in its widest sense. Who did it? And why? The characters are presented in general terms; this is a physical plot, and action is more important than character depth. We find out what we need to know about Bigelow, and that he's a lot like the rest of us: slightly bored with life and looking for a taste of excitement. We easily identify with him. His focus for the rest of the story will be on one thing: finding out who killed him.

THE SECOND DRAMATIC PHASE

The hospital makes arrangements for a room for Bigelow to make his last days comfortable, but he flees in a panic. He cannot die without knowing why someone would want to kill him. His search at first is frantic and disorderly. When he realizes his panic is keeping him from getting anywhere, he settles into a more methodical search with the help of his fiancee. He finds out a man is desperately trying to get hold of him. Bigelow had notarized a bill of sale for a shipment of iridium for the man, and since iridium is radioactive and Bigelow is dying of radioactive poisoning, he knows this is the connection he seeks.

But when he flies to Los Angeles to find the man, Bigelow learns the man has supposedly killed himself. One clue points to another, and Bigelow gradually unravels the plot against him.

Like the structure of the riddle, the second dramatic phase includes the specifics. Having learned what we need to know about the basic cast of characters, the nature of the crime, and the detective's dedication to solve the puzzle, we now begin the pursuit of clues.

It has often been said that the rule of the best mysteries is that they have all their clues in place for the careful reader to find and deduce the culprit, as Sherlock Holmes would. Raymond Chandler claimed that half his books violated this so-called rule. It is certainly more satisfying for the reader to play the game along with the detective, because the whole point of a riddle is to solve it before the protagonist does. We have our suspicions, we infer motives, we make accusations. We enjoy being armchair detectives and outwitting everyone. To do this, we must have all the proper clues so that we can reach the proper conclusions. But the clues shouldn't be so obvious (as with riddles) that we immediately solve the mystery.

Mary Roberts Rinehart's point about a mystery story having two stories in one is good: There's the story of what appeared to have happened, and the story of what actually happened. The same holds true for the riddle itself: There's what the language *seems* to mean, and there's what it *actually* means. The plot derives its conflict from the tension between the two. Appearance vs. reality.

Go back to the concept of casual and causal discussed in chapter two. The casual disguises the causal. As you write, don't give away your hand by telegraphing clues. If a clue sticks out, you've lost the advantage. But if the clue is cleverly disguised in the background so that it seems a natural part of the scene, you've done your job. The problem with many mysteries is that the clues stick out, and the reader reacts by saying, "Ah-hah! A clue! What does it mean?" By making clues obvious, you cheat the reader who wants to discover them for himself. All stones should look alike; only one should contain the diamond.

As you write, figure out the best way to camouflage important information so that it seems a natural part of the action. Otherwise you'll tip your hand. The rule of thumb about "couching" important information is the basic rule of camouflage itself. Make sure whatever you want to hide has the same coloration as the background. Information becomes obvious only when it "sticks out." Information is camouflaged easily when it is a natural part of the environment. A gun hides easily in a gun rack. Hide a chicken in a henhouse, not in a bedroom. Create an environment (background) that is natural to the object/person/information you want to present. You want the reader to notice the information in a passive way. If the information "pops out," you're being too obvious and won't fool anyone.

THE THIRD DRAMATIC PHASE

The riddle has been presented both in its generals in the first dramatic phase and in its particulars in the second dramatic phase. Now it's time to solve the riddle. In *D.O.A.* there's confrontation and chase, as Bigelow uncovers the plot against him. Bigelow avenges his murder and then turns himself in to the police. "All I did was notarize one little paper, one little paper out of hundreds." The antagonists thought he was wise to their scheme when in fact he knew and suspected nothing.

Bigelow dies in front of the police. He is avenged, the riddle is solved. (You might wonder why this isn't a revenge plot. The focus in this story is not getting even but finding out what happened to Bigelow. Revenge is secondary, rather like cleaning house.)

The answer to the riddle must fit both the generals and the particulars. Like pieces of a jigsaw, each piece contributes directly to the picture. Individually, a piece may look harmless and unimportant, but in fact it may be key to understanding the big picture.

PSEUDO-NEO-CRYPTO SYMBOLISM

A story like *D.O.A.* has its story line and its clues, and in the end it isn't that hard to figure out. You're given all the major clues, and they aren't all that subtle. Sometimes the story is more devious, such as the film *Chinatown*, in which there are two riddles, one within another, each relating to the other.

But there is another class of riddle that is impossible to solve. Perhaps they're not meant to be solved, only pondered. Anyone who reads Kafka knows not to ask the question "Why?" because the reader won't get a satisfactory answer. That's Kafka's point: Real life doesn't give whys. Things happen, period. No explanation. One day Gregor Samsa wakes up and he's a bug. Why? Kafka predated the beer commercial, but the slogan could just have easily been his: "Why ask Why?" We're spoiled as readers—we *expect* answers. Good answers. Answers that make sense. And if we don't get them, we feel cheated. We get angry. We want an orderly world that answers our questions. Kafka didn't think that was necessary. In his world, you can wake up a bug and it wouldn't occur to you to ask why.

So it is with Kafka's *The Trial*. Joseph K (he doesn't even get a real name) is accused of a crime he doesn't understand by a court he can't communicate with. There are no clues because there are no particulars, only generalities. There's a riddle, but it doesn't seem to have a solution. Lots of events *seem* to mean something, and we must struggle to make sense out of them. In a sense it's like the princess or the tiger, except at a more abstract level. Kafka seems to say, "Life's that way, there are no clear answers . . . just what you can come up with." Only in fiction is there a godlike figure that can come forward to give the "correct" answer. A philosopher might reply that there are no correct answers, only fabricated ones.

So that's what we must do with riddles like *The Trial*: Construct a meaning. No one will tell us how all this fits together; it's up to us to make it work.

When Stanley Kubrick released *2001: A Space Odyssey* (based on Arthur C. Clarke's story "The Sentinel of Eternity"), audiences were bewildered. The film was filled with objects and events that seemed to have meaning, and we struggled to put it all together. Many dismissed it as psychedelic babble, a sign of an unhinged mind. Critics were unimpressed. And yet the film was clearly a riddle begging solution. What is the rectangular monolith that keeps appearing from the prehistoric past to the future? What happens to David Bowman at the end of the film, when he's suddenly drawn into a Louis XIV drawing room somewhere near the moons of Jupiter? Why does Bowman transform from a decrepit old man in a Howard Hughes bedroom to a celestial embryo? *What does it all mean?* Figuring it out was like trying on new clothes at a department store. If you didn't like how it fit, you tried on something else. Who knew what it meant? Maybe it didn't really matter. The fun was in coming up with possibilities. Of course, for some, that's terribly frustrating and unfulfilling, rather like someone telling you a joke without a punchline.

To present a problem supposes an answer, but that's not always how it is. Writers who are serious about dealing with and reflecting the true nature of existence often find it presumptuous to present life as finite and clear. Your decision as a writer is whether you want to deal with a closed system that offers absolute answers or an open system that is uncertain and may not offer answers.

If you're interested in writing for the widest general audience, your options are more limited. The general audience prefers absolute answers. It wants its riddles solved. So decide whom you're writing for first.

CHECKLIST

As you write, keep the following points in mind:

1. The core of your riddle should be cleverness: hiding that which is in plain sight.

2. The tension of your riddle should come from the conflict between what happens as opposed to what seems to have happened.

3. The riddle challenges the reader to solve it before the protagonist does.

4. The answer to your riddle should always be in plain view without being obvious.

5. The first dramatic phase should consist of the generalities of the riddle (persons, places, events).

6. The second dramatic phase should consist of the specifics of the riddle (how persons, places and events relate to each other in detail).

7. The third dramatic phase should consist of the riddle's solution, explaining the motives of the antagonist(s) and the real sequence of events (as opposed to what seemed to have happened).

8. Decide on your audience.

9. Choose between an open-ended and a close-ended structure. (Open-ended riddles have no clear answer; close-ended ones do.)

Chapter Fourteen

Master Plot #8: Rivalry

An unlearned carpenter of my acquaintance once said, 'There is very little difference between one man and another; but what little there is, is very important.' This distinction seems to me to go to the root of the matter.

— *Henry James*

W
hat happens when an irresistible force meets an immovable object? No question captures the spirit of a plot better than this one.

A rival is a person who competes for the same object or goal as another. A rival is a person who disputes the prominence or superiority of another. Nowhere else is the concept of deep structure more apparent than in a rivalry. Two people have the same goal—whether it is to win the hand of another or to conquer each other's armies or to win a chess game—and each has her own motivation. The possibilities are endless. Whenever two people compete for a common goal, you have rivalry.

Rivalry existed before humanity (at least as presented in certain literary accounts). The struggle for power between God and Satan is a story of rivalry, chronicled best in Milton's *Paradise Lost*. The saga of the gods, Greek and Roman, are stories of rivalry for power on Mount Olympus. And with the arrival of humans, the tradition continued. Rivalry existed in the Garden of Eden in the guise of a serpent. It existed between the children of Adam and Eve: Cain killed his brother Abel out of jealousy when God preferred Abel's sacrifice to Cain's.

In fact, the theme of rivalry of a shepherd for the approval of a deity is as old as literature itself. When the gods weren't busy competing with each other, they were competing with humans (and they usually won); and when humans weren't competing with the gods, they were competing with each other.

A principle rule of this plot is that the two adversaries should have equivalent strengths (although they can have different weaknesses). Having equivalent strengths doesn't mean the precise nature of strengths must be exactly the same. A physical weakling might outwit a muscle-bound giant by virtue of his wit. A wrestling match between hulks can be interesting if they're of equal physical strength, but we prefer stories where wit and cunning match brute strength. (We love it, for instance, when Odysseus outwits the cannibal Cyclops Polyphemus, although theirs is not a true rivalry.) The point is that whatever the strength of one party, the other party has a *compensating* strength that levels the balance. A tug-of-war isn't interesting if one opponent can easily drag the other across the line.

Literature is overflowing with rivalries: Captain Ahab and Moby Dick; the children who revert to savagery in *Lord of the Flies*; The Virginian and Trampas in *The Virginian*. Every Superhero has his nemesis, every Montgomery his Rommel. Some rivalries are the classic struggle between good and evil, as in Herman Melville's *Billy Budd*, and some struggles are between opponents who are both deserving. The tension comes from their opposition. Whether it's a pitcher facing a batter or two politicians squaring off to run for office, two people cannot occupy the same space. One must win, one must lose (with all its variations of winning and losing). Rivalry is competition.

That competition can take many forms. It can be Felix Unger vs. Oscar Madison of *The Odd Couple*; the old man vs. the fish in *The Old Man and the Sea*; or Captain William Bligh vs. Fletcher Christian in *Mutiny on the Bounty*. Rivalries are familiar ground for bedrooms, as well: Literature is filled with comedies about two people competing for the love of a third, everything from the comedies of Shakespeare to *Jules and Jim* by Francois Truffaut. The classic love triangle is a rivalry plot.

Readers like *mano a mano* combat because it's exciting. *Ben-Hur* has been in print for more than a hundred years. As a novel, it was one of the first works of fiction allowed in American homes, and it was the first work of fiction ever carried in the Sears catalogue. The novel was turned into a play in 1899, made into a silent film in 1907, then remade in 1925 and again in 1959. The final film version, directed by William Wyler and starring Charlton Heston, won an incredible eleven Academy Awards.

The story is compelling because of the depth and breadth of the rivalry between its two principle characters, Judah Ben-Hur, a Jew, and Messala, a Roman. Whichever critic described the film as "Christ and a horse-race" wasn't paying attention to the fundamental conflict of the story between Roman and Jew and between two opposite ways of life in the pagan world.

The story starts at the point of conflict. Messala, a boyhood friend of Judah Ben-Hur, returns from his apprenticeship in Rome as an officer in the imperial service. The two men embrace, recalling their childhoods together. Immediately their competitive spirit surfaces as they hurl javelins at a wooden crossbeam. This moment is typical of the first dramatic movement: The two rivals have a common ground. They meet and are perceived as equals. They eat and drink together, and Judah gives Messala a gift that foreshadows what will come later: a beautiful Arabian horse.

There is no conflict up to this point, and the writer shouldn't spend too much time reconstructing the past. Once the common ground has been established, the conflict should be introduced.

Messala wants to return Judah's gift by advancing his friend in the favor of the Emperor. But to do this, Judah must reveal the names of other Jews who have been resisting Roman rule.

Enter conflict: Judah refuses to turn over his friends.

Messala issues an ultimatum: Either you're with me or you're against me. All right, says Judah, I'm against you. The challenge issued, they take sides.

Now it's time for a catalyst episode to occur, something that pits the rivals against each other in action, not just threats.

Shortly after the initial confrontation between Messala and Judah, the Roman governor arrives. As Judah's family watches the procession from a rooftop, a tile slips and crashes onto the governor's head. Messala's men break into Judah's house and arrest the entire family for attempting to assassinate the governor.

Judah makes a daring escape and forces his way to Messala,

threatening to spear him if he doesn't release his family. Messala, being a true macho Roman, swears he'll kill Judah's mother and sister if he doesn't surrender. Judah throws his spear into the wall behind Messala (an action that parallels the spear he threw in friendly competition a little while ago).

Messala knows Judah's sister and mother are guiltless, yet he plans to make an example of them. Messala makes the first move, capitalizing on circumstance to make it work in his favor. As is typical of the plot, one rival moves to gain the advantage over the other. This is a struggle for power. One rival acts to overcome or overwhelm his competition. In this case, Messala manipulates both events and people for his purposes.

Judah's mother and sister are sent to prison and Judah is sent to row in a Roman galley ship. One rival has attained momentary superiority over the other. If we were to look at what we might call the "power curves" of each of the two rivals, we would usually find that they are inversely related to each other. As one rival moves up the power curve (that is, becomes more powerful and has a distinct advantage over his competitor), the other rival moves down the same curve. Messala's rise in power and influence is matched in reverse by Ben-Hur's descent into anonymity and slavery. This matching of opposites is important for developing audience sympathy. Usually that's done by clarifying the moral issues within the story line.

In *Ben-Hur*, Messala is unscrupulous and ambitious; therefore, he's the antagonist. Judah Ben-Hur is conscientious and honest, so he's the protagonist. The antagonist usually takes the initiative in the rivalry and gains the advantage. The protagonist suffers by the actions of the antagonist and is usually at a disadvantage in the first dramatic phase. That is the function of the first dramatic phase: to separate the rivals on the power curve, with the protagonist at the bottom and the antagonist at the top.

In the second dramatic phase, events occur that reverse the protagonist's descent.

Judah spends three years shackled to an oar of a Roman flagship. During a battle in which their ship is rammed, Judah escapes, but not before he saves the life of the Roman commander, Quintus

Arius. Thankful to Judah for saving his life, Arius frees Judah and adopts him as his son.

This is the reversal of fortune necessary for Judah to rise to the level at which he can compete with Messala. Judah goes to Rome, learns the arts of war, and becomes an expert charioteer. Once Judah has gained power, he is in a position to challenge the antagonist. Notice how the motion has reversed itself: In the first phase the antagonist challenges the protagonist; in the second phase the protagonist challenges the antagonist. Judah has ascended on the power curve. The rivals have reached parity; they have equal power, which sets the stage for their conflict.

But the protagonist's house must be in order first (after all, he's a moral person). His mother and sister are still unaccounted for, so Judah goes in search of them.

The antagonist is often aware of the empowerment of the protagonist. (It heightens the tension if the antagonist continually looks over his shoulder, anticipating the inevitable confrontation.) Messala, who's completely forgotten about Judah's mother and sister, knows Judah's back in town and starts to worry. He checks on the two women only to find that they are both lepers. He retires them to a leper colony. Judah's girlfriend hides this fact from Judah, insisting that his mother and sister are dead. This reinforces Judah's intent to avenge his family's wrongful deaths.

The stage is set. The empowered protagonist's motivation is morally justified. The antagonist prepares to defend. Enter the third dramatic phase: the inevitable confrontation.

An Arab sheik convinces Judah to race his team of horses against Messala in the Circus in Rome. The sheik gets Messala to bet his entire personal fortune on the race, thus giving Judah even more reason to beat him.

Anyone who's seen the 1959 film version remembers those eleven minutes as the two men pit strength and cunning against each other. Messala's chariot is outfitted with hubcaps that have revolving blades that chew up the competition. But the hubcaps don't work on Judah, and Messala's chariot crashes. He gets trampled by the other teams behind him and lies in the sand bleeding. Before he dies, Messala tells Judah what really happened to his mother and sister. Now Judah must find his family.

In the movie, Christ comes in and out of the action, affecting Judah and his family. After Messala's death, Christ is crucified, and Judah's mother and sister are cured. The Ben-Hurs have found a new faith. But the film version leaves out the greater depth of the rivalry. Ben-Hur wants Jesus to be the head of a revolution against Rome, and even raises an army for him to lead. The rivalry extends beyond Judah and Messala; it is pagan against Jew, Rome against Jerusalem. The forces that oppose each other extend beyond individuals; they incorporate religions and cultures. The third point of the triangle is Jesus. Jesus doesn't affect Messala, but he does affect Judah, who finally realizes that Jesus isn't the rebel he wants him to be. By the end, Judah and his family have been raised to a higher level of moral consciousness.

AN IMMOVABLE OBJECT

If the basic premise of the rivalry plot is what happens when an immovable object meets an irresistible force, you should structure your characters and situations along those lines.

First, establish two conflicting and competing characters who vie for the same goal. The characters should be equally opposed; if one character has a superior strength in one area, the other character should make up for it in another area. As mentioned at the beginning of this chapter, it's more interesting to the reader if the strengths between characters aren't exactly matched. Your first character may be stronger physically while your other character may be more clever. Then create circumstances that test your characters according to their strengths. In some cases, one character will win, and in the other case, the other character will win. The pendulum swings both ways. This increases the tension and makes the reader wonder who will win.

And don't always be obvious. The physically stronger character may actually lose a contest of strength to her opponent because the opponent is more clever. This adds a twist to the action and keeps it from being predictable.

But this plot isn't just about forces and objects. It's about human nature, too. The intent of the rival is to overcome her opponent. But what is the character's motivation? What fuels her ambition? Is it anger, jealousy, fear? Examine the characters who are involved in the contest. Round out action with an understanding of what motivates your characters. We want to get a sense of the source of their obsession.

CHECKLIST

As you write, keep the following points in mind:

1. The source of your conflict should come as a result of an irresistible force meeting an immovable object.

2. The nature of your rivalry should be the struggle for power between the protagonist and the antagonist.

3. The adversaries should be equally matched.

4. Although their strengths needn't match exactly, one rival should have compensating strengths to match the other.

5. Begin your story at the point of initial conflict, briefly demonstrating the status quo before the conflict begins.

6. Start your action by having the antagonist instigate against the will of the protagonist. This is the catalyst scene.

7. The struggle between your rivals should be a struggle on the characters' power curves. One is usually inversely proportional to the other: As the antagonist rises on the power curve, the protagonist falls.

8. Have your antagonist gain superiority over your protagonist in the first dramatic phase. The protagonist usually suffers the actions of the antagonist and so is usually at a disadvantage.

9. The sides are usually clarified by the moral issues involved.

10. The second dramatic phase reverses the protagonist's descent on the power curve through a reversal of fortune.

11. The antagonist is often aware of the protagonist's empowerment.

12. The protagonist often reaches a point of parity on the power curve before a challenge is possible.

13. The third dramatic phase deals with the final confrontation between rivals.

14. After resolution, the protagonist restores order for himself and his world.

Chapter Fifteen

Master Plot #9: Underdog

So many people have an unconquerable instinct to help an underdog . . .
Many people have a snobbish instinct to deal only with topdogs. There are
these two kinds of people in the world, as unlike as male and female.

—*NBC War Correspondent Tom Treanor*

The underdog plot is a form of rivalry plot (so you should read chapter fourteen before reading this), but it is distinct enough to be a separate category. The premise for rivalry is parity: the matched strengths of protagonist and antagonist. But in the underdog plot, the strengths aren't equally matched. The protagonist is at a disadvantage and is faced with overwhelming odds.

This plot is near and dear to our hearts because it represents the ability of the one over the many, the small over the large, the weak over the powerful, the "stupid" over the "smart."

The rivalry between Nurse Ratched and McMurphy in *One Flew Over the Cuckoo's Nest* is a classic example of the underdog plot. McMurphy struggles with a system against which he has no chance. A lovable rebel, McMurphy would rather fake being crazy than do hard time at a work farm. At the mental institution he meets the embodiment of everything inhumane and unfeeling: Nurse Ratched. Theirs is a test of wills. The reader recognizes the system in Nurse Ratched and, although we would probably detest McMurphy in person, we root for him because he's dedicated to subverting a system that squelches individuality and creativity. It is a fight we want fought.

We also side with Joan of Arc as she struggles against the

hypocrisy of the Church. She is a hero because of her canny ability to probe the problems of life and to formulate independent ethical values, all of which alienate her from mainstream society. And then there are less complicated, transparent underdogs like Rocky Balboa, the man who beats the impossible odds. Rocky isn't very smart (by his own admission), but he has tenacity and a certain native shrewdness. He's also virtuous, and when he takes on the boxing establishment with all its glitter and hype, we find ourselves rooting for him. The audience's connection to the protagonist in the underdog plot is much more visceral than in the rivalry plot. We don't identify with Judah Ben-Hur as strongly as we identify with the poor slob Rocky. Why not? Because Ben-Hur is on a higher emotional and intellectual plane than most of us. We respect what he represents, but he isn't really *one of us*. Rocky is. He's heroic in ways we can *feel*. Most of us come up against some kind of oppression that we feel we have no chance of beating. But the underdog actually *does* beat his oppressor.

If you want your reader to feel empathy for your protagonist, make sure that her emotional and/or intellectual plane is equal to or lower than the reader's. If your reader feels your protagonist is superior, he won't make the psychic connection. Part of this is vicarious; the reader wants your hero to be like *him*, at least symbolically. She's no great genius, she's a common person— someone your reader can relate to.

One of the world's best-known tales, *Cinderella*, is a good example of the underdog plot. It was first written down in China during the ninth century. It circulated the world for centuries, making its appearance in the West most notably in the collections of Charles Perrault and the Brothers Grimm. I'm using the Grimms' version, called *Aschenputtel*.

While most of us know the story, we know the sanitized version created by Disney, who invented the fairy godmother. Disney's version, while endearing and charming, doesn't capture the true spirit of the tale, which has to do with Cinderella's rivalry with her stepsisters, not her romance with the prince.

The structure of *Cinderella*, like most fairy tales, divides itself clearly into three phases, each of which typifies the primary movements of the plot.

In the first dramatic phase, Cinderella, an only child of a rich couple, kneels beside her mother's deathbed. Typically, the story begins at the point of interruption in the protagonist's life, so we can glimpse her life *before* the contest between protagonist and antagonist begins. In this case, the mother's death causes a dramatic, irreparable change in Cinderella's life. Her mother's last words are advice: "Dear child, be good and pious, and then the good God will always protect you, and I will look down on you from heaven and be near you." She has her instructions; her mother will protect her as long as she remains virtuous.

Six months later, Cinderella's father remarries a woman with two beautiful daughters (unlike Disney's three uglies) who are the spiritual opposite of the humble and self-effacing Cinderella: They are vain, selfish, lazy and cruel—a grab bag of the seven deadly sins. They're the mirror reflection of Cinderella.

The nature of the competition isn't obvious in Disney's version, but it is in Grimms'. Although Cinderella possesses great beauty, so do her stepsisters. Their ugliness is strictly internal. Since all are young women of a marriageable age, their ambition is to marry as well as possible. (Obviously this happened in the days before raised feminist consciousness.) To avoid direct competition, the stepsisters actively abuse Cinderella.

Once the rivalry begins in the first dramatic phase, the antagonists have the upper hand. An important attribute of the underdog is disempowerment. The protagonist is overwhelmed by the power of the antagonists. Cinderella is made to work from dawn until dusk carrying water, lighting fires, cooking and washing. The sisters taunt Cinderella by throwing peas and lentils into the ashes of the kitchen hearth and making her pick them out.

This descending action represents the new status quo. The protagonist now finds herself in a lower, suppressed state, under the rule of the antagonists. But the nature of the protagonist is to resist. Thus, the next important action is to do something that would reverse the descending action.

In the case of Cinderella, this happens when the father (who is typical of fathers in fairy tales—he has no real presence or authority—goes to a fair and asks each of the three daughters what they would like as a present. The first sister wants beautiful clothes, the second wants pearls and jewels, and Cinderella, still modest and humble, asks for "the first branch which knocks against your hat on your way home."

The girls get their requests, and Cinderella takes the hazel branch her father has brought back for her and plants it on her mother's grave, watering it with her tears. The branch grows into a tree, and a little white bird (presumably the spirit of her mother) comes to roost in the tree. This bird is no ordinary bird; it grants Cinderella's every wish. Without either strength or allies, Cinderella couldn't compete with her stepsisters, but now she is empowered by both. She is ready to do battle.

The second dramatic phase begins when the empowered protagonist is in the position to challenge her rival and reverse the descending force in the first dramatic phase.

The King, who has a son also of marriageable age, invites the kingdom to a three-day festival, during which his son can pick from the local crop.

The stepsisters make plans to attend, forcing Cinderella to comb their hair, brush their shoes and so on. Cinderella ventures to ask if she can go and is met with derision: "You go, Cinderella! Covered in dust and dirt as you are, and would go to the festival! You have no clothes and shoes, and yet would dance!"

The sadistic stepmother gives Cinderella a "chance" to go to the festival. She throws a dish of lentils into the ashes and tells her if she can pick them out within two hours she can go.

But Cinderella is now empowered, and she enlists the help of all the birds beneath the sky, who come "whirring and crowding in, and alighted amongst the ashes." They pick out all the lentils with time to spare.

Cinderella accomplishes the feat (her first act to counter her suppressed state), but her victory is quickly squelched. The stepmother refuses to honor her promise. "No, Cinderella, you have no clothes and you can not dance; you would only be laughed at." She repeats the lentils trick, this time throwing twice as many lentils in the ashes and gives her half the time to pick them out.

Cinderella again gets the birds to pick the lentils out of the ashes. The stepmother still refuses to honor her promise, again reiterating the basic problems with her going along: She has no clothes and she can't dance. The stepmother sets off for the castle with her daughters, leaving Cinderella behind.

The protagonist attempts to reverse her power position only to fail. As is usual in literature, however, the third time is the charm. After the initial failures, Cinderella must adjust her thinking and her action accordingly if she wants to fulfill her intention: to go to the festival. This represents the real turning point in the second dramatic phase—movement from a position of weakness toward a position of greater strength. The protagonist must get to the point where she can effectively challenge her rivals.

Cinderella goes to her mother's grave beneath the tree and invokes the mother's spirit through the tree and the white bird:

Shiver and quiver, little tree,

Silver and gold throw down over me.

Presto, she's dressed to the tees, overcoming the deficiency of not having clothes. She goes to the festival and dances with the prince, who falls under her spell. While there is no imperative that she return home by a certain time (and have her carriage turn into a pumpkin), she must escape the prince by running away. Her intention is not yet completely fulfilled.

The second night is a repeat of the first. Cinderella is ravishing and the courtship continues, but Cinderella must make her escape by climbing into a pear tree.

The third night (again, three times), the prince devises a scheme of smearing the staircase with pitch so when Cinderella steps in it, it catches her slipper. (The slipper is variously described as gold or fur, never glass.) This part of the dramatic action represents a shift; the prince's interest in her is passive at first, but he must take action now to ensure he doesn't lose her. Cinderella is clearly rising on the power curve. She has done what her stepsisters could not.

End the second dramatic phase. The contest is yet unresolved; Cinderella has yet to fulfill her greater intention: to find freedom from her repressive stepsisters and stepmother, and to find the love of a man. She is leading a dual life: dirty housemaid by day, golden princess by night. She must reconcile these two states.

The third dramatic phase must bring the rivals into equal competition with each other. With Cinderella ascending on the power curve, she now can openly challenge her stepsisters.

The prince has a shoe but no princess to go with it, so he begins his search. The two stepsisters "were glad for they had pretty feet." The first stepsister tries on the tiny shoe but she can't jam in her big toe, so her mother advises her to cut it off, since "when you are Queen you will have no more need to go on foot." This her daughter does, and when the prince sees that the shoe fits, he puts her on his horse and heads back to the castle. On the way they pass Cinderella's mother's grave and the birds in the tree sound the alarm. The prince looks at the stepsister's foot, which is soaked with blood, and realizes she's a fake.

The second stepsister tries on the shoe, but her heel is too wide, and again the mother advises cutting off part of her heel since, well, you know . . .

Again the prince is deceived, and again the birds tip him off. When he sees her stocking is soaked red, he returns her. Finally, it's Cinderella's turn. The stepmother refuses to produce her, saying it's impossible for Cinderella to be the mystery princess, but the prince insists, and the slipper fits. The rest, as they say, is history.

Except for one small detail. Cinderella is now fully empowered and has realized her freedom. But her defeat of her rivals isn't complete. (Since they're both disfigured it would seem to be enough, but apparently not.)

The stepsisters show up at the wedding looking to get into Cinderella's good favor. In a scene reminiscent of Alfred Hitchcock's *The Birds*, the pigeons attack the two sisters and peck out their eyes. "And thus, for their wickedness and falsehood," the story ends, "they were punished with blindness all their days."

The focus at the end of the story is *not* on the prince and princess' living happily every afterward, but on the comeuppance of the two false sisters. The rivalry is over; Cinderella has triumphed over wickedness and falsehood.

AGAINST ALL ODDS

The underdog is a fascinating character. The underdog really wants to succeed. As you develop your character, ask yourself what motivates him to want to achieve his goal. Again, the intent of the character—to win—is clear. But at what cost to himself or others? Don't just concentrate on the competition that pits the underdog against the superior. Give your reader an understanding of what forces propel him.

In some ways this plot is predictable. We identify strongly with the underdog, just as we identify with the protagonist in the rivalry plot. Readers love it when the odds are stacked against the good guy and the good guy wins anyway. But don't make a cartoon out of your characters by creating odds so lopsided and unrealistic that the underdog has no reasonable chance of winning. The final competition should be a real competition, head to head, and as much as the antagonist cheats, the underdog always maintains the true course: courage, honor, strength. (It is permissible, however, to use the antagonist's dirty tricks against him.)

Keep your audience in mind every step of the way. Your underdog has a rooting section. Stay in touch with what your reader is feeling (frustration, anger, exhilaration) and play toward those feelings. At the end, when your hero finally overcomes all obstacles, your audience should feel the same triumph. Don't disappoint your audience by not including it at the finish line.

CHECKLIST

The summary for the rivalry plot also applies for the underdog plot, with the following exceptions:

1. The underdog plot is similar to the rivalry plot except that the protagonist is not matched equally against the antagonist. The antagonist, which may be a person, place or thing (such as a bureaucracy), clearly has much greater power than the protagonist.

2. The dramatic phases are similar to the rivalry plot as it follows the power curves of the characters.

3. The underdog usually (but not always) overcomes his opposition.

Chapter Sixteen

Master Plot #10: Temptation

I can resist everything except temptation.
  — Oscar Wilde

To be tempted is to be induced or persuaded to do something that is either unwise, wrong or immoral. Happily or unhappily, depending on your point of view, life presents daily opportunities for us to be stupid, wrong and immoral.

No one's ever managed to get through life without being tempted by someone or something. Our examples start in the Garden of Eden (we know what price Adam and Eve paid for not resisting temptation) and continue forward to today, without exception, from the rich and powerful to the lowly and powerless. Not even Christ was immune.

We consider it a sign of strength and self-discipline to be able to resist temptation. But temptation isn't something that comes along once or twice in a lifetime and is dealt with; we must fight against it daily. Who hasn't fought off the temptation to do something you knew you shouldn't? Maybe it was something minor, like trying to resist a decadent dessert the day you started your diet. Or maybe it was something more substantially immoral, such as trying to resist having an affair with a married person. Or maybe it was illegal, such as the desire to embezzle money from your company.

The story of temptation is the story of the frailty of human nature. If to sin is human, it is human to give in to temptation. But our codes of behavior have established a price for yielding to temptation. The penalties range from one's own personal guilt to a lifetime without parole in the state penitentiary.

Forces rage within us when tempted. Part of us wants to take the risk for whatever we see as the gain. We convince ourselves we won't be caught. Another part of us is horrified. That part knows what we intend to do is wrong, and it resists the powerful impulse to act incautiously by dragging out every paragraph, sentence, comma and period of the moral code that we have learned through our society. The battle rages: yes and no, pro and con, why and why not. This is conflict, and the tension between opposites creates the tension. *Knowing* what to do and actually *doing* it are sometimes oceans apart.

It's not hard to see how fundamental this plot is to human nature. It may be harder to see that temptation is perhaps the most religiously oriented of all the plots.

Literature has plenty of examples. Temptation is a common theme in fairy tales. Bruno Bettelheim points out that most fairy tales were created at a time when religion was the most important element in life; therefore, many of the tales have religious themes. A particularly beautiful but almost unknown tale by the Brothers Grimm is "Our Lady's Child," a cautionary tale about temptation. "Hard by a great forest dwelt a woodcutter with his wife, who had an only child, a little girl three years old . . ." the story begins. Times are so hard the woodcutter can't feed his wife and daughter. Taking pity on them, the Virgin Mary appears before the father wearing a crown of shining stars and offers to take care of his daughter. The father sees no alternative if his daughter is to survive and agrees.

STRUCTURE

In the first dramatic phase, the nature of temptation is established and the protagonist succumbs to it. As with this tale, the protagonist fights to resist but eventually gives in. She may also rationalize her behavior as if trying to find an easy way to reconcile the forces tearing at her. Oftentimes a period of denial follows the act.

In "Our Lady's Child," Mary then takes the little girl to Heaven, where she grows up in the Virgin's great house eating sugar cakes and drinking sweet milk. One day, when the girl is fourteen, the Virgin takes a long trip and gives the girl a set of keys to the thirteen doors of Heaven. She tells her she may open any door she chooses except for the thirteenth: That one she may not open.

The girl promises to obey.

We don't have to project far to know what will happen. At first, the girl is good. She takes a tour of each of the twelve dwellings of the kingdom of Heaven. "In each one of them sat one of the Apostles in the midst of a great light, and she rejoiced in all the magnificence and splendor. . . ."

But there was that thirteenth door, the forbidden one.

A great hunger to know consumes her. "I will not open it *entirely*," she rationalizes her behavior to the angels, "and I will not go inside, but I will unlock it so that we can see just a little through the opening."

Oh, no, counsel the angels, that would be a sin. That would cause such unhappiness.

The desire grows into an obsession, and when the girl is alone she figures no one will ever know if she just *peeks* inside.

And peek she does. Behind the door she sees the Trinity sitting in fire and splendor. She stares at it in amazement and reaches out to touch the light. As her finger touches it, the finger turns golden.

She is overwhelmed by a great and sudden fear. She tries to wash her golden finger but to no avail.

The Virgin returns home and immediately suspects the girl has violated her promise. She asks the girl, but she compounds her crime by lying. The Virgin asks again, and again she lies. Finally she asks a third time and still the girl denies it. The Virgin ejects the girl from Heaven and sends her back to earth a mute.

In the second dramatic phase, the protagonist must undergo the effects of her decision. She may continue her denial, trying to find a way out of the punishments that are certain to follow. The girl of "Our Lady's Child" has compounded her sin. She not only disobeyed the Virgin, but then she steadfastly lied about it even though the Virgin gave her several chances to recant.

The girl is back on earth, naked and speechless in the desert.

She lives like an animal, eating roots and berries and sleeping in a hollow tree.

After several years a king finds the wild girl and falls in love with her, even though she can't speak. He takes her back to his castle and marries her. She bears him a son. Suddenly the Virgin appears before her and offers to take her back to Heaven if she will confess. If she continues to deny her sin, however, she will take away her child.

The Queen refuses to confess.

The Virgin takes away her child. A rumor travels around the kingdom that the Queen is a cannibal and has eaten her child. But the King loves her so much he won't believe it.

She bears him another child, and the Virgin shows up again and makes the same proposition. Still the Queen refuses to confess. She takes the second child. The people of the kingdom accuse the Queen of cannibalism; the King's councillors demand she be brought to justice, but still he refuses to believe his wife could do such a thing.

Finally she bears the King a third child. The Virgin shows up but this time takes the Queen to Heaven, where she sees her two other children. "Is your heart not yet softened?" she asks. "If you will own that you opened the forbidden door, I will give you back your two little sons."

The Queen refuses, and the Virgin confiscates her third child.

This is more than even the King can take.

The effects of the temptation in the first dramatic phase reverberate through the second dramatic phase. The protagonist tries to deal with the effects of her behavior, but as is typical of moral stories, the more she tries to wriggle free from the burden of her sin, the more it oppresses her. Finally it reaches the point at which it is no longer bearable.

The third dramatic phase resolves these internal conflicts. Everything now comes to a head; the crisis has been forced. In "Our Lady's Child," the protagonist must now not only face her expulsion from Heaven and bear the punishment of being cast down and struck dumb, but because she continues to refuse to acknowledge her sin, she must confront losing the man who loves her and deal with the fury of the people who believe she's been murdering her children. Talk about a snowball effect.

In the third dramatic phase, the people rise up against the Queen, demanding that she be judged for devouring her children. The King can no longer contain his councillors, who condemn his wife to be burned at the stake.

The Queen is bound to the stake and wood gathered around her. The fire is lit. As it begins to burn, the hard ice of the Queen's pride melts, and her heart is moved by repentance. "If I could but confess before my death that I opened the door," she laments.

Her voice suddenly returns to her, and she shouts, "Yes, Mary, I did it!"

A rain falls from the skies to put out the fire, and a brilliant light breaks above her. The Virgin descends with the Queen's children and forgives her. "Then she gave her the three children, untied her tongue, and granted her happiness for her whole life." In this case, the resolution is happy. The Queen is forgiven for her sin.

The temptation plot isn't about action as much as it's about character. It is an examination of motives, needs and impulse. The action supports the development of character, and as such, it's a plot of the mind rather than of the body.

You may notice in "Our Lady's Child" there is no antagonist unless it's the girl herself wavering between two moral states, one representing the protagonist (the "good girl") and the other representing the antagonist (the "bad girl"). But many stories have a more concrete antagonist, such as *Fatal Attraction*, in which the other woman is the temptress and the creator of havoc. In the Garden of Eden the serpent is the antagonist; in many other stories it is Satan himself, in any one of his thousand guises.

Perhaps literature's greatest temptation story is that of Doctor Faustus, a legendary figure and subject of many literary works, not the least of which are a play by Johann von Goethe, a novel by Thomas Mann, and operas by Boito, Busoni and Gounod.

Faustus is actually the subject of a bet between God and the devil, Mephistopheles. God believes his servant Faustus is above temptation, but Mephistopheles bets that Faustus can in fact be tempted from his faithful service to God. Mephistopheles, an eternal student of human nature, knows exactly how to tempt Faustus. Mephistopheles proposes to strike a bargain with Faustus to learn the full meaning of existence. Faustus agrees, but only if he experiences something in life that is so profound that he would wish it would never end.

Mephistopheles tries some cheap tricks with women but they don't work. Then he tries again by restoring Faustus's youth and introducing him to the young, beautiful Gretchen. He's tempted by her but their affair ends in tragedy, including the deaths of Gretchen's brother, their child and Gretchen herself. Mephistopheles must up the ante. Instead of an earthly Gretchen, he brings forth an unworldly Helen, the most beautiful woman who ever lived. Again Faustus is tempted, but he knows beauty is transitory and rejects her.

Faustus, having resisted Mephistopheles, wants to be a productive being and starts a land reclamation project, and it is in this Mephistopheles finally wins his bet. When Faustus sees all the good he has done over the years developing a vast territory of land occupied by people who are making something useful for themselves, he wishes the moment would never end.

The irony is that Faustus doesn't succumb to basic human motives such as lust or greed. He gives in only to achieve the better good of the human race. He had made some tragic mistakes during his life, but he never lost sight of what was true and good. Mephistopheles wins by the letter of the bet, but not by the spirit of it.

The devil, being a stickler for detail, claims Faustus's soul. But God intercedes and the angels carry him to Heaven instead.

The story of Faustus follows the same three dramatic phases as "Our Lady's Child." The difference lies in the continuing temptation of Faustus as opposed to other stories, in which the protagonist gives in to temptation in the first phase. Faustus doesn't give in until the third phase. But he still pays a heavy emotional price along the way, with Gretchen, with Helen, and with the devil's constant need to persuade.

YIELD NOT TO . . .

If you want to write about temptation, think about the nature of "crime" you want your character to commit. What would be the gain? What would be the loss? What is the price the protagonist must pay for giving into temptation? Cost is one of the major factors in this plot. That makes this plot more moral than most, because it carries a message about the cost of giving into temptation. In many ways, this plot creates parables about behavior.

Don't focus your story completely on the temptation and the cost of giving into it. Focus your story on the character who gives in to the temptation. Define the internal struggle raging inside the character. Is it guilt? If so, how does that guilt show itself in the behavior and actions of your character? Is it anger? (Anger is the result of the character being angry at himself for giving in to temptation.) How does that anger express itself? Temptation can reveal a wide range of emotions in your character. Don't create a character who is capable of only one emotional note. Your character will probably go through a variety of emotional states. The result of all the turmoil will be a realization about himself. He will reach a conclusion about giving in to temptation. What is the lesson learned, and how has your character matured (if he has matured at all)? Remember to look at the effect of temptation on your character.

CHECKLIST

As you write, keep these points in mind:

1. The temptation plot is a character plot. It examines the motives, needs and impulses of human character.

2. Your temptation plot should depend largely on morality and the effects of giving in to temptation. By the end of the story, the character should have moved from a lower moral plane (in which she gives in to temptation) to a higher moral plane as a result of learning the sometimes harsh lessons of giving in to temptation.

3. The conflict of your plot should be interior and take place within the protagonist, although it has exterior manifestations in the action. The conflict should result from the protagonist's inner turmoil—a result of knowing what she should do, and then not doing it.

4. The first dramatic phase should establish the nature of the protagonist first, followed by the antagonist (if there is one).

5. Next, introduce the nature of the temptation, establish its effect on the protagonist, and show how the protagonist struggles over her decision.

6. The protagonist then gives in to the temptation. There may be some short-term gratification.

7. The protagonist often will rationalize her decision to yield to temptation.

8. The protagonist also may go through a period of denial after yielding to the temptation.

9. The second dramatic phase should reflect the effects of yielding to the temptation. Short-term benefits sour and the negative side surfaces. The bill starts to come due for making the wrong decision.

10. The protagonist should try to find a way to escape responsibility and punishment for her act.

11. The negative effects of the protagonist's actions should reverberate with increasing intensity in the second dramatic phase.

12. The third dramatic phase should resolve the protagonist's internal conflicts. The story ends with atonement, reconciliation and forgiveness.

Chapter Seventeen

Master Plot #11: Metamorphosis

Why shouldn't *truth be stranger than fiction? Fiction, after all, has to make sense.*

—*Mark Twain*

I f any one plot is truly magical, metamorphosis is it. Most of the master plots are grounded in reality: They deal with situations and people whom we readily recognize because they're based in our experience. Even good science fiction and fantasy stories are ultimately as real in their portrayal of people and events as anything by Henry James or Jane Austen. Science Fiction author Theodore Sturgeon pointed out that a good science fiction story deals with a *human* problem and a *human* solution. Fiction, whether it happens in Middle Earth or in a galaxy far, far away, is always about *us*. Fiction reveals truths that reality obscures.

The metamorphosis plot is about change. That covers a lot of territory. But in this plot the change is specific. It's as much physical as it is emotional. In the metamorphosis plot, the physical characteristics of the protagonist actually change from one form to another. The most common form of metamorphosis has a protagonist who starts out as an animal and ends up as a gorgeous young man of marriageable age. But not always. The reverse process may be true, as in the case of "The Wolfman."

I WOKE UP THIS MORNING . . .

We have always found images of ourselves in other things, particularly in other animals. We're familiar with metaphor and allegory.

The lion and the fox in Aesop's fables represent distinctly human characteristics of strength and cunning. The wolf in *Little Red Riding Hood*, however undeserved its reputation, represents human traits of power, greed and evil. Ditto the snake. We have maintained our animal links through the ages, perhaps as an acknowledgement of our own place in the animal kingdom.

The modern era hasn't diminished our fascination with the connection between beast and human. The fairy tales and fables of the past are very much with us, but so are our modern versions: a man who is a wolf; a bat who is a man; a man who is a giant insect; a prince who is a frog; a man who is a lion; the list is long. The works are among our favorites: "The Wolfman," *Dracula*, *Metamorphosis*, "Frog King" and "Beauty and the Beast." The stories have such a powerful grasp on our imagination that we constantly remake them. No one knows the source of the original "Beauty and the Beast" tale. The version with which we're most familiar first appeared in eighteenth-century France in the works of Madame Leprince de Beaumont. Since then the story has been made into a film four times (including one cartoon version) and a television series. (No one has the time or patience to count the number of wolfman and vampire films made over the years.)

The metamorphosis is usually the result of a curse, which is placed as a consequence of a wrongdoing or offense against nature. The wolfman and the vampire are expressions of evil; Gregor Samsa is cursed by a meaningless existence that turns him into an insect; the frog prince in "Frog King" has been cursed by a witch, as is the beast in "Beauty and the Beast." Whatever shape we take as animals, we metamorphise the human condition the same way Aesop did two thousand years ago.

The cure for the curse, if there is one, is always the same: love. The curative power of love can overcome any curse and conquer any affliction. If the metamorphosis plot teaches us anything, it is that love can salvage us from our basic instincts. Love can correct wrong; it can heal the wounded and strengthen the weak at heart.

Love can take many forms. It can be the love of a child for a parent (or a parent for a child), the love of a man for a woman (or a woman for a man), the love of people for one another, or the love of God. If a curse represents evil (either possession by an evil force or a manifestation of evil's displeasure), it represents the evil *within us*; but we may also possess the chance for salvation, restoring the good that is within us. This story is about the forces of good and evil that wage war within us. Sometimes the evil holds sway, but there is always the chance of restoring the good.

The Dracula created by Bram Stoker is the essence of evil; he's a creature of the night that feasts on the blood of humans. He's also urbane, sophisticated, witty and charming. Women find him irresistible. Like the wolfman, he's one of the few metamorphs who's incapable of being redeemed by love, but he yearns to be free of the curse that condemns him to stalk the earth.

Obviously I'm taking the concept of metamorphosis literally. The metamorph is usually the protagonist, which means there is an antagonist to match the action against. Not all metamorphs are evil. The Beast in "Beauty and the Beast" holds Beauty against her will in his castle as ransom for her father's misdeed. He exhibits loathsome behavior (such as running down his game and eating it raw), but he commits no real crime and is guilty of no real offense, except the one that has transformed him from a man into a beast. The Beast is most commonly portrayed in film as a lion. But to make the Beast a cutesy lion is to miss the point of the curse which was to make him *totally* unlovable. George C. Scott's portrayal of the Beast seems closer to the mark: He was a boar. The frog's only offense in "Frog King" is wanting to crawl into bed and sleep with the young princess. (Forget the Walt Disney version in which the princess kisses the frog. It doesn't happen in the original quite that way.)

The point of the plot is to show the process (or failure) of transformation. Since this is a character plot, we're more concerned with the nature of the metamorph than with his actions. The metamorph represents mystery: What sin has he committed to warrant this change? What must he do to free himself from the curse? The metamorph is an innately sad person, burdened by his affliction.

The terms of the curse not only affect his looks, but they also affect his behavior. His life is complicated by rituals and prohibitions. The vampire can't go out by day; the wolfman dreads the full moon; Gregor Samsa scuttles up the walls of his bedroom and hides behind the furniture; and the Beast is hemmed in by thorns. The metamorph is cornered, looking for a way out.

There's usually a way out. For the vampire, it's daylight or a stake through the heart; for the wolfman, it's a silver bullet; for the frog, it's sharing a princess' bed for three nights; and for Gregor Samsa, the only way out is a slow death.

If the curse is so profound that only death releases the metamorph from his state, he seeks death. The terms of release are usually carried out by the antagonist, but the metamorph welcomes the end even if he resists it in the process. Dracula, the wolfman and Gregor Samsa all welcome death because it is their release.

If the curse can be reversed by getting the antagonist to perform certain actions, the metamorph must wait until the antagonist fulfills the terms of the release. The conditions of release are usually dictated by the person who made the original curse. Both the Beast and the frog must be loved.

The action generally follows three dramatic phases.

The first phase introduces the protagonist, the accursed. We learn the current state of his condition but not the reason for the curse. (That is usually disclosed in the third dramatic phase.) The curse has already been in place a long time; the story begins at the point prior to the resolution of the curse (release).

We also meet the antagonist, who acts as the catalyst that propels the metamorph toward release. The antagonist is "the chosen one," the person for whom the metamorph has been waiting. The antagonist may not know she is the chosen one, however.

The antagonist is often a victim. It's easy to see how she would be a victim for a vampire or a wolfman, but it's harder to understand in other cases. The princess in "Frog King," for instance, resists the frog every step of the way. Her father forces her to comply with the frog's wishes. Beauty isn't a volunteer, either. She goes to the Beast's castle because she is honor-bound to do so by her father. Given a choice, both protagonists would rather be somewhere else.

But fate has cast them together. The first dramatic phase begins the process toward release, but as much as the protagonist wishes to be released, he can do nothing to explain or hurry the process. That's an implicit law of the curse. The frog can't explain and say, "If you sleep with me for three nights, I'll turn into a hunk." Likewise, the Beast can't say, "I'm really rich and handsome and if you would give me a kiss, I'll prove it."

Usually the antagonist is repulsed by the metamorph. She wants out. But she remains a prisoner, either bound physically (by walls of thorns or wild beasts) or mentally (by her promise to remain). And almost always the antagonist at least in some small way falls under the spell of the metamorph. The vampire has immense sexual appeal. The wolfman, one of the few who can explain his curse (always to people who don't believe him), always gains sympathy from his victims, who see him as a deeply troubled man. The princess despises the frog, period. She sees no redeeming value in his green self at all. The Beauty, however, is immediately attracted to certain human (and inhuman) attributes in the Beast.

By the end of the first dramatic phase, however, the curse is evident, and the antagonist has felt the effects of it. It may be gruesome (the vampire sucking her blood), it may be comic (the frog arrives for dinner at the castle), or it may be eerie (Beauty arrives in the kingdom of the Beast, but he is nowhere present). There is a sense, however, that the antagonist is either directly or indirectly a captive of the metamorph.

The second dramatic phase concentrates on the nature of the evolving relationship between the metamorph and the antagonist. The antagonist continues to resist but her will softens, either out of pity, fear or control by the metamorph. At the same time, the antagonist starts to establish control over the metamorph, by virtue of her beauty, kindness or knowledge. The motion of the two characters is toward each other; it is the beginning of love, if it is possible within the terms of the curse. The victim may still be horrified (as in the case of the vampire's victim and the princess in "Frog King"), but the metamorph is infatuated.

The second dramatic phase may have the usual number of complications, but they all center around things such as escape (the antagonist may have the chance to leave and either takes it and is recaptured or doesn't take it at all). The metamorph, who may have what the antagonist considers a vile (animal) side, exhibits the full range of his animalness. He may also exhibit unanimal behavior, such as tenderness, affection and a concern for her well-being. The couple are moving toward fulfilling the terms of the release, although the reader is rarely aware of that. But the initial revulsion of the antagonist gives way slowly toward a variety of feelings, from pity to the beginnings of love.

By the third dramatic phase, the terms of the release reach a critical stage. The time has come for the partners to achieve what fate has intended. This usually requires an incident that acts as the final catalyst for the metamorph's physical change—the culmination of all the other action: what it has been leading toward.

In the case of "Frog King," the princess is so fed up with the insistent frog (who keeps asking her to kiss him) that she picks it up and throws it full force against the wall. When he hits the wall, presto, a beautiful prince appears. (You *must* read Bruno Bettelheim's explanation of this act in *The Uses of Enchantment*; it's almost as entertaining as the story itself. He insists this act of violence is in fact an act of love.) In "Beauty and the Beast," the Beast lies dying, and it's only Beauty's declaration of love that brings him back from death and changes him into a prince.

In the cases where death is the release, the terms are also fulfilled. Since love cannot remedy the curse, the antagonist or the antagonist's agent must perform the proper ritual to ensure release for the metamorph. The metamorph may die, but it's still a relief to be free from the curse.

The third phase usually gives us the explanations for the curse and its causes.

This plot combines the grotesque with the curative power of love, and its appeal is as old as literature itself.

CHECKLIST

As you write, keep in mind these points:

1. The metamorphosis is usually the result of a curse.
2. The cure for the curse is generally love.
3. The forms of love include love of parent for a child, a woman

for a man (or vice versa), people for each other, or for the love of God.

4. The metamorph is usually cast as the protagonist.

5. The point of the plot is to show the process of transformation back to humanity.

6. Metamorphosis is a character plot; consequently, we care more about the nature of the metamorph than his actions.

7. The metamorph is an innately sad character.

8. The metamorph's life is usually bound by rituals and prohibitions.

9. The metamorph usually wants to find a way out of his predicament.

10. There is usually a way out of that predicament, which is called release.

11. The terms of the release are almost always carried out by the antagonist.

12. If the curse can be reversed by the antagonist performing certain acts, the protagonist cannot either hurry or explain the events.

13. In the first dramatic phase, the metamorph usually can't explain the reasons for his curse. We see him in the state of his curse.

14. Your story should begin at the point prior to the resolution of the curse (release).

15. The antagonist should act as the catalyst that propels the protagonist toward release.

16. The antagonist often starts out as the intended victim but ends up as the "chosen one."

17. The second dramatic phase should concentrate on the nature of evolving relationships between the antagonist and the metamorph.

18. The characters will generally move toward each other emotionally.

19. In the third dramatic phase, the terms of release should be fulfilled and your protagonist should be freed from the curse. The metamorph may either revert to his original state or die.

20. The reader should learn the reasons for the curse and its root causes.

Chapter Eighteen

Master Plot #12: Transformation

God changes not what is in a people, until they change what is in themselves.
— *The Koran 13:11*

Another character plot, closely related to metamorphosis, is transformation. If you read the chapter on metamorphosis, you know that I take the term literally: A character literally changes shape. That shape reflects the inner psychological identity of the metamorph. In the work-a-day world, people constantly change, too. We are always in the process of becoming who we are. From day to day and week to week we may not be able to detect change within ourselves (unless we're undergoing some momentous revolution in our life that forces us to change at a faster pace).

The study of humanity is the study of change. We change our perceptions of our universe and that, in turn, colors how we think, feel and react to it. The twentieth-century citizen is much different from the nineteenth- or the twenty-first-century citizen. Time, however, hasn't altered certain aspects of humanity, and we share much with a Greek citizen in Athens three thousand years ago or an Egyptian trader in Memphis five thousand years ago. The denominators of basic human psychology have remained the same. We're born, we grow up and mature and we die.

This shared common experience is the basis for fiction. The plot of transformation deals with the process of change in the protagonist as she journeys through one of the many stages of life. The plot isolates a portion of the protagonist's life that represents the period of change, moving from one significant character state to another.

The key word is *significant*. One of the tests of character plots in general is the change the main character makes in her personality as a result of the action. The protagonist is usually a different person at the end of the story than she was at the start of it. The transformation plot goes one step further by concentrating its attention on the nature of the change and how it affects the character from the start to the end of her experience. This plot examines the process of life and its effect on people. Given a situation, how will this person react? Different people react to the same stimulus in different ways; similarly, people are affected by the same stimulus in different ways. This is the core of interest.

PLOTTING A PLOT

As we near adulthood, we must learn the lessons of the adult world, a new and oftentimes awkward experience for those who have been comfortable in childhood. These issues are addressed in Larry McMurtry's *The Last Picture Show* and John Jay Osborn's *The Paper Chase*. Nick Adams in Ernest Hemingway's "Indian Camp" and Sherwood Anderson's unnamed narrator in "I'm a Fool" are such characters.

War teaches lessons as well. Anyone who's gone into combat cannot help but be changed by the experience. The story may be about learning the true nature of courage, as in Stephen Crane's *The Red Badge of Courage*, Joseph Heller's *Catch-22* or Philip Caputo's *A Rumor of War*.

The search for identity can take a character into the darkest recesses of the human psyche. We always try to understand who we are and what is the essence of human nature, and sometimes we make discoveries about ourselves that horrify us. Such is the case in Robert Louis Stevenson's *Dr. Jekyll and Mr. Hyde*. Dr. Jekyll discovers the dark side of himself and that change can lead to self-destruction. The same is true for other stories, such as H.G. Wells' *The Invisible Man*.

People are also changed by the dramatic moments of transition. Judith Guest's *Ordinary People* explores the troubled Jarrett family. On the outside, the family looks like any upper-middle-class family, comfortable in its affluence. But behind closed doors lurk secrets and an ugliness that has begun to surface. Once the family members are forced to deal with it, it changes them forever. The Kramers in Avery Corman's *Kramer vs. Kramer* are transformed by the trauma of divorce as they seek to reidentify themselves. And in *Siege at Trencher's Farm*, (better known by its movie title, *Straw Dogs*), a timid professor of astrophysics learns there are times when violence is unavoidable. In the process, he discovers a brutal part of himself he never thought possible.

Francis Macomber in "The Short Happy Life of Francis Macomber" is transformed by an incident in the bush after he wounds a lion and is terrified to track it down to kill it. He later finds his courage, during a buffalo hunt. A few minutes later Macomber is murdered by a wife who doesn't like her new husband. Such transformations often do not come without cost.

George Bernard Shaw's play *Pygmalion* is a wonderful example of transformation. In the play (which is very different from the film, titled *My Fair Lady*), Henry Higgins, a teacher of English speech, transforms Eliza Doolittle, a cockney flower girl, into a seeming English lady by teaching her to speak cultivated English.

He doesn't transform her simply by teaching her to speak correctly. To speak like a lady doesn't necessarily *make* her a lady. Higgins tampers with her as a human being by raising her out of her lower class and dressing her up as if she were a member of the upper class. Once Higgins is finished with her, she can't go back to being a cockney flower girl, and she can't go forward as the duchess she's been primed to be. Higgins refuses to accept his responsibility for changing her.

The irony of the story is that Higgins isn't a gentleman, even though he talks like one. Aloof and unapproachable, he refuses to admit that Eliza has made a difference in his own life. He believes he's a self-sufficient man—until Eliza leaves him.

Once he realizes his mistake, Higgins finds Eliza and pleads with her to return to him so they can live together (with Colonel Pickering) as three dedicated bachelors. At the end of the play, he is sure she will come back, even as she tells him goodbye forever. The transformation of Eliza Doolittle also transforms Henry Higgins. But the play does not have a happy ending. Shaw resisted it even when his audiences demanded it. The point of the story wasn't to show two people falling in love, but to show the human costs of meddling in another person's life. But audiences from his day to ours have refused to listen.

SMALL-SCALE TRANSFORMATION

The incident that changes the protagonist doesn't have to be on such a large scale as Hemingway's story or Shaw's play. Anton Chekhov showed that sometimes even the smallest events can reverberate through our lives with the awesome power of an avalanche.

"The Kiss" is set in a small Russian village in the 1880s. The protagonist is an inept lieutenant in the Russian artillery. "I am the shyest, most modest, and most undistinguished officer in the whole brigade!" he laments. He's a lousy conversationalist, a clod of a dancer—altogether a pathetic mix of officer and gentleman.

The occasion is an evening of dining and dancing at the home of a local retired lieutenant general. The protagonist attends but is ill at ease because of his lack of social graces. He wanders away from the gathering into a dark part of the house when suddenly a woman throws her arms around him, whispers "At last!" in his ear, then kisses him on the lips. Realizing her mistake, she runs from the room before the officer can identify her.

Lt. Ryabovich is stunned. The kiss penetrates him to the core. Although the room is too dark for him to identify the woman, he leaves the room already changed. "He wanted to dance, to talk, to run into the garden, to laugh aloud."

This is the heart of the first dramatic phase: the incident that starts the change in the protagonist's life. Since this plot is about character, it's important to understand who the protagonist is before the change takes place. Chekhov does this with a few simple brush strokes. We should understand enough about the character before the transforming event that when it happens, we also understand how it can affect the protagonist in such a profound way. An accidental kiss by a mysterious woman in the dark would be a great source of amusement for most men, but it wouldn't have the profound impact it has on Ryabovich. We know the lieutenant has low self-esteem, that he feels lonely and unloved, out of the mainstream of human affairs. So suddenly, when this woman's kiss makes him feel connected to the world, we understand why. He has been, as they say, primed for this event. To anyone else, it would've been an insignificant moment, but for Ryabovich, it's the moment of a lifetime.

Ryabovich rejoins the party. The kiss has already started to turn into a romantic fantasy. He scans the women at the party and wonders which was the one in the dark room. The mystery excites him. Before he falls asleep that night, the fantasy is rooted deeply in his imagination.

After the transforming incident, we begin to see the first effects of it. Action, reaction; cause, effect. The personality of the protagonist begins its transformation. This is a process plot. We follow the changes in the protagonist as he transforms from one personality state to another. He may pass through several states in the process of becoming what he will ultimately be. There are lessons to be learned, judgments to be made, insights to be seen.

The next day Ryabovich leaves the Russian village for maneuvers. He experiences a rational moment when he tries to convince himself the kiss was meaningless, that he's making too much out of it. But he cannot resist the temptation of the fantasy; he is already hostage to it. He relates the incident to his fellow officers, who react as normal men might. To them it's one of those wonderfully absurd moments we encounter from time to time. Ryabovich is disappointed by their reaction, for in his mind, the mysterious woman is his goddess of love. He loves her and he wants to marry her. He even begins to fantasize that she really loves him, too. He wants to go back to the village to be reunited with her.

In the second dramatic phase we see the full effects of the transforming incident. We might better describe the transforming incident as an inciting incident, because it begins the process of change in the protagonist. It's an internal process, an expression of the human mind. Whatever actions the character takes are a direct expression of what the character thinks. The character's nature determines the action, just as Ryabovich's nature determines his resolution to go back to be reunited with the woman he is convinced waits for him.

The third dramatic phase usually contains another incident that defines the result of the transformation. The protagonist has reached the end of his experience. It's common for a protagonist to learn lessons other than what he expected to learn. The real lessons are often the hidden or unexpected ones. Expectations are baffled; illusions are destroyed. Reality overtakes fantasy.

Ryabovich returns to the village full of anticipation and tortured by questions: "How would he meet her? What would he talk about? Might she not have forgotten the kiss?" He knows that once the old general hears he's in the village he will be invited back to the house. He can go back to the dark room where it all started.

But the closer he gets to the house, the more uncomfortable he feels. Nothings looks right or feels right. The details he remembered with such clarity have vanished. The nightingale that sang in May is silent; the trees and grass have lost their fragile scent; the village looks crude and cold. Ryabovich suddenly realizes the true nature of his fantasy. "And the whole world, all of life seemed to be an unintelligible, aimless jest. . . ."

When the invitation comes from the general, Ryabovich instead goes home to bed. "How foolish! How foolish!" He is saddened by his realization. "How stupid it all is!"

The clarifying incident of the third dramatic phase allows the protagonist true growth. Ryabovich is sadder but wiser for his experience. Oftentimes that is the lesson of life itself: that sadness comes with greater wisdom.

CHECKLIST

As you write, keep the following points in mind:

1. The plot of transformation should deal with the process of change as the protagonist journeys through one of the many stages of life.

2. The plot should isolate a portion of the protagonist's life that represents the period of change, moving from one significant character state to another.

3. The story should concentrate on the nature of change and how it affects the protagonist from start to end of the experience.

4. The first dramatic phase should relate the transforming inci-

dent that propels the antagonist into a crisis, which starts the process of change.

5. The second dramatic phase generally should depict the effects of the transformation. Since this plot is about character, the story will concentrate on the protagonist's self-examination.

6. The third dramatic phase should contain a clarifying incident, which represents the final stage of the transformation. The character understands the true nature of his experience and how it has affected him. Generally this is the point of the story at which true growth and understanding occur.

7. Often the price of wisdom is a certain sadness.

Chapter Nineteen

Master Plot #13: Maturation

Almost all the great writers have as their motif, more or less disguised, the passage from childhood to maturity, the clash between the thrill of expectation, and the disillusioning knowledge of the truth. "Lost Illusion" is the undisclosed title of every novel.

—*Andre Maurois*

Think about all the books you've read and the films you've seen. In what percentage of them does the character change for the *better* during the course of the work? Definitely the majority, right? Writers are free to write about whatever they please in any way they please. So why do an overwhelming number of works show characters improving themselves and their lot? It's a curious phenomenon. Could we say that ultimately the writer's nature is to be optimistic? Sure, Hollywood prefers happy endings—we know that. But that doesn't account for the predisposition of writers to create stories that are socially and morally constructive.

The maturation plot—the plot about growing up—is one of those strongly optimistic plots. There are lessons to learn, and those lessons may be difficult, but in the end the character becomes (or will become) a better person for it.

The maturation plot is a close relative to transformation and metamorphosis plots, and yet it's distinct enough to have its own category. You could argue it's a metamorphosis from childhood to adulthood (from innocence to experience), and it certainly includes a physical change. But this plot isn't a metamorphosis plot in the sense that I've outlined it. You could also argue that maturation is a transformation plot as well, but the maturation plot relates only to the process of growing. One way to look at it, perhaps, is to say the transformation plot focuses on adults who are in the process of changing, and the maturation plot focuses on children who are in the process of becoming adults.

ENTER THE HERO

The protagonist of the maturation plot is usually a sympathetic young person whose goals are either confused or not yet quite formed. He floats on the sea of life without a rudder. He often vacillates, unsure of the proper path to take, the proper decision to make. These inabilities are usually the result of a lack of experience in life — naivete — as in John Steinbeck's "Flight."

This coming-of-age story is often called the *Bildungsroman*, which is German for "education novel." The focus of these stories is the protagonist's moral and psychological growth. Start your story where the protagonist has reached the point in her life at which she can be tested as an adult. She may be ready for the test, or she may be forced into it by circumstances.

Ernest Hemingway wrote a series of short stories called the "Nick Adams" stories, about a young boy in upstate Michigan. These stories are about growing up. In "Indian Camp" the boy goes with his father, who's a doctor, to treat an Indian. The Indian has killed himself and for the first time the boy must confront death. But the boy is too young to grasp the experience and rejects the lesson. That is the point of story: He isn't yet capable of dealing with the adult world. In many of Hemingway's other stories, however, the young protagonist learns quickly the lessons of growing up. In what is arguably Hemingway's most famous story, "The Killers," an older Nick Adams must confront evil for the first time in his life.

"THE KILLERS"

"The Killers" is a template for the maturation story. As a story it is deceptively simple (as is much of Hemingway's work), but it contains the thrust and understanding of the difficulties a young person must confront in the process of growing up.

The story is seen through the eyes of Nick, who remains a

spectator rather than a central character through most of the story. This position of observer is quite common, because the young person isn't old enough to understand or to participate in the action in any meaningful way.

Two Chicago hoods, Al and Max, come to a hick town to kill Ole Andreson, a fighter who's double-crossed them by not throwing a prize fight when he was supposed to. The hoods go into a diner where Nick works. The dialogue takes place among George, the counter man, Sam, the black cook, and Nick. When Nick learns what the hit men plan to do, he decides to try to help Ole. Young and idealistic, he wants to save Ole from his fate. He runs to the boarding house where Ole is staying and warns him, but the old Swede is tired of running and is ready to accept death. Nick doesn't understand Ole's resignation and refuses to accept it. He is too young and too optimistic. By the end of the story, Nick rejects Ole's attitude and decides that one must resist death and evil no matter what the cost.

BEFORE: THE FIRST DRAMATIC PHASE

The actual process of maturation in a young person covers many years. You can pick up at any point, from a young, impressionable child to someone in young adulthood. You may explore one day in the life of the protagonist, or you may follow him for months or even years. Two works that are consummate masterpieces of the maturation plot are Dickens' *Great Expectations* and Twain's *Huckleberry Finn*. We follow Pip and Huck through all the agonies they must confront, and we follow their adventures hoping that they will eventually choose the right course. When they do, we feel a sense of justified satisfaction.

We begin with the protagonist as he is before events start to change his life. We need to see who this character is, how he thinks and acts, so we can make a decision about his moral and psychological state before he undergoes change. Your character may exhibit a lot of negative (childlike) traits. Perhaps he is irresponsible (but fun-loving), duplicitous, selfish, naive—all the character traits that are typical of people who haven't accepted the responsibilities of adulthood or who haven't accepted the moral and social code that the rest of us abide by (more or less).

Your character may be endearing (as are Huck and Pip) but will still lack the virtues that we believe adults should have. The audience will forgive these shortcomings at the beginning (after all, the hero is still just a child), but you will raise the audience's expectations that as the story progresses, your character will respond to the test and eventually come through.

Nick at the beginning of "The Killers" is not prepared to deal with the kind of world that the hit men and Ole represent. He hasn't been exposed to cynicism and what we might call the dark side of human nature. He still leads a sheltered life in small-town Michigan. He looks normal in all respects; and, in fact, he is. But now the ugly outside world will intrude into his peaceable kingdom.

WHEN SUDDENLY . . .

Which brings us to the test. The catalytic event. Your character is merrily sailing through childhood without any real worries when suddenly something comes along and smacks her square in the face. It could be the death of a parent, a divorce, or suddenly being cast out of the home. The event must be powerful enough to get the attention of the protagonist and literally shake up her belief systems. If a child believes (as children do) that the family and everyone in it is immortal, and something happens to prove that isn't the case, the child must reassess her beliefs and reaccommodate herself according to the new events. In the child's eyes this event is apocalyptic, although as adults we may see the event as part of the normal course of life.

You will prove your skills as a writer by making us feel the apocalyptic force of the event on the child's psyche. You want us to feel what the child feels. Don't let your reader react as an adult, because that will undercut the emotional upheaval your protagonist feels. Take us back to when we were young and we felt those same stirrings. Recall those buried emotions. You must be convincing in your portrayal of young people.

Writers often make the mistake of writing about someone or something they know little about. While it's true that at one time we were all young, some of us can't tap the reservoir of feelings and thoughts we had ten, twenty or fifty years ago. If you adopt the persona of a young person, you must convincingly portray what a young person thinks and feels. Hemingway did it in his stories; so did Steinbeck. And Dickens. They make us empathize. If you don't carry us back, your story will lack the emotional zest it needs.

Many authors make the mistake of writing like adults pretending to be children. You must have a feel for what children think and feel without resorting to a primitive level. There is a fine balance between maturity and immaturity of character in writing. In a book like John Knowles's *A Separate Peace* or J.D. Salinger's *The Catcher in the Rye*, the protagonists are a mixture of adult and child. They aren't oversimplified characters, but they are still convincing as young people. If you aren't in touch with the sensibilities of the people you want to write about, don't believe you can be convincing.

Nick's test comes when he overhears the hit men plan to kill Ole Andreson. He doesn't understand a world that will not move to save Ole. He doesn't understand the complacency with which George, Sam, Max and Al accept Ole's fate. He is given two options: Either he does nothing (as George and Sam do) or he becomes actively involved and tries to warn Ole.

I DON'T WANNA: THE SECOND DRAMATIC PHASE

The lesson about growing up rarely just falls into place. A bulb doesn't suddenly go on inside the head of the protagonist. Your protagonist now must react to the cataclysm. Generally the child's reaction is to deny the event, either literally or figuratively. *Mother isn't really dead.* Or *Mom and Dad aren't really getting a divorce.* Or *I don't really have to get a job.* Denial is a strong emotion. It tries to protect the protagonist from reality. It's not unusual for the protagonist to do exactly the wrong thing. He resists; he becomes more difficult, less predictable. His character may even degenerate. Children don't like to be forced into dealing with the cold, cruel world. They prefer the relative warmth and security of childhood.

But like Hansel and Gretel, who are abandoned by their parents in the forest because they can't afford to feed them anymore, they are forced with a do-or-die reality. Fairy tales are short and get right to the point, and Hansel and Gretel, in spite of their lack of maturity, pretty much have the skills it takes to survive (although they become victims of the witch by giving into the childlike behavior of eating her gingerbread house). In longer and more realistic stories, the process of resistance may take longer.

It may be, in fact, that your protagonist is actually trying to do the right thing, but doesn't know what the right thing is. That means trial and error. Finding out what works and what doesn't work. That is the process of growing up, the journey from innocence to experience.

Nick Adams is in this position. He does what he believes is right. He can't conceive of any other action. But what he doesn't understand is Ole's reaction (and in fact all the adults' reactions to what seems like an unwillingness to resist fate). He resists their fatalistic attitude.

The lessons your protagonist learns usually come at a price. The costs may be tangible or intangible. He may lose his sense of confidence or self-worth; he may lose all his earthly possessions. He has moved from a world that was safe to a world that is unpredictable and perhaps even hostile.

You can play this story out on any scale. The lesson may be a small one learned in a day, a small, almost unnoticeable lesson that no one else notices but that is important to the protagonist. Or the lessons may continue over months or years and result in a socially stable, mature individual.

The point of the second dramatic phase is for you to challenge your protagonist's beliefs. Test them. Do they hold up, or do they fail? How does your protagonist deal with change? This character, perhaps more than any other in our repertoire, is *always* undergoing change.

FINALLY: THE THIRD DRAMATIC PHASE

Finally your protagonist develops a new system of beliefs and gets to the point where it can be tested. In the third dramatic phase, your protagonist will finally accept (or reject) the change. Since we've already noticed that most works of this type end on a positive note, your protagonist will accept the role of adult in a meaningful rather than a token way.

Obviously, adulthood doesn't come all at once. It comes in stages, lesson accumulating on lesson. Nick glimpses a world he never knew existed. It is a dark, foreboding world, and it goes against everything he knows and feels. At the same time, he senses the power of this world. George and Sam give in to it. So does Ole. Nick isn't old enough to understand *why* they give in to it, but he knows how he feels, and that is to resist it. The story implies that this experience represents a turning point in Nick's life. He resolves to struggle against what Ole cannot. He has this day seen the world and the people in it in a different way, and it has changed who Nick is and how he thinks about the world.

Don't try to rush all the growing in one day. It doesn't happen that way. In the small event lies hidden the meaning of life. Don't lecture or moralize; let your protagonist slowly peel away one layer at a time. Our focus as a reader is on how your protagonist deals with the event and how she interprets it in the scheme of life. What has she learned? Has she taken another step toward adulthood? Or has she resisted that step?

Don't try to capture all good and evil in your story. Choose your moment carefully. Make it happen in your story as it does in life. Find meaning in the seemingly trivial. Remember that what may seem trivial to an adult may be earth-shattering to a child. That's your key: to tune in at a child's level of consciousness and read the world the way you did years ago.

CHECKLIST

As you develop your story, keep the following points in mind:

1. Create a protagonist who is on the cusp of adulthood, whose goals are either confused or not yet clarified.

2. Make sure the audience understands who the character is and how she feels and thinks before an event occurs that begins the process of change.

3. Contrast your protagonist's naive life (childhood) against the reality of an unprotected life (adulthood).

4. Focus your story on your protagonist's moral and psychological growth.

5. Once you've established your protagonist as she was before

the change, create an incident that challenges her beliefs and her understanding of how the world works.

6. Does your character reject or accept change? Perhaps both? Does she resist the lesson? How does she act?

7. Show your protagonist undergoing the process of change. It should be gradual, not sudden.

8. Make sure your young protagonist is convincing; don't give her adult values and perceptions until she is ready to portray them.

9. Don't try to accomplish adulthood all at once. Small lessons often represent major upheavals in the process of growing up.

10. Decide at what psychological price this lesson comes, and establish how your protagonist copes with it.

Chapter Twenty

Master Plot #14: Love

The course of true love never did run smooth.

— *Shakespeare,* A Midsummer Night's Dream, I,i.

Remember chapter two, when we discussed "Boy Meets Girl"? (Or even the 1990s twist of the same story, "Girl Meets Boy.") Since we know conflict is fundamental to fiction, we also know "Boy Meets Girl" isn't enough. It must be "Boy Meets Girl, But . . . " The story hinges on the "But . . . " These are the obstacles to love that keep the lovers from consummating their affair.

In "forbidden" love, the love affair violates some social taboo, such as race in *Guess Who's Coming to Dinner*; rank in the medieval love romance *Aucassin and Nicolette*; incest in John Ford's *'Tis a Pity She's a Whore*; or adultery in the great medieval romance of *Tristan and Isolde*.

Sometimes the lovers are within what we might call social norms, but situations arise that aren't conducive to love, and people won't condone it. Unlike the lovers in forbidden love, who usually pay for their "folly" with their lives, these lovers have a decent chance of overcoming the obstacles that make their affair such rough sailing.

The obstacles may be confusion, misunderstanding and general silliness such as mistaken identities. Shakespeare's romantic comedies such as *Much Ado About Nothing* and *Twelfth Night* and his tragicomedies such as *Cymbelene* and *Measure for Measure* fall into this category. So does Jane Austen's comedy of manners *Pride and Prejudice*, in which an empty-headed and argumentative mother decides her mission in life is to find a suitable husband for each of her five daughters.

The obstacle may be a simple gimmick, such as R.A. Dick's *The Ghost and Mrs. Muir* (later made into a film and a television series). Mrs. Muir, a recent widow, buys a cottage that's haunted by the benevolent ghost of a sea captain. The two fall in love, but obviously they're incompatible. By the end of the story, however, they find a way to become compatible. Although the television series played it as a comedy, the original story is a serious romantic drama about a woman who chooses one suitor over another and is both literally and figuratively haunted by her scorned lover.

In some cases the story is agonized and tortured, the granddaddy of which may be Emily Brontë's *Wuthering Heights*. Or what about Charlotte Brontë's *Jane Eyre*, in which Jane finds out on her wedding day that her husband-to-be is already married — to a lunatic?

In literature, love is often not easily found, or if it is, not easily kept. Often the story of love is the story of frustration, because someone or something always gets in the way. In the case of forbidden love those barriers are social, but in other love stories, the barriers can come from anywhere in the universe. In *Cyrano de Bergerac*, the obstacle to love is the size of Cyrano's nose. In Ron Howard's *Splash*, the obstacle to love is the size of the woman's flipper: She's a mermaid.

In the case of "Orpheus and Eurydice," fate seems to conspire against the lovers from day one. Orpheus, the tale goes, was such a good musician that not only did the wild animals come out of the forest to hear him play, but so did the rocks and trees.

Orpheus meets Eurydice and falls for her in a big way. He woos her with his music, which is obviously irresistible. He pops the question and she says yes. A good start.

They get married but before they can set up house, a shepherd tries to rape Eurydice. Eurydice fights him off (or, as they said in the old days, "she resisted his advances"). While trying to escape the shepherd, Eurydice steps on a poisonous snake that kills her.

End of love story, right? You can't have a love story if one of the lovers is dead. (Except maybe in stories like William Faulkner's "A Rose for Emily" or Robert Bloch's *Psycho*.)

Orpheus is heartbroken. He mopes around playing sad songs and wrenching everybody's heart. He decides life isn't worth living without Eurydice, so what does he do? No, he doesn't kill himself. Instead, he decides to go to Hades and bring Eurydice back himself.

A neat trick if you can pull it off. We've always been fascinated by the idea of bringing loved ones back from the dead, and I don't know of a single story where it works, including the outrageous *Frankenhooker*.

Orpheus uses his music to charm his way past the security guards to Hades. All Hades stops to listen. Even the ghosts shed tears when they hear him sing. Orpheus makes it to the head honcho, Pluto, and with the power of his lyre convinces the ruler of Hades that he should give back Eurydice.

But on one condition: Orpheus must promise not to turn around and look at her until they get out of Hell.

Orpheus agrees. The two journey back to the Upper World, past the Furies, past the great doors of Hades, climbing out of the darkness. Orpheus knows Eurydice must be right behind him, but he longs to see her for himself. Unlike Lot's wife, who didn't heed God's admonition not to turn around to look or she would turn into a pillar of salt, Orpheus resists the temptation until the moment he steps in the sunlight of the Upper World.

Too soon. Eurydice is still in the shadow of the cavern, and as he holds out his arms to embrace her, she disappears with only a faint "Farewell."

Orpheus desperately tries to follow her back into Hades, but everybody is wise to him and won't let him in a second time.

Obstacles compounded.

If Orpheus was unhappy before, he's impossible now. He must go home alone, in utter desolation. He tortures everybody with his melancholic songs until no one can take it anymore. Some gorgeous Greek maidens try to get him to forget Eurydice, but he rather rudely tells them to go away. In classical Greek fashion, the scorned maidens avenge themselves by ripping off Orpheus' head and tossing it into the river.

As the story begins, we learn the basics: Orpheus loves Eurydice, and Eurydice loves Orpheus. We witness the quality of their love for each other and give them a taste of happiness. But only a taste. Before the wedding cake can get stale, disaster strikes. That disaster could be anything from an automobile crash, to a disease, to the I.R.S. (mistakenly) deciding she owes a zillion dollars in back taxes or the I.N.S. (mistakenly) deciding he's a former guard in a Nazi death camp. It doesn't matter what the obstacle is; what matters is if the lovers can jump the hurdles and make it to the finish line.

The first attempt to solve the obstacle is almost always thwarted. Don't forget the Rule of Three. The first two attempts fail, the third time's the charm. One love is the protagonist (in this case Orpheus), who does all the "doing" while the victim (in this case Eurydice) waits passively for something to happen. Sometimes the victim lover is more active in her own rescue, but her action is secondary to the protagonist's. There may be an antagonist/villain who creates the obstacle; but then again, as in the case of Orpheus, it may just be what we conveniently call Fate conspiring against happiness.

The lesson of fairy tales is the basic lesson of all love stories: Love that hasn't been tested isn't true love. Love must be proved, generally through hardship.

The leap from the myth of Orpheus and Eurydice to C.S. Forester's *The African Queen* isn't that far. The characters in *The African Queen* don't start out as lovers but as opposites. She's a missionary's sister; he's a timid cockney engineer. Together they travel downriver to Lake Victoria on a rickety steam launch called *The African Queen* with the purpose of blowing up a German gunboat. Along the way this unlikely couple falls in love, only to be married as their last request before being hung. (Yes, they live happily ever after.)

A lot of love stories don't have happy endings. *Adam Bede* by George Eliot (a.k.a. Mary Ann Evans) tells the story of Adam, who falls in love with a pretty but shallow woman named Hetty. Hetty doesn't want Adam, who's the absolute picture of propriety. She'd rather marry the local young squire.

The squire seduces Hetty (as squires are wont to do) and then leaves her. Hetty agrees to marry Adam on the rebound but finds out she's pregnant. She tries to find the squire, who's taken off for parts unknown. By the end, Hetty is found guilty of killing her child. Adam finally marries the woman he should've married in the first place, a young Methodist preacher.

Definitely not a happy ending.

It seems the higher up you go in the hierarchy of literature, the more unhappy love stories get. If it's a drama, one of the lovers always seems to die. If it's a comedy, the lovers can ride off into the sunset together. Federico Garcia Lorca was right when he said life is a tragedy for those who feel and a comedy for those who think.

Italian tragic operas are real hanky-wringers. In Puccini's *La Boheme*, Rodolfo falls in love with Mimi; Mimi dies. In Verdi's *La Traviata*, Violetta falls in love with Alfred; Violetta dies. The list seems endless: *Il Trovatore, Rigoletto, Madame Butterfly, I Pagliacci* . . . More women died in Italian opera, it seems, than in the Black Plague.

A LITTLE ROMANCE

What makes a good love story? The answer lies more with the characters than with the actions. That's why the love plot is a character plot. A better way of putting it is by saying that successful love stories work because of the "chemistry" between the lovers. You can create a plot that has plenty of clever turns and gimmicks, but if the lovers aren't convincing in a special way, it will fall flat on its face. We all know what chemistry is, but few of us know how to create it. Chemistry is the special attraction that characters have for each other that lifts them out of the coal bin of the ordinary. Too often, romances are generic: In a formulaic plot, one general-issue man meets one general-issue woman as they pursue their fantasies and desires in the most pedestrian way. This isn't to say that these kinds of plots don't work within their own limited range. The writing and selling of romance novels is big business. The plots are so specific that the publishers insist on certain guidelines, which they coyly call "do's" and "don't's." The publishers have tight perimeters about what a writer can and can't do, and if you're intent on writing for that market, know the rules. But you'll find them confining. The characters must conform to type.

The publishers have their reasons, and the millions of dollars of sales they rack up every year attests to those reasons, at least economically. They know *what* sells and they may even know *why* it sells. It's the same reason fairy tales work for children.

Fairy tale characters, you may remember, also revert to type. The little boy and girl who venture out into the dark forest are like everyboy or everygirl. When they have names, their names are generic, like Dick and Jane. They never have distinguishing marks or characteristics such as tattoos or scars; they're fresh from the mold. They don't come from Buffalo or Biloxi or Bozeman; they come from places like The Kingdom or The Forest. Their parents are defined by what they do for a living rather than by their names ("A woodcutter/fisherman/farmer and his wife").

A child identifies closely with the characters in fairy tales. He casts himself in the role of the poor, abused, unfortunate child, and he takes strength in the fact that he can go out into the world and kill giants (adults) and make his own way by being clever and thoughtful and honest. If Little Hans had been developed so that we knew his father was a stockbroker in Maine and his mother was a pharmacist and his sister was in training as a decathlete, we would lose the chance to identify with him. The more a reader knows about the character, the less the character is a part of the reader's world and more a part of his own world. Since identification is so important in fairy tales (as far as the young are concerned), the tale must conform to the mind and imagination of Everychild.

The same holds true for romance writing. If you as a writer intend to appeal to all readers, you must rely on types that will allow the reader to identify situations and project herself into them. It's like having two blank faces for your main characters, and the reader fills them in according to her own needs.

Literature (with a capital "L") doesn't cater to this crowd. If you want to break away from Everylover and write about two (or more) characters who are unique, you must delve into the psychology of people and love. *A love story is a story about love denied and either recaptured or lost.* Its plan is simple; executing the plan is not. It all depends on your ability to find two people who are remarkable in either a tragic or comic way as they pursue love.

There is a world of difference between the immensely popular but shallow love story of Erich Segal's *Love Story* and the less popular but more enduring stories about the search for love in Eliot's *Adam Bede* or Thomas Hardy's *Jude the Obscure*. All three books are meant to be tragic: They share the same theme of love lost. But *Love Story*, a runaway best-seller and box office hit in its time, was a surface exploration of love denied involving a proto-yuppie couple in ivy league New England. (She gets sick and dies.) They never reach the depth of character and examination of the human soul that Eliot or Hardy's characters do.

But let's face it. The public has a powerful drive for fairy tale (that is, happy) endings. You already know that audiences have universally refused to accept George Bernard Shaw's unhappy ending to *Pygmalion* and turned it into their own version called *My Fair Lady*, which got the Academy Award for best picture. Rudyard Kipling's *The Light That Failed* is about Dick's love for Maisie. But Maisie is shallow and insensitive. Even when Dick starts to go blind (hold on to your handkerchief) and devotes his last days of sight to finishing his masterpiece painting (appropriately entitled *Melancholia*), Maisie ruthlessly rejects him. Brokenhearted, Dick kills himself. Not a very happy ending. But audiences, who cherish Kipling almost as much as they cherish Dickens, refused to stand for it. Kipling buckled under the pressure and rewrote the story with a happy ending, which was published in a later edition. Hollywood demands happy endings *de rigueur* (see Robert Altman's *The Player* for a scathing satire on happy endings).

Thomas Hardy was under no such pressure, and even if he had been, it was unlikely he would've caved in to it. *Jude the Obscure* was his last work, and it's dark and cruel. It doesn't reaffirm the power of love to save or cure all. It is about the tragedy of love. It's a downer all the way. The reader who wants positive, bouncy, "love is wonderful" stories would never get through the first ten pages. But if the reader is interested in an examination of the conflict between carnal and spiritual life, the life of Jude Fawley will deliver. But you must remember, a lot of readers just aren't interested in that kind of close examination of love, especially if it has an unhappy ending. They'll always demand a fairy tale ending, and as long as there's a buck to be made, publishers and film producers will cater to that taste.

Don't get me wrong; there's a place for both kinds of stories. Each fills a distinctive need. The question is, Which story do you want to write?

SOFT RAIN, KITTENS AND MAKING LOVE BY THE FIRE

If you decide to write about love, you are at the slight disadvantage of being in a line that's five thousand years long. Thousands of writers have written about love, and now *you* want to do it? The competition is enough to make anyone pale. What can you hope to say that hasn't already been said?

You can't take that attitude, because it can be applied to any subject you might write about, not just love. But it is true that love can be difficult to write about without relying on the same old, tired clichés. Remember, it's not so much what you say as how you say it. Arguably it's all been said before. But the number of ways it can be said are inexhaustible. We are as much intrigued with the mysteries of love today as some Babylonian was five thousand years ago.

But understand that there's a big difference between creating sentiment and creating sentimentality. Both have their place. Romance novels depend on sentimentality; a love story that tries to be unique depends on sentiment.

What is the difference?

The difference has to do with honest emotion vs. prepackaged emotion. A sincere work—a work of sentiment—generates its own power; a sentimental work borrows feelings from stock. Rather than create characters or events that generate unique feelings, the sentimentalist merely relies on stock characters and events that already have their emotions built in.

Edgar Guest is a good example. At one time, Guest was one of America's most popular poets (proving that there's a big market for sentimentality). His poem "Sue's Got a Baby" isn't exactly a monument to American literature, but it's a first-rate example of sentimentality. The topic of love, in this case, is about mother-hood.

> *Sue's got a baby now, an' she*
> *Is like her mother used to be;*
> *Her face seems prettier, an' her ways*
> *More settled like. In these few days*
> *She's changed completely, an' her smile*
> *Has taken on the mother-style.*
> *Her voice is sweeter, an' her words*
> *Are clear as is the song of birds.*
> *She still is Sue, but not the same—*
> *She's different since the baby came.*

Sentimentality is subject-ive, meaning you write about the *subject* of love rather than create a story in which the unique relationship between writer and subject evokes genuine sentiment. Take a look at Guest's poem and you'll see what I mean.

"Sue's got a baby now . . . " All right, we have a tiny bit of context. We don't know anything about Sue (who she is, where she lives, how she feels about the whole thing) but we know she's just given birth (we assume) to a baby. *Because we know so little about Sue and her circumstances, we must reach our own conclusions about how she feels.* So we draw on our own feelings. Motherhood is a good thing, therefore Sue must be happy, right?

". . . an' she / Is like her mother used to be;" What exactly does that mean? There's no way to tell, because the author is so vague that we can only guess. Again, based our own experience and *the subject of motherhood*, we assume that her mother was as happy about having Sue as Sue is about having her own baby. Right?

"Her face seems prettier, an' her ways / More settled-like." Her face seems prettier than *what*? And I still have no idea what "more settled-like" is supposed to mean. Did Sue used to run around with bikers?

What sentimentality does is rely on the reader's experience rather than the fictional experience created by the writer. *You* fill in the blanks. *You* remember what it's like. The reader, not the writer, does the work. If you go through the poem line by line, you'll see that Guest never says anything specific about being a mother. He just piles cliché upon cliché and lets you bask in your memories of what it's like. There is no real character and no real situation in the poem.

Sentiment comes out of context. With sentiment, you have the portrayal of real people and real situations. That makes sentiment object-ive, because it relates to objects (people, places and things) rather than generalized emotions. If you're going to write about love, think about whether you want to be sentimental (which has its place in certain types of writing, such as melodramas and romances) or if you want to go for the real thing and create a world that has its own feelings and doesn't rely on the reader's.

Stephen Spender wrote a short poem called "To My Daughter," in which he writes about a walk he takes with his little girl. It's a simple poem (five lines), but it packs a lot of feeling. His little girl is grasping his finger with her hand, and the speaker knows that even though they are walking together at this moment, he will someday lose his daughter. So he holds the moment dearly. The personna of the poem realizes that he will always remember how his daughter's hand clasps his finger. Her tiny hand is like a "ring" around his finger. The ring becomes a metaphor for the emotional bond between father and daughter.

Can you tell the difference between the two poems? Spender works with two people we can see *and feel*. We see the two of them walk down the road, and we understand the feeling the man has for his daughter, both having her and yet losing her. The ring (the object) is a metaphor, rather like a wedding ring between father and daughter. Spender's poem goes much deeper in five lines than Guest's does in all ten. Guest relies on the feelings I already have toward motherhood and taps into that reservoir. Spender creates a moment and feeling in time.

We never feel so alive as when we are emotionally aroused. It's not easy to accomplish that in writing, but when we take a short-cut by faking those emotions—by building them up into more than what they are—we're guilty of sentimentality. Sentimentality is the result of exaggerating any emotion beyond what the context of the moment can express.

I don't want to sound overly critical of sentimentality, because it definitely has its place. Most of us like a good sentimental book or movie now and then. The point is to know the difference between sentiment and sentimental, and to know when to use one and not the other. If you're trying to write standard formula romance, sentimentality (to some degree, anyway) is expected of you. If you're trying to be sincere and authentic as a writer, you need to develop feelings that are in line with the action, and avoid exaggerating them. In other words, don't just talk about love, show it!

I LOVE YOU SO MUCH I HATE YOUR GUTS

Since most of us spend much of our lives searching for and fantasizing about love, we forget love has two sides: the up side (falling in love) and the down side (falling out of love).

For every thousand stories about falling in love, there may be one story about falling out of the love. For obvious reasons, it's not a real popular theme in love stories. Yet it's produced some incredibly dramatic works. I suppose the optimist thinks about the possibilities that lie ahead, whereas the pessimist broods on the realities that lie behind. That's not to say that princes and princesses can't live happily forever after. They do — sometimes.

Falling out of love is about people, too. It's about the end rather than the beginning of a relationship. The success of your story depends on an understanding of who your characters are and what has happened to them. By the end of your story, the situation is driven to crisis, which results in some kind of resolution: resignation to perpetual warfare, divorce and death being the most common resolutions.

I can give you three stunning (and depressing) examples to read and study. The first is August Strindberg's *The Dance of Death*, which is about a love-hate relationship between husband and wife. Alice is a virtual prisoner of her tyrannical husband of twenty-five years, Edgar. As the play opens, Edgar is gravely ill, and yet he continues to try to dominate his wife. They battle it out to the death.

So do George and Martha in Edward Albee's *Who's Afraid of Virginia Woolf?* (which has its roots in Strindberg's play). And finally, on a more psychological level, Georges Simenon's *The Cat* (also made into a film starring Jean Gabin and Simone Signoret).

In *The Cat*, Emile and Marguerite have reached the point of mutual hate at the beginning of the novel. They share nothing else — they don't eat, sleep or even talk together. With consummate skill, Simenon relates the circumstances that led first to their union and, gradually, to its bizarre devastation.

The emotional focus of these works isn't love so much as it's love/hate. This is the stormy side of love, but it's still every bit as much a part of reality as its sunny side.

THE STRUCTURE OF THE LOVE PLOT

In the other plots, I set out what were the commonly used plot phases. But in this plot, major sets of phases depend on the nature of the plot you intend to use. You must adapt accordingly.

The exception is the plot about two lovers who find each other in the beginning and then are separated by circumstances. In that case the three dramatic phases are:

1) **Lovers found.** The two main characters are presented and their love relationship begins. The first phase deals primarily with establishing that relationship. By the end of the first phase they are deeply in love and are committed either by marriage, "troth," or some symbol of connection. Close to the end of the first phase, however, something happens to separate the lovers (as in the case of Eurydice's death). This may come from an antagonist who does something to deny the lovers each other. (She is kidnapped. His parents make him move to Cincinnati with them. Her ex-husband doesn't like the fact that she's taken up with another man.) Or the lovers may be separated as the result of circumstances, or Fate. (He must go off and fight in a war. She gets brain cancer. He has a skiing accident and is crippled.) However it happens, the first phase usually ends with the lovers' separation.

2) **Lovers split.** In the second dramatic phase, at least one of the separated lovers makes an attempt to find/rescue/reunite with the other lover. Usually the focus is on one of the lovers who must put forth all the effort while the other either waits patiently to be rescued or actively resists those efforts. For example, Jack has been crippled in a skiing accident. The doctors say he will never walk again. Jack is depressed; he tells Jacqueline he wants

to get a divorce so she can find a "real man" (you know the speech). Jacqueline is too much in love with Jack to leave him or to let him drown in his own self-pity, so she fights the battle for him until he comes around and fights the battle for himself.

But the path to salvation is never clear. There are always setbacks. These setbacks are the guts of the second dramatic phase. One step forward, two steps back. The protagonist, the active lover, may have to fight a battle with the antagonist (if there is one), and for the short term, the protagonist only wins minor victories.

3) **Lovers reunited.** By the third dramatic phase, the active lover has found a way to overcome all the obstacles of the second dramatic phase. As is often the case with most plots, the obvious rarely succeeds. Opportunity presents itself to the diligent, and the active lover finally finds an opening that allows her either to overcome the antagonist or the preventative force (illness, injury, etc.). The final effect for all this is the reunion of the lovers and a resumption of the emotional intensity of the first phase.

The love, now tested, is greater, and the bonds have grown stronger.

CHECKLIST

As you write, keep in mind the following points:

1. The prospect of love should always be met with a major obstacle. Your characters may want it, but they can't have it for any variety of reasons. At least not right away.

2. The lovers are usually ill-suited in some way. They may come from different social classes (beauty queen/nerd; Montague and Capulet) or they may be physically unequal (one is blind or handicapped).

3. The first attempt to solve the obstacle is almost always thwarted. Success doesn't come easily. Love must be proven by dedication and stick-to-it-iveness.

4. As one observer once put it, love usually consists of one person offering the kiss and the other offering the cheek, meaning one lover is more aggressive in seeking love than the other. The aggressive partner is the seeker, who completes the majority of

the action. The passive partner (who may want love just as much) still waits for the aggressive partner to overcome the obstacles. Either role can be played by either sex.

5. Love stories don't need to have happy endings. If you try to force a happy ending on a love story that clearly doesn't deserve one, your audience will refuse it. True, Hollywood prefers happy endings, but some of the world's best love stories (*Anna Karenina, Madame Bovary, Heloise and Abelard*) are very sad.

6. Concentrate on your main characters to make them appealing and convincing. Avoid the stereotypical lovers. Make your characters and their circumstances unique and interesting. Love is one of the hardest subjects to write about because it's been written about so often, but that doesn't mean it can't be done well. You will have to feel deeply for your characters, though. If you don't, neither will your readers.

7. Emotion is an important element in writing about love. Not only should you be convincing, but you should develop the full range of feelings: fear, loathing, attraction, disappointment, reunion, consummation, etc. Love has many feelings associated with it and you should be prepared to develop them according to the needs of your plot.

8. Understand the role of sentiment and sentimentality in your writing and decide which is better for your story. If you're writing a formula romance, you may want to use the tricks of sentimentality. If you're trying to write a one-of-a-kind love story, you will want to avoid sentimentality and rely on true sentiment in your character's feelings.

9. Take your lovers through the full ordeal of love. Make sure they are tested (individually and collectively) and that they finally deserve the love they seek. Love is earned; it is not a gift. Love untested is not true love.

Chapter Twenty-One

Master Plot #15: Forbidden Love

Love looks not with the eyes, but with the mind, And therefore is winged Cupid painted blind.

— *Shakespeare*, A Midsummer Night's Dream I, i

C haucer said it before Shakespeare, and it has been said many times before and since: Love is blind. We believe in the power and strength of love to overcome all obstacles. It is the supreme achievement of human emotion. In the perfect world there is only love, and all the petty meanness that holds human beings down to such an earthly plane is left behind. Love is a transcendent state, and we spend our lives seeking it.

In our romantic imagination we believe love has no bounds. We are familiar with the strangeness of it: how it matches together those who seem unmatchable, how it creates its own miracles. We know its power to soothe and heal. Love is more powerful than any other human strength.

But we are earthbound. We're imperfect creatures who can only aspire to the perfection of a world filled with love. In the meantime we must suffer with our shortcomings as we muddle through our lives, taking our turn to try grasping the brass ring.

The truth is that we have written volumes on the rules of love. Although our hearts know love shouldn't have any tethers, we learn the lessons of what constitutes "proper" love every day and diligently pass those lessons on to our children. We define love and make judgments about it. One shouldn't marry above or below one's station. One shouldn't marry outside one's own faith. One should marry only a person of the same race. One shouldn't fall in love with a person from another social class or a person who's already married or a person who's too old or too young. Our society makes these demands, and most of us abide by them. But the power of love — or just the idea of being in love — is enough to make some cross "the line" and enter forbidden territory. And since fiction often acts as our social conscience, there are plenty of stories to warn us about the penalties of crossing that line. Occasionally a story comes along that flies in the face of social taboos and shows that love can sometimes be more powerful than the disapproval of an entire society. Love sometimes thrives in the cracks.

The first written version of *Romeo and Juliet* appeared in 1476, more than a hundred years before Shakespeare wrote his play. In fact, Shakespeare's version is the fourth, and it wasn't the last. Gounod made it into an opera and Jean Anouilh wrote a bitter and realistic version of it called *Romeo and Jeanette*. The story has a powerful hold on our imagination primarily because the two lovers defy their feuding families' prohibition that the Montagues and Capulets should have nothing to do with each other. Although their love is real, so is their tragedy.

The love between *Heloise and Abelard* follows the same tragic path. Abelard, a French scholastic philosopher and theologian, fell in love with and seduced his student, Heloise. She got pregnant and had a son, after which the pair was secretly married. When Heloise's uncle, who was the Canon of Notre Dame Cathedral, found out about their illicit love affair, he had Abelard castrated.

Society has always been uncomfortable with people who are particularly ugly or grotesque. We pretend they don't exist, and we deny that they have feelings and desires like the rest of us.

Victor Hugo created Quasimodo, the hunchback bell ringer in *The Hunchback of Notre Dame*. I doubt there's anyone in literature who's uglier. (One of his eyes is buried under a huge tumor, his teeth hang over his lower lip like tusks, his eyebrows are red bristles, and his gigantic nose curves over his upper lip like a snout.) But Quasimodo is as beautiful on the inside as he is ugly on the outside.

His passion is for Esmeralda, a beautiful gypsy dancer, a woman clearly beyond his reach. And yet he becomes her protector and champion against the hypocritical archdeacon of Notre Dame who denounces Esmeralda as a witch when she won't surrender herself to him sexually. Like most impossible loves, it ends in tragedy: It's a love that cannot be realized except in the heart and imagination of Quasimodo. But he avenges her death by killing the archdeacon.

ADULTERY

The most common type of forbidden love is adultery. Some of the classics of modern literature that deal with the subject include *The Scarlet Letter* by Nathaniel Hawthorne, *Anna Karenina* by Leo Tolstoy, and *Madame Bovary* by Gustave Flaubert. Despite that these are all novels written by men about women with cheating hearts, they're still first-rate works.

Madame Bovary is about a woman who feels trapped married to a husband who has no romantic imagination. Love hasn't been the many-splendored thing she'd read about, so she decides to go out into the world and find it on her own. Emma Bovary is afflicted with a bad case of sentimentality, and she thinks the world awaiting her outside her door (outside her little Norman village, actually) is like a Harlequin romance waiting for her to step into it.

What she finds isn't what she expected. Love with strangers turns out to be something other than what she hoped. By the end of the book, Emma Bovary has poisoned herself and died an agonizing death.

Anna Karenina doesn't seem to have any better luck. She isn't a naive, star-struck woman like Emma Bovary. But she's love-struck by a handsome young officer and impetuously leaves her husband and child to run off with him. Eventually, however, her lover leaves her to join his army buddies when they go off to fight a foreign war. Disconsolate, Anna throws herself in front of a train. (Tolstoy got the idea for *Anna Karenina* after he saw the body of a woman who killed herself the same way.)

Hester Prynne of *The Scarlet Letter* starts out marked as an adulteress by the puritanical society of seventeenth-century Boston. She's forced to wear a red "A" on her breast so everyone knows who and what she is. Even worse, she has had a child, Pearl, out of wedlock.

The Boston clergy, being the sanctimonious stuffed shirts that they were, are intent on finding out who Hester's lover was, but she refuses to tell them. Her husband comes back from a long trip abroad and assumes a disguise so he can carry out his revenge against his wife's lover. He suspects a respected young minister, Arthur Dimmesdale. He bears in on Dimmesdale, trying to get him to confess. Finally Hester, Arthur and their child try to escape, but they're caught. In the final scene, Dimmesdale climbs up the stairs to the pillory with Hester and Pearl and has his own red letter embroidered on his chest. He escapes the husband's nearly satanic vengeance, and dies in the arms of his beloved. Again, forbidden love has ended in tragedy.

The character triangle in stories about adultery is always the same: the wife, the husband and the lover. The strict moral codes of the nineteenth century would never allow an adulterous affair to be a *happy* one, and since the wage of sin is death, Emma Bovary, Anna Karenina and Arthur Dimmesdale all die. In the case of Bovary and Karenina, they find that the passion they've been seeking is a lie. In the case of Hester Prynne, the love is real, but it comes at the cost of shame and death.

Writing about adultery wasn't always such stern stuff. Before we became so serious-minded, it was often treated casually. The French *fabliaux* (short, humorous tales written between the twelfth and fourteenth centuries) and English Tudor drama often played on the theme of the cuckolded husband. "The Miller's Tale" from Geoffrey Chaucer's *Canterbury Tales* is a wonderful example. The story reads more like a Marx Brothers script than high-brow literature. (Alison, the young wife of an old fart, scorns the attentions of the local parish clerk, but has the hots for the young stud at the local boarding house.) If you tried to write that story today you'd get angry letters from the church, women's groups, and all the crusaders of the world who think it's in bad taste to write such scurrilous trash that, to their mind at least, would encourage widespread immorality. Scurrilous? Of course it is. It's also an important part of our literary past. The world still

prizes the scurrilous humor of Geoffrey Chaucer, Giovanni Bocac-
cio, Ben Jonson and William Shakespeare.

The person committing the adultery is often the protagonist.
The betrayed spouse is often the antagonist and frequently seeks
revenge. The plot easily reverses itself and has the adulterers
turn into murderers by killing or trying to kill the spouse, as
in *The Postman Always Rings Twice*. Or, as in the French film
Diabolique, the wife joins forces with her husband's lover to kill
him. In most cases the point of the plan to kill the spouse is to
free the lovers to marry (although in *Diabolique* the point was
simply to get rid of an insufferable man).

INCEST

Other, darker forms of forbidden love deal with incest. We remain uncomfortable with this taboo, and I doubt the comedy
has been written that deals lightly with the subject. Incest is one
of nature's strongest and most terrifying taboos. Poor Oedipus,
the great riddle solver, ends up marrying his own mother. When
he finds out, the horror is so great he puts out his own eyes.

The subject comes up infrequently, but it's always considered
aberrant behavior. We can forgive Anna Karenina and Emma
Bovary for their sins, but we can't forgive the crime of incest,
whether or not it involves the passion of love. In William Faulkner's *The Sound and the Fury*, one of the major characters, Quen-
tin, is a moody, morose boy whose only passion is his sister,
Candace, who returns his love.

HOMOSEXUAL LOVE

The theme of homosexual love has often been treated as forbidden
love. In pre-Christian times, homosexuality wasn't seen as deviant
behavior, but with the scriptural admonition against homosexuality and the rise of a puritanic frame of mind, we became less
tolerant. Our literature reflects this intolerance by making stories
about homosexual lovers tragedies. The best case in point is
Thomas Mann's *Death in Venice*. The main character, an older
man named Aschenbach, falls in love with a fourteen-year-old boy,
Tadzio. The action takes place during a scourge of cholera, and

Aschenbach is so taken by Tadzio that he can't leave the city and eventually dies of the disease.

The connection of homosexuality with cholera and death suggests strongly the connection between the two characters. Aschenbach's "unnatural" love for Tadzio leads directly to his death. Mann includes obvious symbols of Hell, including being ferried across the river of death, which supports the connection even more.

MAY-DECEMBER ROMANCES

Rather than use these older, more traditional stories that dote on a heavy-handed morality, I have chosen to explore a more modern story that frees itself from the convention of these other tales.

Harold and Maude was written by Colin Higgins. It is the story of a twenty-year-old rich boy who's in love with death and whose hobby is staging mock grisly suicides for the sake of his mother. Harold also likes to go to the funerals of complete strangers. At one such funeral he meets a seventy-nine-year-old woman, Maude. Harold is charmed by Maude's vitality and wit. He visits her in her apartment (which is an old railroad car) where she teaches him the meaning of life and love. She exposes him to the joys of the five senses—everything from learning yoga and how to play the banjo to drinking oatstraw tea and eating ginger pie. Maude is a free spirit; she hates conformity and has no patience for a repressive society.

Harold is thoroughly taken with Maude. Gradually he falls in love with her as he develops a positive attitude toward life. The two become lovers. In one fleeting scene, we glimpse a number tattooed on Maude's forearm, so we know she's survived the horrors of a concentration camp. The brilliance of the scene is that it says so much by saying so little. There's no discussion about it. Maude doesn't launch into the horrors of Nazism and concentration camps. She doesn't get on a soapbox and deliver any of the dozens of "survivor" speeches we've heard so many times. She doesn't have to. Her actions as a woman who has a fierce attachment to life say everything in the context of that one shot of her tattoo.

Harold announces, to his family's utter horror, that he plans to marry Maude. He plans to propose to her on her eightieth birthday. Harold has been transformed by Maude's power of life; it has converted him and brought him out of his fatalistic depression. But when he goes to Maude on her birthday, he finds that she's taken an overdose of sleeping pills and is waiting for death.

Harold is devastated. He can't understand why she would want to kill herself. Maude's explanation is simple: She didn't want to live past eighty. She refused to live a life compromised by infirmity. She wanted death to come on her terms, not on anyone else's.

Harold rushes Maude to the hospital. In the ambulance Harold tells Maude he loves her. She replies she loves him too, but he must "go out and love some more." Maude dies shortly afterward.

At the end of the story we see Harold's car plummet over a cliff and crash into the rocks below. For a moment it seems Harold has met death on his terms as well, but as the camera pulls back, we see Harold at the top of the cliff, playing a tune Maude had taught him on the banjo.

The difference between *Harold and Maude* and other examples of forbidden love is that the couple's relationship is affirmed. Love has healed. Although Harold's family is mortified by the idea that he should marry a woman four times his age, society doesn't win this round. Maude's suicide is tragic but it's also triumphant. It's an act of self-determination that affirms the quality of her life and, more important, the act is consistent with Maude's intent.

The first dramatic phase of the story starts with the beginning of their relationship. We learn first who Harold is, but Maude comes into the story quickly. She has an immediate and profound impact on him. Usually society, if it knows about the forbidden love, expresses its disapproval or takes direct action to stop it. The lovers either pursue their affair in secret or in open defiance of what everyone else thinks. The secret affair is almost always found out. Society is always ready to punish those who don't abide by its rules.

The second dramatic phase takes the lovers into the heart of their relationship. It starts out on a positive note: The lovers are on the front end of their affair and all is well. But by the middle of the second phase the seeds that will lead to the destruction of their relationship have already been planted. We have no hint that Maude is going to kill herself, but we do know the love affair cannot go in the direction Harold wants. Harold is naive and in love; he doesn't understand or fear consequences. Maude is worldly and in love; she understands the consequences but refuses to concede the pressures of society. She must be the one to find the way out.

By the second half of the second dramatic phase, the relationship between lovers may be on the decline. In *Madame Bovary* and *Anna Karenina*, the affairs are rapidly dissolving; the illusion of love has been shattered. Reality and the force exerted by society is taking its toll.

In the third dramatic phase, the lovers must pay their overdue bill to society. Death seems just about the only way out. Romeo and Juliet die. So do Emma Bovary and Anna Karenina and Esmeralda and Arthur Dimmesdale and Aschenbach. Only Abelard is spared — he just gets castrated.

The love may continue to burn in the heart of one of the partners, as in the case of Quasimodo for Esmeralda, Hester Prynne for Dimmesdale and Harold for Maude. Or the survivor may surrender to disillusionment and despair. The remaining lover often has lost everything. Society, it seems, never loses.

CHECKLIST
As you write, keep the following points in mind:

1. Forbidden love is any love that goes against the conventions of society, so there is usually either an explicit or implicit force exerted against the lovers.

2. The lovers ignore social convention and pursue their hearts, usually with disastrous results.

3. Adultery is the most common form of forbidden love. The adulterer may either be the protagonist or antagonist, depending on the nature of the story. The same is true for the offended spouse.

4. The first dramatic phase should define the relationship between partners and phrase it in its social context. What are the taboos that they have broken? How do they handle it themselves?

How do the people around them handle it? Are the lovers moon-struck, or do they deal with the realities of their affair head-on?

5. The second dramatic phase should take the lovers into the heart of their relationship. The lovers may start out in an idyllic phase, but as the social and psychological realities of their affair become clear, the affair may start to dissolve or come under great pressure to dissolve.

6. The third dramatic phase should take the lovers to the end point of their relationship and settle all the moral scores. The lovers are usually separated, either by death, force or desertion.

Chapter Twenty-Two

Master Plot #16: Sacrifice

The value of a sentiment is the amount of sacrifice you are prepared to make for it.

    —*John Galsworthy*

O riginally the concept of sacrifice meant to offer an object to a god to establish a relationship between yourself and that god. The days of blood offerings are pretty much gone. But the days of divine offerings are still with us, in forms such as the Eucharist, in which bread and wine taken during Holy Communion are transubstantiated into the body and blood of Christ.

We know the story about the patriarch Abraham, whose faith God tested by commanding him to sacrifice his son Isaac. The tension mounts when Abraham raises a knife to kill his son. (Genesis 11-25)

The Greeks also put great stock in sacrifice. Stories like Euripides' *Alcestis* were common: When Admetus offends the gods and is sentenced to death, Apollo gives him an out: Find someone to die in your place, and you can live.

Admetus goes to his elderly parents and asks if either of them would die in his place. They decline. But Admetus's devoted wife, Alcestis, pledges herself to die in his place—a model of a wife, at least as far as Greek men were concerned. She sacrifices herself out of love. (Hercules later rescues Alcestis when he challenges Death to a wrestling match and wins.)

Modern day literature, as I noted earlier, pretty much took the gods out of the equation. If a person made a sacrifice, it wasn't to or for a god, but to or for a concept such as love, honor, charity or the sake of humanity. When Sydney Carton takes the place of Darnay on the guillotine in Dickens' *Tale of Two Cities*, he does so because of his great love for Darnay's wife. When Terry Malloy in *On the Waterfront* breaks the code of silence of the docks and informs on the union racketeers, he does so because of his belief that he must do the right thing, no matter what the personal cost. When Norma Rae (in the film by the same name) takes her stand against management and for unionism in the cloth mill where she works, she too is motivated by a higher purpose. The characters sacrifice themselves for an ideal. They subscribe to the belief that the needs of the many outweigh the needs of the individual.

One of the best Westerns ever made, Stanley Kramer's *High Noon*, deals dramatically with the issue of sacrifice in a particularly moving way. The story is simple. Will Kane (played by Gary Cooper) is the marshall of a small western town in 1870. He's just retired and is waiting for the new marshall to get into town. He's also getting married to Amy (played by Grace Kelly). Together they plan to move to another town, open a small store and have a family. In the middle of their wedding party, word comes that a killer Will Kane sent to jail has been pardoned and is due to arrive on the train at noon.

It's 10:40 A.M. The train platform is deserted except for some of the killer's cohorts, who are waiting for him to arrive. Together they plan to gun down Kane.

Amy is a Quaker. She hates violence. She wants her husband to leave town with her before the killer arrives. She tries to convince her husband it's the new marshall's problem. Even his friends urge him to leave. No one else takes any chances either: Even the judge who had sentenced the killer leaves town. Clearly there would be no shame in leaving. After all, Will has already turned in his badge.

But Will Kane is a moral man. The showdown is a challenge he can't walk away from, even if it means his death.

The train arrives at noon. The killer joins up with his gang, and they walk into the deserted town to confront Kane. The clock ticks off the minutes after twelve.

The climax is famous and many Westerns have copied it since.

It's the classic showdown, four against one. Will Kane has no chance, and there's no one left in town to help him.

In the face of such odds, Kane's wife takes up a rifle to protect her husband even though it goes against her beliefs. Although feminists would object that the wife must give up her beliefs to support her husband's, the story takes place more than a century ago, when attitudes were less than enlightened (by our point of view). The film portray's Amy's decision as a surprise, rather than show us her internal struggle to overturn a lifetime of belief and resort to violence. Her love for her husband was stronger than her beliefs against violence, and she knew if she wanted to see him alive again, *she* must be the one to make it happen. Will Kane was ready to sacrifice himself for his code of honor. By doing so, he forces his wife to sacrifice her own code of honor instead. Talk about being between a rock and a hard place! It's a no-win situation that seems to come out all right: The last scene of the film shows them riding off together to their new life. But at what cost to her? Or their marriage? We're only left to wonder.

That may be the point of sacrifice: It always comes at a great personal cost. It may cost your character her life, or it may cost in profound psychological ways. Your character should undergo a major transformation.

Your protagonist may begin this transformation from a lower psychological state, in which she's unaware of the nature and complexity of the problem that confronts her. But circumstances (or Fate, if you prefer) suddenly propel your character into a dilemma that demands action. She must make a decision. She can take the low road, which is the easy way out (run, play it safe, etc.), or she can take the high road, which is the hard way and comes at a great personal cost (Terry Malloy's brother is killed and he's temporarily ostracized by the dockworkers; Norma Rae is fired; and Sydney Carton has his head chopped off). Generally, your character will balk at doing the right thing. Sacrificing yourself is never easy.

Of course, we've all read books and seen movies in which the hero valiantly gives his life to save another person's (he steps in front of her to take a fatal bullet, and vice versa), but those kinds of sacrifices are instantaneous and intuitive. They may make a nice dramatic twist, but we're more intrigued by the profound internal struggle of a person who must make a decision that will either result in shame (for taking the easy way out) or honor (even though it may cost him his life). And, as in the case of Amy Kane, sometimes you must sacrifice honor for love.

In the early 1940s there was a play called *Everybody Comes to Rick's* by Murray Burnett and Jean Alison. The play is filled with improbable situations and bad dialogue, and it would've been buried and forgotten in the dung hill of literature if it weren't for Julius and Philip Epstein and Howard Koch, who adapted the play to the screen.

The production was just as big a mess. The script was constantly being revised, and the director and cast didn't know from minute to minute what the story was about or what the motivations of the main characters were supposed to be. Because of delays and script troubles, the film was actually shot in story sequence (whereas most films are not). The film was cast with Ronald Reagan and Ann Sheridan and then changed to Ingrid Bergman and Paul Henreid and Humphrey Bogart.

Somehow the resulting film — *Casablanca* — not only took home three Academy Awards (for best picture, best director and best screenplay) but has become one of the all-time American movie classics. How did they do it?

In spite of all the confusion, the writers concocted a story that works. The story is about love, but more important, it's a story that climbs to a higher plane, sacrifice for the sake of love, the same sacrifice that Amy Kane makes for her husband in *High Noon*. But where *High Noon* doesn't explore the characters that make these difficult decisions, *Casablanca* does.

The foundation of sacrifice as a plot is character; the act of sacrifice itself is a manifestation of character, and so it's secondary to it. *Casablanca* is about four people and the dynamics among them. The events that surround them are reflections of their characters, and when Rick Blaine makes his sacrifice at the end, everything that has happened before, during and after both shapes and is shaped by his sacrifice.

RICK'S CAFE AMERICAINE

The story takes place in the North African city of Casablanca during World War II. Refugees from Europe choke the city as they search anxiously for exit visas to Lisbon while Nazi agents plot their capture. Some of the refugees pass their time drinking at Rick's Cafe Americaine. We don't range all over the city grabbing glimpses of the refugees and their plight; it all takes place in Rick's cafe. We get the full flavor of the backdrop of the war and its tensions without going out into the street. Rick's bar, in effect, is a microcosm of the world outside. As mentioned earlier, if you want to increase tension, limit the geographical space available to your characters. Make the setting *claustrophobic*. Block all the exits. Put the protagonist and the antagonist within arm's length of each other. By separating them across town, you dilute the tension. One of the reasons for limiting the action to Rick's bar may have been financial—it was cheaper to shoot than going on location—but the effect is what's important. You don't have to circle the globe. You can still capture the feeling of the exotic and strange without including seventeen different cities in eight different countries.

THE FIRST DRAMATIC PHASE

We meet Rick. He's definitely not the sort of person we would suspect of having any higher ideals. He's stubborn and out for himself. That makes his transition—from a person with all the morals of a slug to a person who makes a decision of real conscience—truly worth following. If your character already has high ideals, sacrifice would come easily (unless, as with Amy Kane in *High Noon* the sacrifice goes against those ideals). What makes Rick interesting is that he's so selfish, withdrawn and hard—and yet vulnerable.

Flashback: Paris. Rick is now Richard, and he's desperately in love with Ilsa (Ingrid Bergman). He's so flushed with love that he wants to get married and flee Paris before the Nazis move in. But Rick doesn't notice Ilsa's hesitation, so he's stunned when he finds out that she's gone. She leaves a farewell note. Parting shot:

a crushed Rick holding the note in his hand as the rain symbolically blurs the ink on Ilsa's note.

Back to scene: Rick's Cafe Americaine, 1941. We know something about his secret life. He's been badly hurt in love. We understand him a little better.

Even though Rick says, "I stick my neck out for no one," we learn otherwise during the course of the story. We learn he's fought against the fascists in Spain. We know he left Paris to avoid the Germans who would've been after him. Even after his bitter experience in love, Rick still hates Germans. He orders one away from his gambling tables, and in a particularly rousing scene, he orders the band to play "La Marseillaise" to drown out some Germans who are singing "Wacht am Rhein." And he helps out Ugarte (played by Peter Lorre) after he kills two Germans and steals their signed visas. Rick hides the visas for Ugarte, in spite of the danger of being caught with them. Thus we have a deeper insight into Rick's character. He *is* a man of principles, even if time and circumstances have muted them.

By setting the foundations of character, you will make believable the transition from a selfish state to a selfless state. You can't just turn a character around 180 degrees and reverse her attitudes and actions by a simple event. You must show convincingly how the character *could* get from point A to point Z. Rick claims he won't help anyone; but we also know why he says that (he's tried in the past and been hurt), and we know at least he has the *potential* to help someone. The plot question is, Who will he help? And how? What will make him change his mind and come out of his shell?

A woman, of course.

Which brings us back to being caught between a rock and a hard place. If you have established your character properly, we should understand these underlying tensions as real expressions of character, not just some gimmick you've tried to paste onto your character. To do that, we must know the character's past. That's why the flashback in *Casablanca* is so important. If you take it out, we wouldn't understand Rick's internal conflict. In a plot like this one, you can't get away with cardboard characters. They must be convincing. We must understand their motivations for acting. We don't know anything about Ilsa or her husband yet, other than what we know through Rick, so we have that to look forward to in the second dramatic phase. Why did Ilsa leave Rick in Paris? How will it affect him? How much of a grudge does he hold? He literally controls their destinies.

THE SECOND DRAMATIC PHASE

As you develop a character, keep in mind your character's motivation. People always do things for a reason, and as much as we would like to think of the world as a place in which people give for no reason other than to give, with no expectation of return, we know from personal experience this is rarely the case. (Although there is the rare exception, and stories about these people, which are often inspirational, fascinate us.) We all have our motives. Sometimes those motives are high-minded and sometimes they're not. If you have a character make a sacrifice as the pivoting point in your plot, you commit yourself to that character. That means we should understand the basic nature of the character and why she would make that kind of sacrifice. Don't pull rabbits out of your hat. Show the line of action through your character's line of thought.

In the second dramatic phase the character should be confronted with a moral dilemma that has no easy solution. Your character may try to find that easy solution at first—he may avoid doing the right thing—but eventually the truth and the choices become obvious. That doesn't mean you should be obvious, because that will make your story predictable and uninteresting. We shouldn't ever be entirely sure what your protagonist will do. There may be a real chance that he *won't* do the right thing. People do rationalize. They do find easy ways out that salve their conscience. In this plot, doing the right thing often comes at a high price.

Have your character play for big stakes. Otherwise you won't capture the interest of the reader. You don't have to go overboard and have life as we know it hang in the balance, but you should focus the stakes at a level that is meaningful both for your protagonist and for the other characters nearby. Trivial events and trivial people usually make for trivial stories. Certainly the fate of at least one person should hang in the balance. That fate may be literal in the sense that it's a life-or-death proposition, or it may be figurative in the sense of your protagonist's self-esteem or any psychological change that will affect him in the future.

Sacrifice usually entails a clash between what Freud called the id and the superego. In a caricatured way, the id stands for that part of the personality that wants to do what it wants to do; it's selfish and always puts itself first. Popular depictions of the id usually show it as a devil perched on your shoulder. The superego is the other side of the psyche. It's the part of us that knows the right thing to do. It's the angel sitting on your other shoulder. And you're the poor character in the middle with a voice in one ear saying, "do this, do this," and a voice in the other ear saying, "don't do that, it's not right." Somehow, whether we're guided by one voice or the other, we do make a decision about how to act. The character that makes a true sacrifice is guided by the superego, because the whole idea of sacrifice is to give up something about yourself. In a story about sacrifice, that something should come at a substantial cost. Maybe it's personal safety, maybe it's love, maybe it's life itself. Sacrifice entails our higher selves, so it's a good place to show the human spirit at its best. Even outwardly selfish, greedy and hurtful people sometimes become saints when it comes down to that all-or-nothing moment, when either you put yourself or others first. Self-preservation is a strong impulse in all of us, and sacrifice goes against that instinct.

These are powerful forces at play. In stories about sacrifice, we usually see a character who seems totally incapable of any kind of meaningful sacrifice make that sacrifice when the chips are down. The story gives us confidence in the essential rightness of people.

THE THIRD DRAMATIC PHASE
The idea of sacrifice is to give up something in return for accomplishing a higher ideal. We attain a higher state of being when we put others before ourselves. This plot has the ability to show people at their best.

But, as I already pointed out, the meaningful sacrifice is the costly sacrifice. If the sacrifice is made at leisure and at no real expense to the giver, it is of less value than the sacrifice made at great personal cost. For a millionaire to write a check to a charity for a thousand dollars is no great sacrifice (it's probably not a sacrifice at all, since it's tax deductible). But for a poor person to give everything he owns to help someone else is a much greater sacrifice.

Sacrifice shouldn't be judged only in financial terms. More important are the sacrifices people make of their lives. We consider giving your life the greatest sacrifice of all if it's given for the sake of your country or your family. There are hundreds of other sacrifices a person can make, material and spiritual.

As you develop your third dramatic phase, focus on the payment your character must make to make his sacrifice. Most stories about sacrifice build up to this point: It is the moment of truth for your character. Will he or won't he do the best thing? (Sacrifice often means doing more than the right thing, it means doing the "best" thing.) In this phase you should concentrate on two major aspects:

- the actual sacrifice of your character and how it affects him.
- the effect of the sacrifice on the other characters.

As readers, we're as interested in the effect of the sacrifice as in the sacrifice itself. We want to know if the protagonist's action has had the result he intended it to have. And if not, why?

As you might expect, the third dramatic act tends to be emotional. Watch how you develop the emotions of your characters; avoid being sentimental or melodramatic. Don't exaggerate the emotions of your characters and don't exaggerate the act of the sacrifice. It is far better to underplay those scenes than overplay them.

You might also want to avoid trying to make a saint out of your character. Just because she makes a sacrifice doesn't guarantee admission into Heaven's Hall of Fame. Let the reader determine the value of the sacrifice. If you're clear in your writing and your character's intent, the reader will reach the decision you want her to reach.

CHECKLIST

As you develop this plot, keep the following points in mind:

1. The sacrifice should come at a great personal cost; your protagonist is playing for high stakes, either physical or mental.

2. Your protagonist should undergo a major transformation during the course of the story, moving from a lower moral state to a higher one.

3. Make the events force your protagonist's decision.

4. Make sure you lay an adequate foundation of character so the reader understands his progress on the path to making sacrifice.

5. Remember that all events should be a reflection of your main character. They test and develop character.

6. Make clear the motivation of your protagonist so the reader understands why he would make that kind of sacrifice.

7. Show the line of action through the line of your character's thought.

8. Have a strong moral dilemma at the center of your story.

Chapter Twenty-Three

Master Plot #17: Discovery

Eureka! I found it!

—*Archimedes*

We are in constant search to find out who we are. The questions of "Who am I?" and "Why am I here?" ring endlessly in the ear of humanity. Philosophers have filled volumes considering the question; the answer seems as slippery as soap.

Various thinkers have various answers for us to choose from, as if we were reading a giant menu in a celestial restaurant. Arguments ricochet through the air around us, but none seems entirely satisfactory.

While philosophers tackle the question in abstract terms, writers try to tackle it concretely, by using characters who seem real in situations that seem real. That is part of the great appeal of literature: It tries to translate the meaning of life.

In one sense this plot is closely related to the riddle plot because life is, in a sense, a riddle that begs to be solved. But this plot dedicates itself more to the pursuit of learning about the self than uncovering an assassination conspiracy or figuring out the mystery of the pyramids.

The possibilities of this plot are endless, but all the stories share a certain focus. It is a plot of character, and to this effect perhaps it's among the most character-oriented plots in this collection. Discovery is about people and their quest to understand who they are.

As we discussed earlier, the human condition constantly

changes and yet never changes. The fears, hopes and desires of a Babylonian five thousand years ago probably match closely our fears, hopes and desires. Times change, but people don't.

This sameness allows us to share human experience and seek the meaning for ourselves through the experiences of others. Literature is one of the great sources of examining other people's lives.

Discovery isn't just about characters. It's about characters in search of understanding something fundamental about themselves. In the normal course of events it takes seventy or eighty years for life to present itself fully to us, and if we're really lucky we have insights about the value of our life somewhere along the way. But literature has this great ability to condense a complete life into five hundred pages. It presents to us the scan of a generation—or generations—in the time it takes to read that many pages. And if the writer understands something about the nature of his characters and the effect of certain circumstances on those characters, she will share with us what may be valuable insights.

LEARNING THROUGH DISCOVERY

The lure of literature is discovery. Sure, we read to enjoy because we don't want to think; we want to escape the crushing reality of everyday life as it closes in on us. But we also read to learn, not only to discover about the characters in a book but to understand something about ourselves. Life's lessons can come from life as we live it or from books. Reading is a form of vicarious experience, and in some ways it's just as valid an experience as if we'd actually gone through it.

Your task as a writer is to make that world and the people in it so real that the reader can bridge the fantasy of words with the reality of belief. You've heard so many times that good characters come to life; they inhabit the imagination; they have a power of their own. You have also probably experienced a time when a character you were writing about seemed to take on a will of his own, directing you rather than your directing him. Something is fundamentally honest and real about such characters. They aren't momentary inventions; they are projections of life.

The discovery plot can take many forms. It's an important

children's plot, because children are more involved in the process of discovery about themselves than adults are. They constantly go through major upheavals in their lives and must learn to readjust. If you write children's literature, keep in mind that a good writer doesn't preach ("This, dears, is what you should know and how you should behave"). A good writer allows the reader to extract meaning from her own consideration of the circumstances. You should allow the child to *discover* for herself the effect of life on your characters. No one wants to be force fed. Children, like adults, want to turn over the rocks for themselves to discover what lies beneath. If you write well, your intention will be clear.

The same is true for writing for adults. Readers won't tolerate a writer on a crusade to tell the world the *real* meaning of life. What we will tolerate, however, is your sincere attempt to present a character struggling through the difficulties of life.

We need to make a distinction between the maturation plot and the discovery plot here. The maturation plot focuses on the process of becoming an adult. The protagonist of a maturity plot will probably make a discovery about himself or the world, but the point is not the discovery itself but the *effect* of the discovery on growing up. The maturation plot is about the journey from innocence to experience. The discovery plot, however, doesn't deal so specifically with that process; it deals with the process of interpreting and dealing with life.

Take Eudora Welty's *Death of a Traveling Salesman* (not to be confused with Arthur Miller's play, *Death of a Salesman*). Set in rural Mississippi in the 1930s, the plot is about a shoe salesman in the last hours of his life. Stricken with influenza, R.J. Bowman seeks shelter in the home of a country couple who live in the middle of nowhere. He realizes, as he gets sicker and closer to death, that these simple people possess virtues he never had. As a man who'd spent his life on the road, he begins to realize that his life has never been emotionally whole. He had never regretted not settling down and raising a family, but as he watches this young couple go about their personal lives, he begins to understand what he's missed. But it is too late; death is at hand.

YOU WERE, YOU ARE, YOU WILL BE

The process of discovery generally goes through three movements. To understand what a character is to become, we should understand what she was before the unique circumstances propel her on her journey. You don't want to delay the catalyst that initiates the plot of your story, but you also want to give a strong sense of what life was like for your character before events start to move her toward revelation. Typical of many plots, we generally meet the main character moments before she loses equilibrium.

A common mistake many beginning writers make is to dwell too much on this "pre-catalyst" phase of the character's life. The rule about beginning the story as late as possible (up to the point when things are going to change) is a good one to remember. Don't overwhelm the reader with tons of detail about what the character's life is like before events start to change him. Don't spend too much time setting the stage, because you'll lose the interest of the reader. The early action of your story is critical, not only because you must involve the reader, but because you have only a short time to give the reader a sense of your character's entire life.

As *Death of a Traveling Salesman* begins, Bowman has recently recovered from influenza (or so he thinks). We find him on the road, anxious to get back to work selling shoes to country bumpkins. Note that Welty doesn't dwell on the scenes with the hotel doctor. She gets Bowman on the road very quickly and lets us know through flashback what has happened. But Bowman is weak and he drives his car to the edge of a ditch. Fortunately, he gets out before the car topples over.

In these opening scenes we learn a lot about Bowman's character: who he is, what's important to him, what he wants to accomplish.

This first movement gives way to the second movement, which initiates change. Very often the main character is satisfied with his life and isn't looking to change it. But then life happens. Events force change. The character may be forced to look at his life closely for the first time and learn that everything wasn't as good as it was cracked up to be.

Bowman stops at the first farm down the road in search of help and meets the farm couple who try to help him get his car out of the ditch. Perhaps because he's approaching death (although he doesn't know it), he starts to notice things he'd never noticed before. He begins to envy the young couple's strength and purposefulness. The wife is pregnant and radiates calm and comfort. Bowman finds himself wanting to return to a totally different life, but "his heart began to give off tremendous explosions like a rifle, bang, bang, bang." Death is at hand.

The third movement of the story begins when Bowman starts to understand the nature of his revelation. Although he doesn't know he's dying yet, he has begun to understand that he hasn't lived life the way he really wanted. He realizes that he has missed love. And yet his final experience with the farm couple brings him a measure of peace before he dies. He doesn't go to the grave totally bankrupt.

MOVING AROUND THE MIDDLE

Of the three movements, the most complicated is the middle because it requires that you examine the character in depth. Oftentimes the character will resist change because it brings uncertainty and pain. After losing balance, the character struggles to regain equilibrium, but events force her to confront aspects about herself that she may have always avoided. The process for the character can be healthy or unhealthy. She may end up a better person (as in the case of Bowman) or a worse person. The struggle is the important thing.

Make sure you develop a struggle for your character that is meaningful. Don't make it trivial. No one will care about your character if the turmoil is over some little domestic tragedy. You would hardly expect someone to reevaluate her life as a result of the death of her goldfish.

Nor do you want to make the revelation trivial. If the character goes through a monumental struggle, then realizes that she needs to go to church more regularly, your audience won't buy it. There should be a sense of proportion between the degree of the upheaval and the depth of the revelation. It takes the advent of death to get Bowman there.

Henrik Ibsen's play *Ghosts* is about a similar realization. The main character, Mrs. Alving, must learn the painful lessons about her dead husband's past. By the end of the play, Mrs. Alving realizes that by basing her actions on duty rather than love, she has been indirectly responsible for her family's tragedies. Bitter medicine.

If you start to get the drift of this plot, you can see that its focus is self-realization. The characters move from a state of unawareness (Bowman and Mrs. Alving don't understand what has happened to them during their lives) to a state of revelation in which they begin to understand the truth of their lives. This process of revelation often takes a painful toll: They learn things about themselves they might not want to know. Bowman still has a chance to reconcile himself to his lost past before he dies, but Mrs. Alving is left at the end of the play contemplating a gigantic mess: a son about to go insane from syphilis, an illegitimate daughter, and a tarnished image of a husband.

In this sense *Oedipus Rex* by Sophocles is a classic discovery plot. Even though an oracle has warned Oedipus that he will kill his father and marry his mother, he tempts fate with the somewhat arrogant attitude (for a Greek anyway) that he can change fate. The point of the story is that it's not nice to fool Father Fate, and Oedipus becomes the unwitting victim in spite of all his efforts to avoid his fate.

An absolute master at this kind of plot was Henry James. As a writer he was concerned with people learning about themselves, exploring their nature. For readers with a taste for lots of action and intrigue, James isn't your man. But for readers who are interested in the human condition, for readers who don't mind taking time to explore the psyche of people, few writers can top Henry James.

The Portrait of a Lady is about Isabel Archer, a young, romantic New England woman who inherits an English fortune. She turns down several suitors for Gilbert Osmond, an impoverished dilettante living in retirement in Italy with his daughter Pansy. Osmond is scornful of what he considers the crudities of the modern struggle for survival. He is a selfish, uncaring man who cares more for himself than for anyone else.

Isabel must learn about herself the hard way, through revelation, about the real nature of Osmond's character and her own circumstances. After she makes the mistake of marrying Osmond, she finds out she has been duped by Madame Merle, Osmond's mistress (and the mother of Pansy), who brought Osmond and her together so she could get her hands on Isabel's money. Older, poorer, but more important wiser, Isabel must deal with the undisguised reality of life and her own character.

The novel contains the same basic three movements as Eudora Welty's story. In the first movement we find out who Isabel is and we understand her flaw, which is her romantic nature. She is a woman in search of ideal love. But the world is not an ideal place. The catalyst comes in the guise of her inheritance. Now she has the means to move out into the world and meet other people; she has the means to start her search for love. But that which frees her also enslaves her. It's one of those paradoxes that makes for great tension and irony. Money can free or it can enslave.

Isabel is cruelly manipulated by Osmond and Madame Merle, and when she finally gets to the point at which she is ready to understand what is happening to her — once she is willing to lift the veil of romanticism — she must learn cruel lessons about life, other people and herself.

These stories tend to be dramatic, even melodramatic. That may be because they deal with such extremes of emotion: love, hate, death. Try to imagine writing a story today about a young man who kills his father and marries his mother (although we're still fascinated with those so-called Freudian twists). It would be easy for a writer to fall into the trap of melodrama.

When does a story become melodramatic? When the emotion being expressed is exaggerated beyond the subject matter's ability to sustain that level of emotion.

We're back to the idea of proportion.

Once the plot (action) takes over character, you lose proportion. If you want to be sincere and deal with complicated emotions, you must spend the time it takes to develop a character who is strong enough to carry those emotions. Otherwise, all you're trying to do is glue feelings onto a cardboard cutout of a character.

This plot is a character plot. Action is completely a function of character. What a character does depends on who that character is. This plot supports Aristotle's claim that character *is* action.

CHECKLIST

As you develop your discovery plot, keep the following in mind:

1. Remember that the discovery plot is more about the character making the discovery than the discovery itself. This isn't a search for the secrets of the lost tombs of some Incan king; it's a search for understanding about human nature. Focus your story on the character, not on what the character does.

2. Start your plot with an understanding of who the main character is *before* circumstances change and force the character into new situations.

3. Don't linger on your main character's "former" life; integrate past with present and future. Place the character on the cusp of change. Start the action as late as possible, but also give the reader a strong impression of the main character's personality as it was before events started to change her character.

4. Make sure the catalyst that forces the change (from a state of equilibrium to disequilibrium) is significant and interesting enough to hold the reader's attention. Don't be trivial. Don't dwell on insignificant detail.

5. Move your character into the crisis (the clash between the present and the past) as quickly as possible, but maintain the tension of past and present as a fundamental part of your story's tension.

6. Maintain a sense of proportion. Balance action and emotion so that they remain believable. Make sure your character's revelations are in proportion to the events.

7. Don't exaggerate either your character's emotions or the actions of your character to "force" emotions from her. (This maintains proportion.) *Avoid being melodramatic.*

8. Don't preach or force your characters to carry your messages for you. Let your characters and their circumstances speak for themselves. Let the reader draw his own conclusions based on the events of the story.

Chapter Twenty-Four

Master Plot #18: Wretched Excess

The road to excess leads to the palace of wisdom.
— *William Blake*

Aristotle cautioned us about the dangers of resorting to extremes. Everything in moderation, he said. It certainly is the safe path. But life doesn't always follow the straight and narrow. We are fascinated with people who push the limits of acceptable behavior, either by choice or by accident.

This fascination for people who inhabit the margins of society is what makes this plot so interesting. You and I and most of middle America fall into a kind of comfort zone. What we do, although important to us, falls neatly into acceptable categories of behavior. We know how we're supposed to act and, to maintain civil calm, we are content to live within those confines. We're comfortable and happy (or some reasonable imitation of happiness, anyway). We have food, clothing and shelter, and the rest is gravy.

But life sometimes throws us a curve that we can't handle. Twenty years on the job and suddenly you're jobless. You can't find another job and suddenly you're homeless. Your spouse and your children leave you and you're alone in the streets without any idea where your next meal is coming from and where you'll spend the night. Now you're on the margins of society and probably on the margins of acceptable behavior.

The scary thing about wretched excess is that it can happen to anyone under any circumstances. It doesn't just happen to people who are on the edge; it can happen suddenly to people who seem to be the rock of respectability. It doesn't really take much to unravel someone.

The real tension inherent in this plot comes from convincing the readers that whatever the excess, it could happen to them, too. Which of us knows what evil lurks in the hearts of those around us? Which of us can see the fatal flaws in our behavior or the behavior of others that lets us become unglued in an instant? True horror, authors like Stephen King have pointed out, lies in the commonplace. Vampires are easy (although fascinating), but to make horror from everyday people and everyday events strikes to the core. I don't expect to meet a vampire any time during the rest of my life, but a good writer could convince me that there are terrors just as great lurking in all our lives. All it takes is the right turn of events.

I don't want to give the impression that there is an evil scheme afoot, that some mastermind is spearheading a plan to take over our lives (although that wouldn't be such a bad interpretation of the Christian fear of Satan). The wretched excess plot is about people who have lost the veneer of civilization either because they are mentally unbalanced or because they have been trapped by circumstances that made them behave differently than they would under "normal" circumstances. Another way to put it: normal people under abnormal circumstances, and abnormal people under normal circumstances.

Knut Hamsun (sometimes called the literary father of Ernest Hemingway) wrote an extraordinary novel, called *Hunger*, about a normal man under extraordinary circumstances. The book chronicles a man's descent into madness as a result of his gradual starvation. The protagonist, a writer, slowly gives up his literary aspirations as finding something to eat becomes more and more his focus. As he descends into madness (because of his starvation), his perceptions of the world and the people in it get increasingly distorted. *Hunger* is stunning because of its feeling of authenticity; we actually witness the hero's descent by stages, from a normal young man with dreams of success to a deranged man who is capable of almost anything to get food.

Hollywood has always been fascinated with the extreme. William Wyler directed *The Little Foxes* with Bette Davis (written by Lilian Hellman and Dorothy Parker) about the Hubbard clan, a ruthless, upwardly mobile family in the American South. Or what about Michael Curtiz' direction of *Mildred Pierce*, a story about ambitious people with shadowy motives who live in a world of fear and violence. You could probably name a dozen films yourself, everything from *Lost Weekend* to *Monsieur Verdoux* (Charlie Chaplin's only talkie, in which he plays a mass murderer—it wasn't a hit) to Paddy Chayefsky's *Network* to John Milius and Francis Ford Coppola's *Apocalypse Now* to *Wall Street*. The battleground can be alcoholism, greed, ambition, war or any number of other difficulties. These characters have been pushed to extremes, and almost any one of them, under the right circumstances, could be us.

ALL RIGHT, SO DON'T DO THE RIGHT THING

We can't talk about wretched excess without talking about one of the most perfectly written plots of this type, Shakespeare's *Othello*.

I know what you're thinking: Oh, no, not more Shakespeare. I can defend my choice by saying the author is just so good that you *can't* ignore him. In all fairness, as I pointed out earlier, his storics were derived from a variety of sources, but he made those stories distinctly his. If you go back and read the sources that he took from, you'd realize the real quality of his genius. *And* he could rhyme.

Othello was written during what historians called Shakespeare's period of despair. Besides *Othello* he also wrote *King Lear*, *Hamlet* and *Macbeth*—all of them about wretched excess when you get down to it. But none of the stories captures the character of excess better than Othello's jealousy.

ENTER, VILLAIN

The villain of a wretched excess plot can be a person (as in the case of *Othello*'s Iago) or it can be a thing, such as a bottle of whiskey (to the alcoholic in *Lost Weekend*). Iago is the epitome of villain. He has no redeeming characteristics. From beginning to end, this guy is bad news.

An ensign in the armed forces of Venice, Iago's superior is a Moor (that is, a black man). When Othello passes over Iago for promotion, Iago decides to get revenge. (This isn't a revenge plot, because the focus of the story isn't Iago's revenge, but Othello's paranoia.) Iago is clever and knows how to manipulate people, but the tragedy is Othello's. Iago is merely the instrument that pushes Othello beyond the boundaries of proper behavior.

Iago is a sadist: He enjoys giving pain (revenge ultimately is just an excuse for him to do what he wants to do anyway) and he doesn't care who gets hurt along the way. (A test of this is that, when Iago's punishment at the end of the play is to be tortured to death, we feel that's too good for him.)

Iago starts off by telling Brabantio, Desdemona's father and a powerful politician, that Othello has stolen his daughter and forced her to marry him. Not good.

Brabantio confronts Othello, who denies forcing his daughter to do anything she didn't want to do. Desdemona backs him up. Not much the father can do. But Othello must go off to fight a battle, so he leaves his bride in the care of Iago's wife. Not a smart move, although he doesn't have any reason to suspect Iago yet.

Iago is busy plotting against Othello, who doesn't have the faintest idea that Iago's "mad" at him. The fact that Othello is unaware of Iago's feelings toward him is a plus because it heightens the tension for the audience. Think of how many first-, second- and third-rate films you've seen — ranging from psychological thrillers to cheap slasher flicks — that involve a person who's *unaware* of being stalked. (Iago's quest for revenge is out of balance for the slight against him. He's just mean. If he does have a strength, it's his deviousness.)

Iago cooks up a clever plan to get Cassio, the man who has gotten the promotion Iago believes he deserved, fired. Then he sidles up to Cassio and says he'll put in a good word with Othello's wife to help him get his job back.

Iago sets up a meeting between Desdemona and Cassio, then makes sure Othello sees the two of them together while he — as they say — casts aspersions about them. He even suggests that the officer and Desdemona had an affair before Othello married her.

Iago is an excellent judge of character. He finds people's soft spots and exploits them. Othello's soft spot is his insecurity about his wife. Iago feeds that insecurity, and jealousy, the "green-eyed monster" (the phrase comes from this play) raises its head.

Iago is on a roll now that he sees Othello has taken his bait. He even plants Desdemona's handkerchief—which had been a wedding gift from Othello—in Cassio's bedroom, then tells Othello he saw the two of them in bed together. Othello goes crazy and orders Iago to kill Cassio and promotes Iago to Cassio's rank.

It's all downhill for Othello from there. He demands Desdemona show him the handkerchief, which, of course, she can't do because Iago's stolen it. Othello goes into deep depression and becomes increasingly unstable. Meanwhile, Iago is busy covering his tracks, stabbing people who know too much.

THE NOT-SO-GOOD GUY

Othello's descent into madness is the play's real focus. It's not about power or treachery or revenge. It's about the extreme of emotion that dooms Othello and his wife. A psychiatrist would've had a great time analyzing Othello, trying to get at the root of his suspicions and inadequacies. But Othello can't deal with the fact that his wife might have been fooling around when even common sense would've told him Desdemona loved him dearly. He loses reason and gives in to jealousy and rage. Everything gets out of proportion. He continues his spiral into madness and loses control, finally smothering his wife beneath a pillow.

When Iago's treachery finally comes to light, Othello tries to kill Iago but fails. He has only one option left: suicide.

Iago is certainly a sick man, but he alienates us. We don't feel for him; he is a villain. Othello commits sins that are arguably just as bad if not worse, and yet we feel for him. Why?

The reason has to do with character development and the attitude the writer takes toward his characters. Shakespeare wasn't sympathetic to Iago. The character was a rotten apple, and rotten apples need to get thrown out. But Othello's psychology is more complex. Shakespeare felt a lot more for Othello than he did for Iago. Othello has a tragic flaw (as do MacBeth and Lear) that leads to his downfall. Othello's fear (that his wife was cheating on him) and his jealousy (that she might have eyes for anyone else) take him out of control. When you write about someone like Othello, you're writing about aberrant behavior. In his jealous rage he even lies to his wife that her so-called lover had confessed to him.

Othello's descent into madness horrifies us, yet we feel the depth of his tragedy, especially when the truth is revealed and he must confront the horror of his actions. It is a horror he can't overcome, so he kills himself. It's his only way out.

VICTIMS AND VILLAINS

We also feel deeply for Desdemona. She is the real victim of Iago's plot. Othello is only the tool. True, it's Othello that Iago's after, but we see the effect of Othello's jealousy on poor Desdemona, whom we know all along is innocent.

Shakespeare was clever enough not to play the game of "did she do it or not?" That's a common game today. Maybe she's fooling around and maybe she isn't. We must wait until the end to find out. The problem with playing that game is that the audience gets no chance to feel sympathy for the character. If we *know* she's innocent and is being falsely accused, we can *feel* for her. But if we're not sure, we hold off making any kind of commitment and avoid any emotional connection to the character. Shakespeare wants us to feel for Desdemona. It's one of the strongest emotions in all of literature: an innocent character unjustly accused. *Othello* works because the playwright allows us to feel for both Othello and Desdemona. We feel for his loss of control and the horrible consequences of it, and we feel for her because of the undeserved treatment she gets from all the men around her.

There's a good lesson in this that you should keep in mind while writing: Don't be coy about your characters by hiding sympathetic information about them until the end of the story. You give up too much that way. The name of the game of this plot (like many others) is sympathy—making us feel for your characters. But if you withhold too much sympathetic information so we can't make a judgment about them (whether they're victims or villains), then neither can we.

BASIC STRUCTURE OF THE PLOT

This plot is about character driven to extremes and the effects of those extremes. As you conceptualize your story, consider moving your character from a stable state to an unstable state. That means your reader will see the main character in what we might describe (or what might appear) to be "normal." She's living her everyday life without major complications. The reason to give us a picture of your major character in normal circumstances is so that we can see her as if she were like one of us. That's the implied horror of excess: that it isn't just the realm of totally crazy people, but that it happens to ordinary people, and the implication is that it might even happen to you, the reader. We try to dismiss people who have gone off the deep end by separating them from the mainstream of society. They're not any of us. But the truth is, in most cases, they *are* part of us. By showing your character living a normal life in normal circumstances, you allow the reader to understand that this character is an ordinary person under extraordinary circumstances.

Of course, you don't want to dwell on this aspect because in terms of the plot, little may happen. Tension, you may remember, is the result of the conflict of opposites, and if you're busy showing a normal person enjoying a normal life, your story probably lacks sufficient tension.

Ask yourself, how would you tell the story of the temptation in the Garden of Eden? At what point would you begin the story? Would you spend a lot of time talking about the idyllic life sitting around eating fruit and watching the animals play? It may sound great, but in terms of literature, it's boring. Why? Because the situation is static.

Introduce the serpent. Now you have the tension of opposites, and the story gets interesting. The best place to begin the story might be a day or two before the serpent tries to seduce Eve. We get a good picture of what life is like *before* the serpent, but we're also immediately introduced to the conflict.

As you develop the plot of wretched excess, keep the same thought in mind. In the first movement, give the reader an understanding of what life was like before things started to change. But don't dwell on them.

Then introduce the serpent.

The serpent is the catalyst—an event that forces change in the life of the main character. Ultimately, the change will result in a total loss of control. The change may be gradual—maybe hardly noticeable at first—but we watch in horror and fascination as the character begins the decline toward whatever his obsession is.

The second movement of the plot develops this gradual loss of control. How does it affect the character? How does it affect those who are near him? Each successive complication takes him deeper into a well that seems to have no escape.

The point at which the character loses control—when he can no longer contain himself—is the start of the third movement. It is the turning point of the plot. Clearly things cannot get worse. In Othello's case it ends with the murder of his wife and his own suicide. (As I said before, once Othello kills his wife, there's no other way out for him.)

Of course, your story doesn't have to be a tragedy. Your character may find a more constructive way out and start back on the road to healing. But something important must happen to resolve the excess. That "something" either leads to a destructive end (because a person cannot live long with such emotional excess) or it leads to a turnaround and the beginning of reconstruction. An alcoholic, for instance, after destroying herself and her family, reaches rock bottom and desperately realizes that unless she gets help she will die.

Think of your plot in terms of tracing the stages of a disease. (Wretched excess is in fact an emotional disease.) Symptoms: The character's behavior indicates that she isn't normal. Diagnosis: realizing there is a problem and correctly identifying it. Prognosis: the prospect of recovery. Your patient may or may not be cured. But in either case the disease is resolved—either happily with a cure, or unhappily, as the disease overcomes the patient.

CHECKLIST

As you write, keep in mind the following points:

1. Wretched excess is generally about the psychological decline of a character.

2. Base the decline of your character on a character flaw.

3. Present the decline of your character in three phases: how he is before events start to change him; how he is as he successively deteriorates; and what happens after events reach a crisis point, forcing him either to give in completely to his flaw (tragedy) or to recover from it.

4. Develop your character so that his decline evokes sympathy. Don't present him as a raving lunatic.

5. Take particular care in the development of your character, because the plot depends on your ability to convince the audience that he is both real and worthy of their feelings for him.

6. Avoid melodrama. Don't try to force emotion beyond what the scene can carry.

7. Be straightforward with information that allows the reader to understand your main character. Don't hide anything that will keep your reader from being empathetic.

8. Most writers want the audience to feel for the main character, so don't make your character commit crimes out of proportion of our understanding of who and what he is. It's hard to be sympathetic with a person who's a rapist or a serial murderer.

9. At the crisis point of your story, move your character either toward complete destruction or redemption. Don't leave him swinging in the wind, because your reader will definitely not be satisfied.

10. Action in your plot should always relate to character. Things happen *because* your main character does (or does not) do certain things. The cause and effects of your plot should always relate either directly or indirectly to your main character.

11. Don't lose your character in his madness. Nothing beats personal experience when it comes to this plot. If you don't understand the nature of the excess yourself (having experienced it), be careful about having your character do things that aren't realistic for the circumstances. Do your homework. Understand the nature of the excess you want to write about.

Chapter Twenty-Five

Master Plots #19-#20: Ascension & Descension

The road up and the road down is one and the same.

    —Heraclitus

Real drama, they've been telling us, is a story about a person who falls from a high place because of a tragic flaw in character. Something on the order of greed, pride or lust. The classic Greek plays have plenty of examples, from *Agamemnon* to *Oedipus*. These days there aren't a lot of kings and queens to choose from, but still we have a fascination for stories about people who fall from high places.

We have an equal fascination with people who rise from humble beginnings to great prominence, the so-called rags-to-riches scenario made famous by Horatio Alger in stories like *The Ragged Dick Series* and the *Luck and Pluck Series*. In these stories, the hero is either a shoeshine or newsboy whose virtue was always rewarded with riches and success.

These two plots—ascension and descension—occupy different positions in the same cycle of success and failure. One plot deals with the rise of the protagonist, and the other deals with her fall. Some stories capture the complete cycle, as in "The Rise and Fall of . . . " stories. Usually the personality traits that allowed the character to reach prominence (ambition, aggressiveness, etc.) are the same traits that cause her downfall.

These are stories about people, first, last and foremost. Without a centerpiece character, you have no plot. The main character is the focus of the story. One way of thinking of the main character (who can be an antagonist or a protagonist) is to think of her as the sun in the solar system of characters; all of the other characters revolve around her.

That means you must develop a main character that is compelling and strong enough to carry the entire story, from beginning to end. If you fail to create a character that can carry the story, your plot will collapse.

Such a main character is usually larger than life. She will dominate the other characters. In fact, all your other characters may pale in comparison. The main character is magnetic: Everyone and everything relates to her.

The main character also tends to suffer from an over-blown ego, which may be her ultimate downfall. Too big for her shoes. Cocky. Joseph Conrad's *Heart of Darkness* (later adapted into Frances Ford Coppola's *Apocalypse Now*) is about a man's journey into the blackness that is central to the heart and soul. In any of these cases, the story has at its core what we might call a "moral dilemma." The main character is involved in a struggle that creates a vortex that sucks everyone else in the story into it.

That moral dilemma may be short and bittersweet, as in the case of Flannery O'Connor's story, "Parker's Back," in which a profane and shiftless man finds the meaning of grace when he has a picture of Jesus Christ tattooed onto his back. Or the moral dilemma may take up the span of a life, as in Jake La Motta's biography (later made into a film by Martin Scorsese) *Raging Bull*. It may even take place over the course of generations, as in the case of the film trilogy, *The Godfather* or Gabriel Garcia Marquez' *A Hundred Years of Solitude*.

Compare the rise and fall of Willie Stark in Robert Penn Warren's *All the King's Men* to the fall and rise of John Merrick in Sir Frederick Treves's book *The Elephant Man and Other Reminiscences* (made into a film by David Lynch). Willie Stark starts out the champion of the underdog, willing to fight political injustice at every turn, but he turns into that which he despises most: a drunk and a demagogue. What character flaws lay the foundation for his failure? We watch him shape events, and we watch the events shape him. That is the core of this plot, perhaps more so than in any other: the intimate connection between character and events. You can't take the main character out of the stream of action because everything the main character does is the mainstream of action.

This means understanding who your main character is, what he thinks and why he thinks that way. It means working out intent and motivation. Willie Stark wants to be a man of the people. Why? What drives him? And why does he crack? *All the King's Men* is a powerful story about political and personal corruption, but more than that it is the story of a man who is consumed by himself.

OF MICE AND ELEPHANT MEN

The story of John Merrick, *The Elephant Man*, reverses the cycle. He moves from a lower state to a higher state of consciousness, the reverse of Willie Stark. These stories are less common, which might say something about ourselves, but the ascension plot (the character's spiritual movement from sinner to saint rather than from saint to sinner) is uplifting. Whereas the descension plot serves as a cautionary tale, the ascension plot serves as a parable. *The Elephant Man* is a stirring ode to the dignity of the human spirit. It is a story of seeming transformation and redemption, an uncovering of the beauty within the beast. (If you wonder why this isn't a metamorphosis plot, it's because Merrick never changes from one physical state to another. He is simply "discovered" for who, not what, he is.)

Merrick is presented to us as a monster, and we understand only what we see — a hideous monster. But gradually we begin to see the man beneath the disfigurement. There is a scene in the film that brings his humanity to the surface in a touching way. The surgeon who has taken on Merrick's cause brings him home for tea. The surgeon's wife is horrified by the sight of him, but when Merrick sees the family photographs sitting on the mantel, he points to them and says, "They have such noble faces." He then reaches into his own pocket and pulls out a picture of his mother. "She had the face of an angel," he says, adding, "I might have been a great disappointment to her. I tried so hard to be good. . . ."

Merrick must suffer tremendous personal physical and mental anguish in his quest to be a "human being." But he is absolutely dedicated to being accepted as human, not animal; and his search is finally rewarded, if only momentarily.

Stories like *The Elephant Man* are uplifting because they ultimately explore the positive aspects of human character. Your main character should overcome odds not just as a hero who has obstacles to conquer but as a character in the process of becoming a better person. Obviously it's easier to accomplish this task if your character starts out in something of a sorry state. The 1939 melodrama *Dark Victory* by George Emerson Brewer, Jr., and Bertram Bloch (which was later made into a film starring Bette Davis) is about Judith Traherne, a rich young socialite who is dying of a brain tumor. As the story starts, she's portrayed as a self-centered, spoiled, intolerable little rich girl. But as the disease progresses and humbles her, she begins to change.

But the change doesn't come suddenly, like someone turned on a faucet. Human character is complicated, and to be believable as a writer, you need to explore the human psyche as it might really behave in such circumstances. In *Dark Victory*, when Judith learns that her brain tumor is inoperable, she reacts with rage and cuts off her relationship with the doctor (which has been developing along personal lines). She parties hard and starts drinking heavily; she refuses to go to bed because she doesn't want to waste whatever time is left in her life. At a horse show she takes reckless risks to win because she knows she has nothing to lose. She turns cynical and bitter.

But she realizes that she cannot depart the world such a person, and she knows she must make her peace with the world and with those people who care for her. The transformation now takes a positive turn. (In psychology, her behavior would be characterized as going from denial of death to its acceptance.) Judith finally faces death with dignity — "beautifully, finely, peacefully." (I would recommend renting the video and watching this film because Bette Davis' performance is absolutely believable and first-rate.)

Leo Tolstoy's novella *The Death of Ivan Ilyich* is arguably one of the finest examples of the ascension plot (and one of the finest short works in all of literature). Ivan Ilyich is a man who, like Judith Traherne, is confronted by the prospect of death. (The threat of death you no doubt have noticed is a great catalyst.) Unlike Judith, however, Ivan is an ordinary man. Nothing distinguishes his life. In many ways he appeals to us as readers because we can see ourselves in him. He thinks life should be smooth, pleasant and routine. No surprises. He is a conscientious man who is responsible to his family and his employer. He is, from afar, boring.

But Tolstoy doesn't bore us with the details. We meet Ivan at his funeral and overhear people talking about him and wondering who will be promoted in his place, and we wonder why this poor dead man is being treated so irreverently.

Tolstoy then takes us back to the beginning of Ivan's decline, when he falls off a ladder and bruises his side. The accident seems trivial but his condition worsens. The story concentrates on Ivan's awareness of the meaning of life (and death) and finding love in the least expected places. Tolstoy's portrayal overwhelms us with its sensitivity and honesty. His portrayal of Ivan is so accurate that even if you apply the clinical standards of the five stages of dying (which were conceived long after Tolstoy wrote the story), they fit perfectly. We follow Ivan in his process step by step as death approaches. Fear is replaced by acceptance and, finally, peace. In an ironic way, Ivan's physical decline allows his spirit to ascend the mundane and the trivial.

This was Tolstoy's genius. He was an incredible observer of human character, and he knew how to bring it to print. Ivan's journey from life to death is a journey from slavery to freedom. It is the journey from a lower character state to a high spiritual state. This common man dies a quiet hero.

There is a lesson for writers in Tolstoy's story. You don't have to be outrageous in your selection of subject matter by having a story about someone as exotic as the Elephant Man. Your story can be about ordinary people. This story is harder to write because it lacks a lot of the easy mileage you can get out of stories like *The Elephant Man*, in which the main character is a monster on the outside but a gentle, intelligent person on the inside.

This isn't to slight *The Elephant Man*, which is a superb story. But *The Death of Ivan Ilyich* moves more deeply and explores human character more convincingly. It doesn't rely on gimmicks.

It relies on understanding human character at the ultimate turning point of life. Now *that's* powerful stuff.

WHO KNOWS WHAT EVIL LURKS IN THE HEARTS OF MEN . . .

Now for the flip side. Just as the ascension plot examines the positive values of human character under stress, the descension explores the negative values of human character under stress. These are dark tales. They are tales about power and corruption and greed. The human spirit fails in its moment of crisis.

People like Charles Foster Kane in *Citizen Kane*, Michael Corleone in *The Godfather* trilogy and King Richard III in Shakespeare's play of the same name fascinate us. So do characters like Elmer Gantry (in *Elmer Gantry*), Willy Loman (in *Death of a Salesman*) and Jake La Motta (in *Raging Bull*). The characters in these stories may range in character from evil (such as Michael Corleone—although we start to develop a smidgen of sympathy for him in *Godfather III* when he tries to atone for his sins) to a sort of wonderment (such as for Charles Foster Kane, who can't be characterized as a "bad" man). As the writer you must focus on what might be loosely called "the journey of life," the rise and fall of your main character. We follow Kane from the moment he is separated from his mother (and father) as a young, carefree boy. Now that he is rich, he has responsibilities. We see him as a young man full of idealism and energy and a desire to make the world a better place. We follow him through the twists and turns of a complicated life. Gradually he becomes disillusioned and bitter about what life has offered him and his lack of power to make the changes he wants to make. Kane isn't an ordinary person. As you develop your central character, you will find that she will quickly become extraordinary. Your main character may start out average, but events (Fate, if you prefer) lift the character above the ordinary and the trivial. The question that ultimately backs most of these stories is simple: How will fame (or power, or money) affect this character? We see her before the change, during the change and after the change, and we compare the phases of character development she has gone through as a result of these circumstances. Some handle it well; others don't.

This doesn't mean your main character must crash morally. The tension, as in *Citizen Kane*, comes as a result of the ocean of difference between what Kane hoped to do with his money and his life and what he actually does. The effort may be valiant, but it fails in this scenario. And because it fails, it leads to disillusionment, unhappiness and even ruin. The lesson seems to be that having fame (power, money) isn't everything—it may not even be enough. These things sometimes (although not always) corrupt, or at least they are forces that are stronger than the people who have them.

Depending on the message you want to present to the reader, you should understand clearly the moral or social implications of the chain of events in your story. If power or money ultimately corrupts your hero, what are you saying about power or money? That these forces are stronger than any of us? This message would be particularly strong if your character is basically good before coming into power and is transformed into a character of dubious values as a result of the power. That would make a strong statement about the corruption of values as a result of power or money. You may be saying that these things in and of themselves are evil. Is that the message you want to give?

The normal effect of these forces (fame, power, money) is a struggle between your character in his previous state (that is, how he was before the catalyst changed things) and the character as he develops into a new person being shaped by events. (Note the difference between this and the transformation plot, which opens with the change.) How easily does your character give in to the abuse of power? Does he resist? In a meaningful way? Or does he just cave in? There's so much human psychology for you to deal with that you should have a goal (that is, a definite idea of what you want to say about the subject matter) to work toward.

As you fashion your character, keep in mind that it's important for the reader to know and understand the stages of development that your character is going through. We should know what he was like *before* the great change in his life so we have a basis of comparison. This constitutes the first movement of your plot.

In the second movement, we should experience the change that propels your character from his previous self into his emerging self. This may be a gradual progression over months or even years, or it may be instantaneous (a sudden stroke of good fortune such as winning the lottery or suddenly being thrust into a position of power). These events make it impossible for your character to remain the same.

The third movement is the culmination of character and events. If the character has a flaw, we will see the expression of the flaw and how it affects him and those around him. Your character may overcome that flaw after some drastic event forces him to confront himself, or he may succumb to the flaw. Usually (but not always) some catastrophe—the result of your character's behavior—forces a realization of what he has "become." Again, it depends on what you want to say about this kind of character in this kind of circumstance, and what you want to say about human nature. Is it strong? Or weak? Are we but the playthings of the universe? Or can we take Fate in our hands and fashion a future for ourselves?

If a character abuses other people during his trip to the top, oftentimes we expect to see that character get his comeuppance. Pride goeth before the fall. We prefer to see haughty people taken down a notch or two. But if the human spirit must overcome great odds, as in the case of the Elephant Man, and that character demonstrates that he deserves to achieve his goal, we want the character to move to a higher spiritual plane. We want him to triumph. But he must prove to us his worthiness. Wanting it isn't enough; even deserving it isn't enough; your character needs to *earn* it.

The story is about your main character; events start and finish with him. He should overwhelm others by virtue of his larger-than-life attributes (positive or negative). He should be charismatic, fascinating and strong. We should be drawn to him, hero or villain.

A lot of the other plots examine human nature and how character is affected under stress, but few plots do it as thoroughly as these two. We recognize that life has its ups and downs and these plots characterize just those fluctuations in human events. For some people the rises and falls are much more dramatic than for the rest of us, and those meteoric people fascinate us. They aren't like us, and yet they're very much like us. They love and hate the same way we do, with the exception that theirs seems more exaggerated. The rises go much higher, and the falls plunge much lower.

Once you've found the moral center for your character and decide whether he will win or lose the struggle, you will see more clearly how to achieve those goals. We are often told we should write with an end in mind, though this is easier said than written. With these plots, however, it's almost an absolute necessity to know how you intend to draw the character. (Notice I said "almost"—nothing is absolute when it comes to writing.) The dramatist would have us believe there is a tragic flaw in each of us waiting for an opportunity to express itself. If it's true, most of us don't have much to worry about. But there are those who step into the limelight of attention (and power) who are tested. Some hold up and are heroes. Others do not—and perhaps they're only human.

CHECKLIST

As you write, keep these points in mind:

1. The focus of your story should be about a single character.

2. That character should be strong-willed, charismatic and seemingly unique. All of your other characters will revolve around this one.

3. At the heart of your story should be a moral dilemma. This dilemma tests the character of your protagonist/antagonist, and it is the foundation for the catalyst of change in her character.

4. Character and event are closely related to each other. Anything that happens should happen because of the main character. She is the force that affects events, not the reverse. (This isn't to say that events can't affect your main character, but that we are more interested in how she acts upon the world than how the world acts upon her.)

5. Try to show your character as she was *before* the major change that altered her life so we have a basis of comparison.

6. Show your character progressing through successive changes as a result of events. If it is a story about a character

who overcomes horrible circumstances, show the nature of that character while she still suffers under those circumstances. Then show us how events change her nature during the course of the story. Don't "jump" from one character state to another; that is, show how your character moves from one state to another by giving us her motivation and intent.

7. If your story is about the fall of a character, make certain the reasons for her fall are a result of character and not gratuitous circumstances. The reason for a rise may be gratuitous (the character wins $27 million in LottoAmerica), but not the reasons for her fall. The reasons for a character's ability to overcome adversity should also be the result of her character, not some contrivance.

8. Try to avoid a straight dramatic rise or fall. Vary the circumstances in the character's life: Create rises *and* falls along the way. Don't just put your character on a rocket to the top and then crash. Vary intensity of the events, too. It may seem for a moment that your character has conquered her flaw, when in fact, it doesn't last long. And vice versa. After several setbacks, the character finally breaks through (as a result of her tenacity, courage, belief, etc.).

9. Always focus on your main character. Relate all events and characters to your main character. Show us the character before, during and after the change.

Chapter Twenty-Six

Parting Shots

I am obliged to remind you that this book is not gospel. It is a guideline for some of the most common applications of major plots. In no way does this forbid you from violating what might be loosely called groundrules for each of the plots. Remember, plot is a process, not an object, and as you fashion your plot, think of it in terms of a wad of clay that needs constant molding.

For some writers, plot comes easily. If that were true for you, you probably wouldn't be reading this book. But since you did, it must mean you are still put off by the prospect of creating a plot. That's good news and it's bad news.

It's good news because every writer should worry about his plot. Don't ever take it for granted. Fashion it now or fashion it later, but it must be fashioned. We envy those who have a strong intuitive sense of structure and understanding of the human dynamics of plot. For the rest of us who worry to death that our form is mangled, lopsided or no-sided, we constantly survey what we have done and ask ourselves, "Is it right?"

As you fashion your plot, ask yourself how you want to go about it. There are two main ways that I know of. The first is to bulldoze your way through the work without ever looking back. *Get to the end and then worry whether or not you got it right.* Don't let intellectual concerns about plot get in the way of the emotional thrust of writing a book. Lots of writers work that way. They put full stock in the power of rewriting. Write it first and then figure out what's wrong with it. If you worry along the way, you can't focus on the real guts of the work.

But there are those who say this approach wastes too much time and invites major disasters. It may end up so cockeyed that you can't fix it. This school says, *Know along the way what you're doing and where you're going.* That way you will avoid major midair collisions by making constant corrections during your writing.

Ask yourself which approach you would feel comfortable with. If you think that constantly applying the elements of plot will stunt your expression of ideas, just get it all on paper. If you know which plot you want (and that may change in the middle of writing your story as you become aware of other possibilities), read over the guidelines and see if they stick in the back of your mind while you write. If not, don't worry.

If you are a control freak and must have your flight plan filed before you taxi down the runway, you will have your markers all along the way. Feel free to veer off course some if it feels right to you, but keep your final objective in mind. Wander too far off course and you may not find your way back, ending up with two or three competing plots grafted onto each other. You should only have one major plot—that's your master flight plan. Any others that you include should be minor plots that support the major plot. But if you aren't sure of your major plot, you'll spend page after page wandering from one to the next, until you find it. By then you'll have wasted weeks or months and have only a rat's nest of ideas to unravel. Knowing your major focus early is important. Then you'll understand how to better include other plots in support of your major plot.

The idea of this book is to give you a *sense* of what each plot looks and feels like. Don't feel you must copy any of them down to the smallest detail. Apply the standard sense of the plot you have picked to the particular circumstances of the story you want to write. On the one hand, don't force your story to fit, and on the other hand, don't get so loose that nothing fits. Plot is the form your idea will take; give it shape and substance as you write. Whatever you do, however, don't be a slave to the plot. You are not in the service of it; it is in your service. Make it work for you.

There are twenty plots in this book. You could spend your life recalculating other plots that you could argue belong in the base twenty. I've picked the most common plots, that's all. The *major-*

ity of the writing that's out there will fall into one of these twenty plots. But not all. So just because it isn't here doesn't mean it doesn't exist.

Also, don't be afraid to combine plots. Many great stories have more than one plot. But make sure that you have a major or primary plot and that any additional plot is minor or secondary. You can stack plots to your heart's delight, but don't get too complicated or you won't be able to effectively juggle all of them. Keep one plot foremost in your consideration. The other plots are just satellites.

I have seen plots for books and screenplays sketched out on a napkin. Nothing elaborate. Maybe fifty words. Sometimes that's all it takes if you have a solid sense of your story. When you can get to that point — where you can lay out your story in fifty words or less — you have all you need to create a plot. Sometimes coming up with those fifty words is easy and sometimes it stubbornly resists you. If it does resist you, keep trying to discover it.

STRAYING FROM THE PATH

Some people feel locked in once they plan their plot and are afraid to make changes. It would be nice if I could say, "Don't feel locked in. Make whatever changes you feel like making." But I can't. I also can't say, "Stick with the plan 100 percent." A tension always exists between staying on the path and wandering off it. Try to find a middle ground to travel on. If you stray too far off the path laid out by your plot, you may end up altering the story in fundamental ways that will require you to totally rethink your story. (This may not be such a terrible thing. If you discover the plot isn't working for you, you should get off the path.) If you hold absolutely to the plot path and resist any temptation to change or add, you may be denying yourself some powerful ideas.

So how do you know when to yield and when to resist? There is no hard-and-fast rule. I would say that if you are writing and you feel good about how your story is developing, don't jeopardize it by wandering too far off course. If, on the other hand, you don't feel satisfied with its development, you ought to start looking for other ideas.

Many times I've had the experience of writing pages that I

knew were brilliant but didn't really fit into the scheme of things as they were developing. I said to myself, "This is really good, I'll find a way to *make* it fit." I was right in one respect: The pages would be really good. But I was totally wrong in my thinking that I could find a way to make them fit. Those brilliant pages had no more home in the work than a worm in a bird's nest. No matter how much I tried to make them fit, they always stuck out.

Feel free to push the envelope of the boundaries of these plots if you think it's important to do so for your work. (I wouldn't suggest, though, doing it solely for the purpose of being different.) Every work has its own demands, and you can't artificially impose rules on a work that can't accommodate them. If you feel the desire to be creative and different, plot may not be the place to start. It's hard (if not impossible) to create a story that hasn't yet existed. The cast of characters remain the same (because people are fundamentally the same) and the situations remain the same (because life remains fundamentally the same). Where your creativity comes in is in the *expression* of your ideas. If you use painting as an analogy, it should be clearer. Paint is paint. It hasn't changed much over the centuries. But look at what painters have done *with* paint. The expression is new; the fundamental tools remain the same. Words are words. But look at what you can do with them!

A FINAL CHECKLIST

As you develop your plot, consider the following questions. If you can answer all of them, you have a grasp of what your story is about. But if you can't answer any of them, you still don't know what your story is and what you want to do with it.

1. In fifty words, what is the basic idea for your story?

2. What is the central aim of the story? State your answer as a question. For example, "Will Othello believe Iago about his wife?"

3. What is your protagonist's intent? (What does she want?)

4. What is your protagonist's motivation? (Why does she want what she is seeking?)

5. Who and/or what stands in the way of your protagonist?

6. What is your protagonist's plan of action to accomplish her intent?

7. What is the story's main conflict? Internal? External?

8. What is the nature of your protagonist's change during the course of the story?

9. Is your plot character-driven or action-driven?

10. What is the point of attack of the story? Where will you begin?

11. How do you plan to maintain tension throughout the story?

12. How does your protagonist complete the climax of the story?

INDEX